KU-185-873

Acceptable risk

Acceptable risk

BARUCH FISCHHOFF,
SARAH LICHTENSTEIN, PAUL SLOVIC,
STEPHEN L. DERBY, AND RALPH L. KEENEY

CAMBRIDGE UNIVERSITY PRESS
Cambridge
London New York New Rochelle
Melbourne Sydney

Published by the Press Syndicate of the University of Cambridge
The Pitt Building, Trumpington Street, Cambridge CB2 1RP
32 East 57th Street, New York, NY 10022, USA
296 Beaconsfield Parade, Middle Park, Melbourne 3206, Australia

First published 1981
Reprinted 1983
First paperback edition 1983

Printed in the United States of America

Library of Congress Cataloging in Publication Data

Main entry under title:

Acceptable risk:

Bibliography: p.

1. Risk. 2. Risk management—Decision
making. I. Fischhoff, Baruch 1946–
HD61.A24 658 81–9957 AACR2
ISBN 0 521 24164 2 hard covers
ISBN 0 521 27892 9 paperback

Contents

Figures

Tables

Preface

Risk is an ever-present aspect of life, and its management occupies a prominent position among society's concerns. Citizens, jurists, politicians, regulators, and developers all spend some portion of their time asking, What risks must I cope with? How large are they? Can they be reduced? When are they acceptable? These questions arise both in the course of mundane decisions and in such large-scale interventions as social reforms and new technologies. Providing answers to these questions is often the weak (or missing) link in the management of hazards; the absence of an adequate decision-making methodology often leads to indecision, inconsistency, and dissatisfaction.

This book offers a critical analysis of possible approaches to making acceptable-risk decisions. In doing so, we focus on what these approaches try to do and how likely they are to achieve the goals they set for themselves. We have tried to provide a conceptual guide rather than a methodological primer or a detailed explication of specific applications, for which other sources are available. The approaches are evaluated relative to one another and by contrast with the absolute standard of what one would want from an ideal method. Within this framework, recommendations aimed at improving society's ability to make acceptable-risk decisions are offered in the areas of policy, practice, and research. Although our focus is on technological hazards, this analysis could readily be extended to managing the risks associated with such areas as child rearing or criminal justice.

Our attempt to examine approaches to acceptable risk has included the following steps.

1. Defining acceptable-risk decisions and identifying some frequently proposed but inappropriate solutions.
2. Characterizing the features of acceptable-risk problems that make resolving them so difficult, including uncertainty about how to define problems of decision, difficulties in ascertaining crucial facts, problematic value issues, unpredictable human responses to hazards, and problems of assessing the adequacy of decision-making processes.
3. Classifying decision-making approaches according to how they attempt to address the features of acceptable-risk problems. The major approaches discussed here are (a) *professional judgment:* allowing technical experts to devise solutions; (b) *bootstrapping:* searching for historical precedents to guide future decisions; and (c) *formal analysis:* theory-based procedures for modeling problems and calculating the best decision.
4. Specifying the objectives that an approach should satisfy in order to guide social policy, including comprehensiveness, logical soundness, practicality,

openness to evaluation, political acceptability, institutional compatibility, and conduciveness to learning.

5. Assessing how well the approaches meet these objectives.

Conclusions

The following conclusions emerge from our analysis:

1. Acceptable-risk problems are decision problems, that is, they require a choice among alternatives. That choice is dependent on values, beliefs, and other factors. Therefore, there can be no single, all-purpose number that expresses the acceptable risk for a society. At best, one can hope to find the most acceptable alternative in a specific problem, one that will represent the values of a specific constituency.
2. None of the approaches considered here is either comprehensive or infallible. Each gives special attention to some features of acceptable-risk problems but ignores others. As a result, not only does each approach fail to give a definitive answer, but it is biased toward particular interests and particular solutions. Hence choosing an approach is a political act that carries a distinct message about who should rule and what should matter. The search for an objective method is doomed to failure and may obscure the value-laden assumptions that will inevitably be made.
3. Acceptable-risk debates are greatly clarified when the participants are committed to separating issues of fact from issues of value. Nonetheless a clear-cut separation is often impossible. Beliefs about the facts of the matter shape our values; those values in turn shape the facts we search for and how we interpret what we find.
4. The determining factor in many acceptable-risk decisions is how the problem is defined (i.e., which options and consequences are considered, what kinds of uncertainty are acknowledged, and how key terms are operationalized). Until definitional disputes are settled, it may be impossible to reach agreement regarding what course of action to take.
5. Values, like beliefs, are acquired through experience and contemplation. Acceptable-risk problems raise many complex, novel, and vague issues of value for which individuals may not have well-articulated preferences. In such situations, the values one expresses may be greatly influenced by transient factors, including subtle aspects of how value questions are posed by interviewers, politicians, or the marketplace. The conflicts in each individual's values are above and beyond the conflicts between different individuals' values and require careful attention.
6. Although a distinction is often made between perceived and objective risks, for most new and intricate hazards even so-called objective risks have a large judgmental component. At best, they represent the perceptions of the most knowledgeable technical experts. However, even such experts may have an incomplete understanding. Indeed, their professional training may even have limited them to certain traditional ways of looking at problems. In such cases, nonexperts may have important supplementary information or viewpoints of their own on hazards and their consequences.

Recommendations

No one solution to acceptable-risk problems is now available, nor is it likely that a single solution will ever be found. Nonetheless, the following recommendations, addressed to regulators, citizens, legislators, and professionals, should, if implemented, enhance society's ability to make decisions.

1. Explicitly recognize the complexities of acceptable-risk problems. The value judgments and uncertainties encountered in specific decision problems should be acknowledged. More generally, we should realize that there are no easy solutions and not expect society's decision makers to come up with them.
2. Acknowledge the limits of currently available approaches and expertise. As no approach is infallible, we should at least avoid the more common mistakes. Our aim should be a diverse and flexible approach to decision making that emphasizes comprehensiveness.
3. Improve the use of available approaches. Develop guidelines for their conduct and review. Make them sensitive to all aspects of the problem and to the desires of as many stakeholders as possible. Analysis should proceed iteratively in order to sustain its insights and absorb its criticisms.
4. Make the decision-making process compatible with existing democratic institutions. The public and its representatives should be involved constructively in the process both to make it more effective and to increase the public's understanding of hazard issues.
5. Strengthen nongovernmental social mechanisms that regulate hazards. Decisions reached in the marketplace and political arena provide important guidelines for most approaches. Those mechanisms can be improved by various measures including reform of the product-liability system and increased communication of risk information to workers and consumers.
6. Clarify government involvement. Legislation should offer clear, feasible, and predictable mandates for regulatory agencies. The management of different hazards should be coordinated so as to build a legacy of dependable precedents and encourage consistent decisions.

If followed, these recommendations will help society to learn from its day-to-day experience in making acceptable-risk decisions and to live with their consequences. The last chapter of this book provides an agenda for scientific research with which to complement this experiential learning.

Intended audience

We have written this book for a broad readership, including technology promoters, public servants (regulators, legislators), professionals who manage risks (e.g., risk analysts, engineers, physicians), academics (and their students), and the growing number of lay people concerned about technological risks. Consequently, there are no mathematical or technical prerequisites for this book. We hope that the ideas presented will be particularly useful to those acceptable-risk decision makers already embroiled in setting regulatory standards.

Acknowledgments

The magnitude of this project has gone beyond the resources we originally allotted to it. Its breadth has gone beyond the disciplinary training of each of us, or that of anyone we know. We have been fortunate enough to receive advice and constructive criticism from many talented people. They include William Bordas (University of Oregon); Bruce Bowers (University of Oregon); Adrian Cohen (Health and Safety Executive, United Kingdom); David Dorfan (University of California, Santa Cruz); Ward Edwards (University of Southern California); F. R. Farmer (Warrington, Cheshire, England); Joseph Fragola (Institute of Electrical and Electronics Engineering); John Gardenier (U.S. Coast Guard); John Graham (American Nuclear Society); Harold Green (George Washington University); Michael Griesmeyer (Advisory Committee on Reactor Safety); Ronald Howard (Stanford University); Roger Hurwitz (Massachusetts Institute of Technology); Herbert Inhaber (Atomic Energy Control Board, Canada); John Jackson (University of Pennsylvania); Daniel Kahneman (University of British Columbia); Roger Kasperson (Clark University); Robert Kates (Clark University); Howard Kunreuther (University of Pennsylvania); John Lathrop (International Institute of Applied Systems Analysis); Lester Lave (The Brookings Institute); Joanne Linnerooth (International Institute of Applied Systems Analysis); Don MacGregor (Decision Research); Alan Manne (Stanford University); James March (Stanford University); Allan Mazur (Syracuse University); Dorothy Nelkin (Cornell University); Harry Otway (Joint Research Center, Ispra, Italy); Talbot Page (California Institute of Technology); William Rhyne (Science Applications, Inc.); Paolo Ricci (Electric Power Research Institute); William Rowe (American University); Romano Salvatori (Westinghouse Electric Co.); Thomas Schneider (Basler and Hofman, Zurich); Zur Shapira (Hebrew University, Jerusalem); Michael Spence (Harvard University); Sonia Stairs (British Columbia Inquiry into Uranium Mining); Ola Svenson (Stockholm University); Amos Tversky (Stanford University); Detlof von Winterfeldt (University of Southern California); John Ward (Sargent and Lundy); Stephen Watson (Cambridge University); Chris Whipple (Electric Power Research Institute); Richard Wilson (Harvard University).

Neither these individuals nor their institutions are in any way responsible for the content of this report. We thank them all for their stimulating and often provocative contributions to our thinking, even where we have chosen to disagree with their views.

The research for this book was supported by the Nuclear Regulatory Commission under subcontract from Union Carbide Corporation, Nuclear Division, Inc. to Perceptronics, Inc. This book was prepared as an account of work sponsored by the United States Government. Neither the United States nor the Department of Energy nor any of their employees makes any warranty, expressed or implied, or assumes any legal liability or responsibility for the accuracy, completeness, or usefulness of any information, apparatus, product, or process disclosed, or represents that its use would not infringe privately owned rights. Although written for the Nuclear Regulatory Commission, this book is not limited to or focused on risks associated with nuclear power. Many individuals from the Nuclear Regulatory Commission and Oak Ridge National Laboratory provided administrative support and invaluable scientific assistance. Specifically, we wish to thank Anthony Buhl, Raymond DiSalvo, George Flanagan, Reg Gotchy, Steven Hanauer, Allan Kenneke, Saul Levine, Fred Maienschein, Fred Mynatt, Harold Peterson, P. Riehn, David Rubinstein, John Sullivan, and William Vesely. Finally, we offer our thanks to Nancy Collins, Gerry Hanson, and Peggy Roecker for their administrative, clerical, and secretarial help.

1 How safe is safe enough?

Definition of the acceptable-risk problem

As human beings develop from infancy to maturity, they go through alternating periods of acquiring behavioral capabilities and learning how to manage them. They learn first to crawl and later where it is safe to go; they learn to speak and then struggle to have something meaningful to say. In the first stage of these processes, their decision-making costs are minimal; they just do what they can. In the second stage, their investment in managing their own behavior greatly increases; with luck the effort spent on decision making will be recouped by avoiding costly mistakes.

Society generates and masters new means of production and destruction in an analogous way. Building codes, labor unions, Underwriters Laboratories, regulatory agencies, and the Geneva Convention are all social institutions that have evolved, at least in part, to control the harmful potentials of new technological developments. The essential question with which each of these entities must grapple is, How safe is safe enough? It takes such forms as: Should there be additional containment shells around nuclear power plants? Is the carcinogenicity of saccharin low enough to allow its use? Should schools with asbestos ceilings be closed? At times, the answers are expressed in performance standards (e.g., emissions must be lower than 0.5 ppm); at times, economic formulations are used (e.g., the expected benefits of a control strategy must outweigh its expected costs); at times, specific solutions are mandated (e.g., install airbags); at times, solutions are negotiated through political processes (e.g., allowing the Tellico Dam to be completed, thereby avoiding a direct test of the Endangered Species Act); at times, the issue is finessed to avoid making an explicit decision (e.g., reducing hydrofluorocarbon emissions by stigmatizing the users of aerosol products).

Of late there has been a growing concern that however well these institutions may have served us in the past, the answers they provide to "how safe" questions are often inadequate. Some acceptable-risk decisions are simply not being addressed, in part because of vague legislative mandates and cumbersome legal proceedings, in part because there are no clear criteria by which to decide. As a result, the nuclear industry has ground to a halt while utilities wait to see if the building of new plants will be feasible, the Consumer Product Safety Commission has been unable to produce more than a few standards, observers wonder whether the new Toxic Substances Control Act can be implemented, and the Food and Drug Administration is unable to resolve the competing claims that it is allowing undue risks and stifling innovation.

Those decisions that are made often appear inconsistent. Our legal statutes are less tolerant of carcinogens in our food than in our drinking water or our air. In the United Kingdom, 2,500 times more money per life saved is spent on safety measures in the pharmaceutical industry than in agriculture (Sinclair, Marstrand, & Newick, 1972). According to some calculations, U.S. society spends about $140,000 in highway construction to save one life and $5 million to save a person from death due to radiation exposure (R. A. Howard, Matheson, & Owen, 1978).

We seem to have undergone a revolution in the creation and identification of technological hazards and in our commitment to bringing them under societal control. As a result, thousands of new chemicals, drugs, foods, machines, treatments, and processes have swamped our decision-making capability. Even taken individually, many of these hazards have imponderable features: irreversible consequences, threats to the resilience of social units, or impacts on "silent" groups (e.g., future generations, biota) that can be protected only through the largesse of powerful others. Many hazards take us into hazy areas where the facts of the matter, the shape of the problem we should be managing, and even the outcomes we want are unclear. Coping with these problems demands a decision-making revolution commensurate with the technological revolution of the last 30 years.

Acceptable risk as a decision problem

Acceptable-risk problems are decision problems; that is, they require a choice among alternative courses of action. What distinguishes an acceptable-risk problem from other decision problems is that at least one alternative option includes a threat to life or health among its consequences. We shall define *risk* as the existence of such threats.

Whether formal or informal, examination of the options in a decision problem involves the following five interdependent steps:

1. Specifying the objectives by which to measure the desirability of consequences
2. Defining the possible options, which may include "do nothing"
3. Identifying the possible consequences of each option and their likelihood of occurring should that option be adopted, including, but not restricted to, risky consequences
4. Specifying the desirability of the various consequences
5. Analyzing the options and selecting the best one

This final step prescribes the option that should be selected, given the logic of the process; thus, it identifies the *most acceptable* option. If its recommendation is followed, then that seemingly best alternative will be adopted or accepted. Of course, one need not do so unless one feels that the decision-making process was adequately comprehensive and defensible.

The act of adopting an option does not in and of itself mean that its attendant risks are acceptable in any absolute sense. Strictly speaking, one does not accept risks. One accepts options that entail some level of risk among their consequences. Whenever the decision-making process has taken into account benefits or other (nonrisk) costs, the most acceptable option need not be the one with the least risk. Indeed, one might choose (or accept) the option with the highest risk if it had enough compensating benefits. The attractiveness of an option depends upon its full set of relevant positive and negative consequences.

Deciding which of a set of options is most attractive is inherently situation specific. That is, *there are no universally acceptable options* (or risks, costs, or benefits). The choice of an option (and its associated risks, costs, and benefits) depends on the set of options, consequences, values, and facts examined in the decision-making process. In different situations, different options, values, and information may be relevant. Over time, any of a number of changes could lead to a change in the relative attractiveness of any given option: Errors in the analysis may be discovered, new safety devices may be invented, values may change, additional information may come to light, and so forth. Even in the same situation and at a single time, different people with different values, beliefs, objectives, or decision methods might disagree on which option is best. In short, the search for absolute acceptability is misguided.

Thus, the acceptance of a risk is contingent on many different things, including the other features of the option with which it is associated, the other options considered, and so forth. One could use the term *acceptable risk* to refer to the risk associated with the most acceptable option in a particular decision problem. However, it may be quite difficult to bear in mind the context upon which such a choice is based in its full richness. Fearing that the term "acceptable risk" will tend to connote absolute rather than contingent acceptability, we have chosen to use it only as an adjective, describing a kind of decision problem, and not as a noun describing one feature of the option chosen in such a problem. Hence, we shall refer to "acceptable-risk problems" and not to "acceptable risks."

Illustrations

A decision-making perspective offers a common language for treating some recurrent issues in acceptable-risk problems, as shown in Figures 1.1 to 1.4. Assume that a single individual is empowered to make each decision, that all risks and costs can be identified, characterized, and assessed with certainty, and that the benefits of all the options are identical. The options differ only in

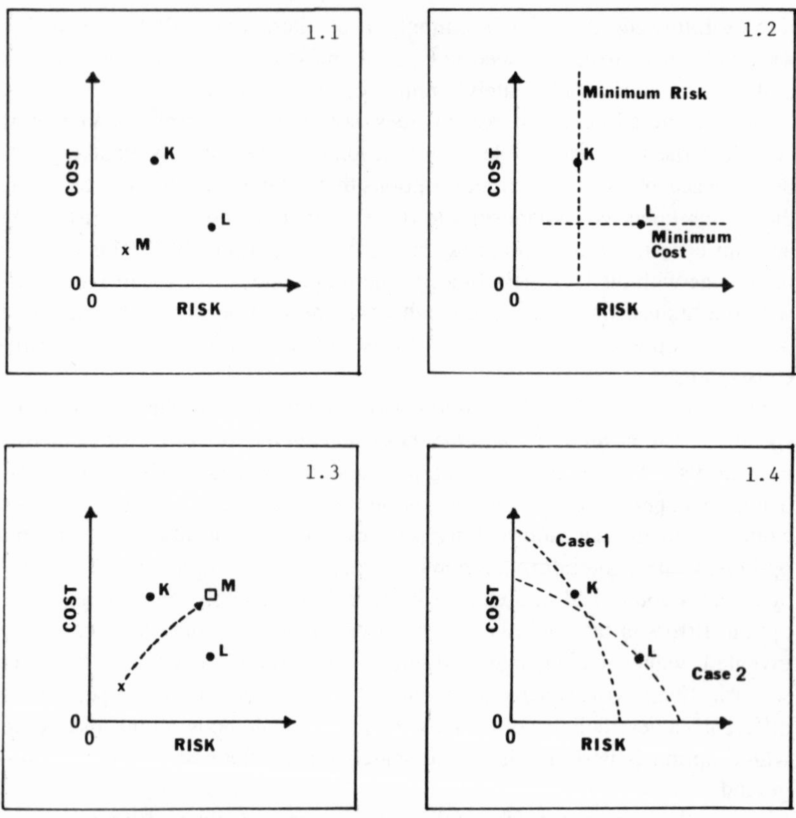

Figures 1.1–1.4. Exemplary choices among alternative risky options. Figure 1.1 shows the effect of the options considered on the choice made; Figure 1.2 shows the effect of the decision makers' values; Figure 1.3 shows the effect of changing information; Figure 1.4 shows the effects of more complicated preferences.

their cost and level of risk; 0 is the best level for each of these dimensions. As concrete examples, consider an individual choosing among automobiles or among surgical procedures that differ only in cost and risk.

Figure 1.1 shows how the set of options considered affects the choice of the most acceptable option. If K and L are the only options available, then the choice is between high cost with low risk (K) and low cost with high risk (L). The level of risk accepted would then be that level associated with either K or L, depending on which was chosen. If another option having lower cost and lower risk (M) became available, then it should be preferred to either K or L. The risk accepted would then be the level associated with the new option.

Figure 1.2 illustrates how determination of the most acceptable option depends upon decision makers' objectives. If the goal is minimizing risk, then option K would be chosen. Minimizing cost, on the other hand, entails the choice of option L and its higher level of risk.

Figure 1.3 relaxes the assumption of perfect knowledge. New information drastically alters the decision maker's appraisal of the costs and risks of M. Had M already been selected, then the accepted level of risk would prove to be much higher than that originally anticipated. If the decision had yet to be made, then the choice would revert to K or L, with their associated risk levels.

The decision rules used in Figure 1.2, minimize cost and minimize risk, were rather simplistic. The two broken-line indifference curves in Figure 1.4 present more believable preferences. Each point on such a curve would be equally attractive to an individual whose preferences it represents. Case 1 reflects a willingness to incur large costs in return for small reductions in risk. By this criterion, option K is preferred to L; the cost saving of L is achieved at the price of too great an increase in risk. Indeed, this individual would prefer K even if L's cost was zero. Case 2 reflects less willingness to increase costs in exchange for reduced risk; option L is now the best choice.

Apparently easy solutions

Viewing acceptable-risk problems as decision problems also helps illuminate the flaws in some simplistic solutions. For example, it may be tempting to claim that no risk should be tolerated. However, the decision-making perspective forces one to ask, What is the cost of absolute safety? Applied strictly, total abhorrence of risk could lead to rather dubious decisions, such as preferring option A to option B in Figure 1.5, thereby incurring great cost for a minor reduction in risk.

Rather than paying for safety, one might propose doing without the substance, activity, or technology in question. A decision-making perspective requires one to ask what option is to be chosen in its stead. When that option has risks of its own, the gain in safety may prove illusory. For example, if diabetics have a need for sweeteners, banning saccharin may eliminate one possible cancer risk in return for increased risk from the consumption of sugar.

A variant of the desire for absolute safety is the unqualified insistence that the chosen option be as safe as possible. Option C in Figure 1.6 provides less risk than option D, but at a large incremental cost. Most people would tolerate some small increase in risk for a large reduction in cost (at least if those bearing the risk also received the cost savings).

Another simplification calls for expressing the answer to, How safe is safe enough? by a small number (like 10^{-7}) representing the maximum allowable probability of some important adverse consequence. Figure 1.7 illustrates one situation in which this solution would appear inappropriate. Suppose that

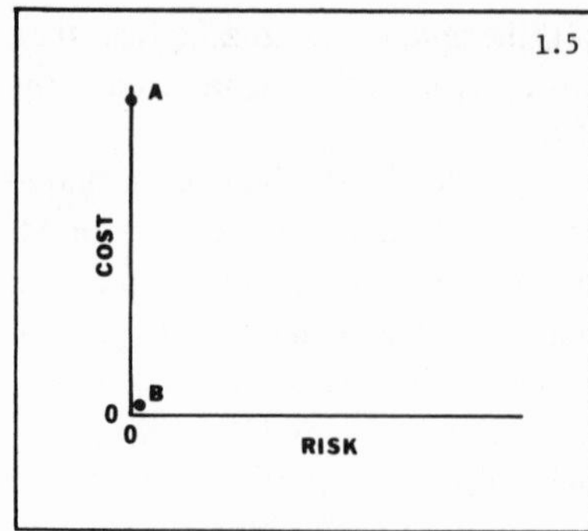

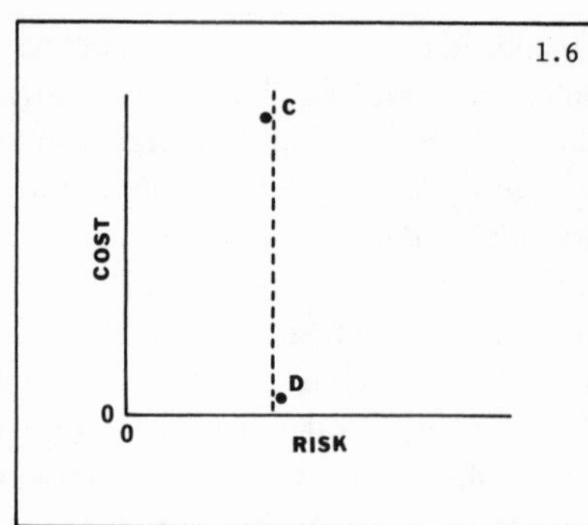

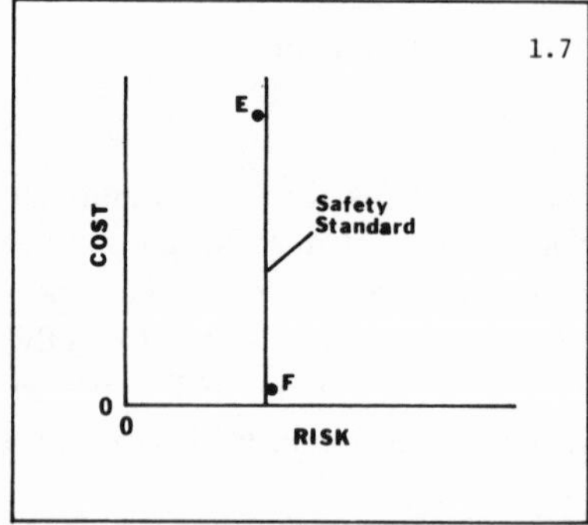

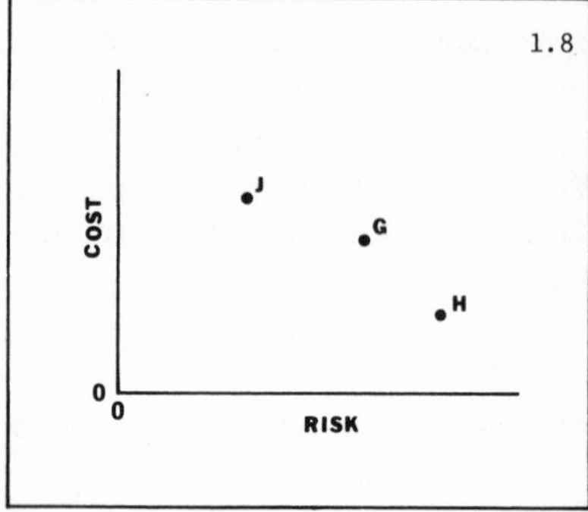

Figures 1.5–1.8. Exemplary choices among risky options, clarifying the pitfalls of some seemingly easy solutions. Figure 1.5 shows an implication of wanting no risk; Figure 1.6 shows an implication of deciding that the option adopted should be as safe as possible; Figure 1.7 considers the adoption of an absolute standard for maximum allowable risk; Figure 1.8 shows an implication of specifying fixed risk-benefit tradeoffs.

options E and F lie just on opposite sides of the designated standard, and that E costs substantially more than F. In practice, most people might prefer F to E despite the fact that F is above the safety standard.

A more sophisticated solution is to specify fixed value tradeoffs between cost and risk. For example, one could adopt any safety measure costing less than $1 million per expected life saved. But Figure 1.8 suggests that that, too, could be an oversimplification. When risk is very high, one might be willing to incur great cost to reduce it. Thus, one might prefer G to H even though the shift to G doubles the cost in order to reduce the risk by only one-fourth. At the same time, one might be more reluctant to pay for added safety when the risks are low. Thus one might not prefer J to G even though that shift buys more safety for less cost than the change from H to G. Such preferences are consistent if one feels that different value tradeoffs are appropriate at different levels of risk.

Overview

There are many candidates for the role of *the* approach to choosing among risky options. In this book we seek to focus the debate over the alternative approaches by presenting each approach in a common conceptual and evaluative framework, and to provide a critical guide clarifying (a) the political and epistemological assumptions made by each approach, (b) the manner in which each approach copes with the generic problems confronted in risk-related decision making, and (c) the degree to which each approach fits into the real world within which hazards are managed, with its vested interests, fallible humans, and institutional stodginess.

Chapter 1 has offered a basic framework for conceptualizing acceptable-risk questions as decision problems. Chapter 2 analyzes the generic complexities of acceptable-risk problems with which any approach must contend; in doing so, it defines our universe of inquiry. Chapter 3 develops a set of criteria for evaluating approaches; it also presents a taxonomy of approaches based on the different notion of rationality underlying each. Chapters 4, 5, and 6 first characterize a specific family of approaches by how it addresses the generic complexities described in Chapter 2, and then apply to it the evaluative criteria of Chapter 3. Chapter 7 assesses the overall strengths and weaknesses of the approaches, as well as their relative ability to meet the challenges posed by particular kinds of acceptable-risk problems. Chapter 8 summarizes our findings; Chapter 9 presents recommendations for public policy. Finally, Chapter 10 offers an agenda for research needed to improve society's decision-making capacity.

Defenders of government regulation often argue that one of its main benefits is *technology forcing,* that is, creating challenges for developers and encouraging them to produce technical innovations sooner rather than later. The analogous claim is made that hazardous technologies have the hidden benefit of *society forcing,* or stimulating new institutional forms and managerial techniques. By giving society new capabilities, technologies may prompt it to be more sophisticated about where it is going.

Summary

Answering the question, How safe is safe enough? means making a choice among alternatives. Thus, acceptable-risk problems are decision problems.

The risk associated with the most acceptable option might be defined as an acceptable risk. However, that definition ignores the conditional, context-dependent nature of the choice. Decision makers using different decision rules, believing different information, or considering different options could make quite different decisions regarding what options (and associated risks) to accept. As a result, there are no universally acceptable options (or risks). In particular, no level of risk can be specified such that risks less than that level are acceptable and risks greater than that level are unacceptable.

2 Why is it so hard to resolve acceptable-risk problems?

Five generic complexities

Chapter 1 used a decision-making framework to conceptualize acceptable-risk problems. The specific examples given (in Figures 1.1 to 1.8), however, were abstractions designed to illustrate basic principles rather than to represent actual decision-making problems. Chapter 2 attempts to characterize real acceptable-risk decisions by identifying five generic complexities that they present: (a) uncertainty about how to define the decision problem, (b) difficulties in assessing the facts of the matter, (c) difficulties in assessing the relevant values, (d) uncertainties about the human element in the decision-making process, and (e) difficulties in assessing the quality of the decisions that are produced.

The discussion of these problems indicates that even the most straightforward aspects of decision making (e.g., defining the problem or assessing the decision maker's values) are often fraught with difficulties if not technically impossible. These complexities are the facts of life for acceptable-risk problems, and any formal or informal approach designed to resolve such problems must contend with them. Later chapters will assess various approaches to acceptable-risk decisions according to how, if at all, they address these five complexities.

Uncertainty about problem definition

The problem definition establishes the universe of discourse for the decision-making process. It determines the options and consequences to be considered and the kinds of information and uncertainty to be taken into account. In many cases, the decision has effectively been made once the definition is set. Unfortunately, however, problem definition is often given only cursory attention in discussions of acceptable risk.

Where is the decision?

Decision-making methodologies often assume that decision problems have clear definitions and that the problems are resolved at fixed points in time by identifiable individuals. Case studies of actual decisions suggest that, more typically, decisions evolve over time as various actors make incremental changes in existing policies or create new options (e.g., March & Shapira, in press; Peters, 1979). Some observers would argue that decisions *should* be made in this decentralized, trial-and-error fashion. For example, by leaving the problem definition fluid, one is better able to incorporate the insights one may have while thinking about the problem (Comar, 1979a). Vague definitions may also help opposing parties to reach compromises that would be impossible were they forced to be more explicit. On the other hand, without an explicit definition, it is hard to apply deliberative decision-making methods or to know just what (or whose) problem is being solved.

What is the hazard?

The decision to decide whether a technology's risks are acceptable implies that, in the opinion of someone powerful, it may be too dangerous. Such issue identification is itself an action with potentially important consequences. Putting a technology on the decision-making agenda can materially change its fate by attracting attention to it and encouraging the neglect of other hazards. For example, concern about carbon-dioxide-induced climatic change (Schneider & Mesirow, 1976) changes the status of fossil fuels vis-à-vis nuclear power.

After an issue is identified, the hazard in question must still be defined. Breadth of definition is particularly important. Are military and nonmilitary nuclear wastes to be lumped together in one broad category or do they constitute separate hazards? Did the collision of two jumbo jets at Tenerife represent a unique miscommunication or a large class of pilot–controller impediments? Do all uses of asbestos comprise a single industry or are brake lining, insulation, and so forth to be treated separately? Do hazardous wastes include residential sewage or only industrial solids ("A look at human error," 1980)? Grouping may convert a set of minor hazards into a major societal problem, or vice-versa. Lead in the environment may seem worth worrying about, but lead solder in tunafish cans may not. In recent years, isolated cases of child abuse have been aggregated in such a way that a persistent problem with a stable rate of occurrence now appears as an epidemic demanding action.

Often the breadth of a hazard category becomes apparent only after the decision has been made and its implications experienced in practice. Some categories are broadened, for example, when precedent-setting decisions are applied to previously unrelated hazards. Other categories are narrowed over time as vested interests gain exceptions to the rules applying to the category in which their technology once belonged (Barber, 1979). In either case, different decisions might have been made had the hazard been better defined in advance.

A hazard, however, cannot be defined merely by its breadth. As shown in Figure 2.1, hazards begin with the human need the technology is designed to satisfy, and develop over time. One can look at the whole process or only

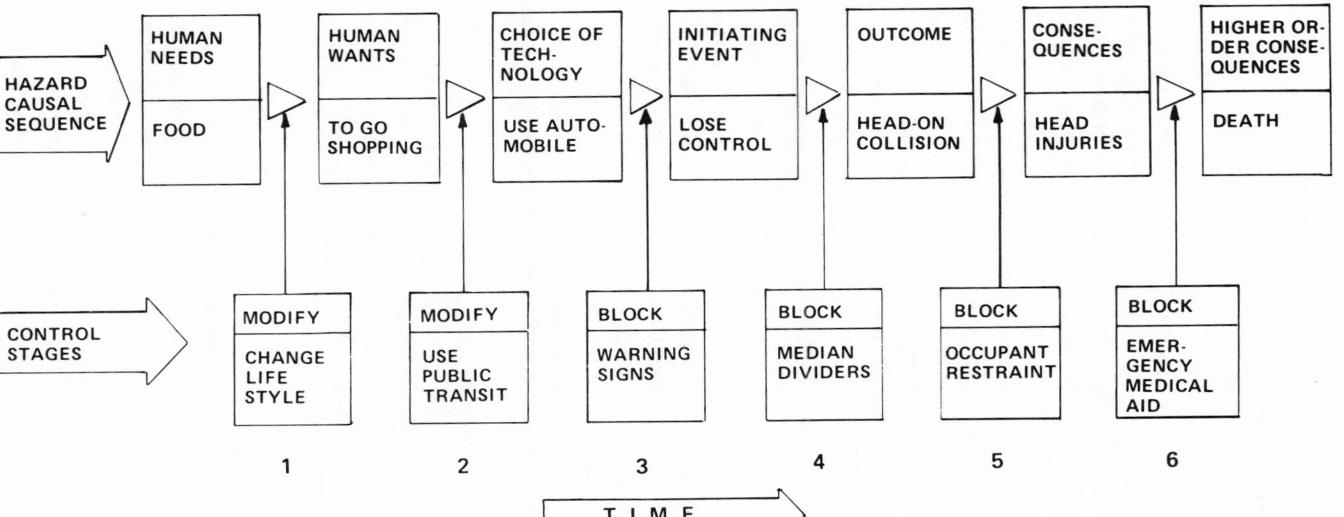

Figure 2.1. Illustration of the causal chain of hazard evolution. The top line indicates seven stages of hazard development, from the earliest (left) to the final stage (right). These stages are expressed generically in the top of each box and in terms of a sample motor-vehicle accident in the bottom. The stages are linked by causal pathways denoted by triangles. Six control stages are linked to pathways between hazard states by vertical arrows. Each is described generically as well as by specific control actions. Thus, control stage 2 would read: "You can modify technology choice by substituting public transit for automobile use and thus block the further evolution of the motor-vehicle accident sequence arising out of automobile use." The time dimension refers to the ordering of a specific hazard sequence; it does not necessarily indicate the time scale of managerial action. Thus, from a managerial point of view, the occurrence of certain hazard consequences may trigger control actions that affect events earlier in the hazard sequence. (Source: Bick, Hohenemser, & Kates, 1979)

its conclusion. The more narrowly a hazard's moment in time is defined, the fewer decision options can be considered.

What are the consequences?

In the simple decisions discussed in Chapter 1, the alternatives were evaluated on two dimensions of consequence, cost and risk, and assumed equal on all other dimensions, including benefits. The problematic, subjective aspect of the decision process appeared to be the task of determining what value tradeoffs to make.

Yet one might ask, Just what do those terms mean? With a little imagination, any consequence can be interpreted as a cost, a benefit, or a risk. Before proceeding, the set of relevant consequences must be defined. Table 2.1 lists a few possible consequence candidates. Each can readily be tied to a particular constituency; each is more compatible with some definitions of "hazard" than others; each can enhance or detract from the attractiveness of various decision options.

There are norms for selecting consequences. These reflect the balance of power at the time of their adoption and shift as the parties lobby to have their concerns better represented. The environmental movement legitimated a few new dimensions; the current "regulatory-reform" movement would like to reinterpret those dimensions or at least ensure that the traditional dimensions of corporate profit and loss are not forgotten. Some observers are worried about the neglect of consequences that are too general or far-reaching to enter the definition of any particular decision, such as genetic diversity, societal resilience, or the opportunity for experimentation (Dyson, 1975; Lepkowski, 1980; Svenson, 1979).

Removing a consequence from the official problem definition need not remove it from the agendas of the participants. Only self-confidence and self-awareness are needed to generate such thoughts as, They won't let me talk about how this option affects my freedom of choice (or the freedom of the chemical industry or my professional liability), so I'll do whatever I can to throw a wrench into the proceedings.

What action options are available?

If decisions involve choices among alternatives, much has already been decided when one defines the set of options to take seriously. In principle, one has, at the very least, a choice between adopting and rejecting a technology, keeping in mind that rejection may effectively mean going with another technology. Promoters may tend to prefer an agenda that includes only alternative versions of "go," such as Go as planned, Go after encountering opposition, and Go after cosmetic changes. Gamble (1978) describes proponents of the MacKenzie Valley pipeline as acting as though "if enough studies were done, if enough documentation presented, somehow all would be well

Table 2.1. Some possible dimensions of consequences for characterizing the attractiveness of options

Economic	Ecological
Compliance costs	Species extinction
Market efficiency (e.g., monopolization, capital formation)	Altered ecosystem balances
Innovation	Changed gene pools
Growth rate	Habitat destruction
Opportunity costs (i.e., How else could the money be used?)	Political/ethical
Physical	Centralization
Death	Inter- and intragenerational equity
Genetic damage	Personal freedom
Injury	International relations
Sickness	Societal resilience
	Psychological
	Worry, anxiety
	Confidence in the future
	Alienation

and the project could proceed as originally planned'' (p. 951). Another dimension of options opens up when one considers the possibilities of making no choice, or many incremental trial-and-error choices, or deferring one's choice to a time when more options or information may be available (Corbin, 1980).

If the hazard is defined in the broad temporal sense of Figure 2.1, one may evaluate additional options directed at each stage of hazard evolution, including modifying wants, changing the technology, and preventing initiating events. Some of the consequences in Table 2.1 suggest that instead of making decisions about individual hazards, we should be setting fundamental social policy and deriving specific hazard decisions from those general principles.

In addition to becoming unavailable practically, excluded options tend to fade from view conceptually, as facts relevant to them are not incorporated into the decision-making process. Even options that are listed can be denied serious consideration by a number of standard ploys. One is to invoke noble alternatives beside which the option pales (e.g., we can feed the starving masses or balance the budget with the money saved by rejecting that option). Another is not to study the option's properties, making them uncertain quantities from which many decision makers will shy away. A third is to invest in a competitor so heavily that the public cannot afford to let it go under; Fay (1975) calls this strategy the overcapitalization rip-off. Indeed, even modest investments in an option may be sufficient to exploit people's unwillingness to walk away from sunk costs (Teger, 1980). The fact that no major dam in the United States has been left unfinished once begun shows how far a little concrete can go in defining a problem (U.S. Government, 1976).

Implicit in any decision problem is a default option that will be adopted if the proceedings reach an impasse. When go and no-go are the only options considered, one common resolution seems to be to assume that the risks of an existing technology are acceptable until proven otherwise, whereas new technologies are denied the benefit of the doubt (Dorfan, 1980).

How should the particulars be specified?

The need for definitions does not end once the broad outlines of the problem are laid down, nor does the power of definitions to determine decisions. For example, the stringency demanded by U.S. air-quality laws hinges on how one operationalizes the "adverse health effects" they are designed to prevent (Feagans & Biller, 1979). The American Public Health Association (1980) accused the Occupational Safety and Health Improvement Act of 1980 (S.2153) of defining "'workplace' in a specious manner [allowing] employers . . . to exempt as many activities and workers from coverage as possible." Guidelines specifying that a safety option should be adopted as long as it costs less than *X* dollars per expected life saved seldom specify what year's dollars are to be used. Weinberg (1979) worries that society may be measuring the safety of nuclear power plants in terms of the absolute number of accidents of the magnitude of Three Mile Island rather than their rate per reactor-year. New and old technologies may be subject to different standards, even though the legal definition of "newness" is often moot (Krass, 1980). One can evaluate an option as it is defined by its proposers or as it is likely to emerge from the implementation process. Because many things about actual hazards are hard to prove, it may make a big difference in effective safety levels whether one has to prove compliance or noncompliance with the safety standard implicit in the proposed option. Even such seemingly unambiguous terms as dose and employed (as in "workers employed in pollution abatement" or "unemployed due to the costs of compliance") are subject to shifting definitions and uncertain interpretations (Brooks & Bailar, 1978; Walgate, 1980). In each of these cases, attention to detail is part of a winning strategy and can make an appreciable difference in the choices made and the risk accepted.

Summary

Before they can be resolved, decision problems must be defined. That process involves deciding whether a decision is to be made at all and, if so, what options and consequences are to be considered. The terms of the decision must then be further elaborated into operational form. Each of these predecision decisions can affect the choices that emerge, so much so that the outcome of the decision process may already be determined once its ground rules have been laid.

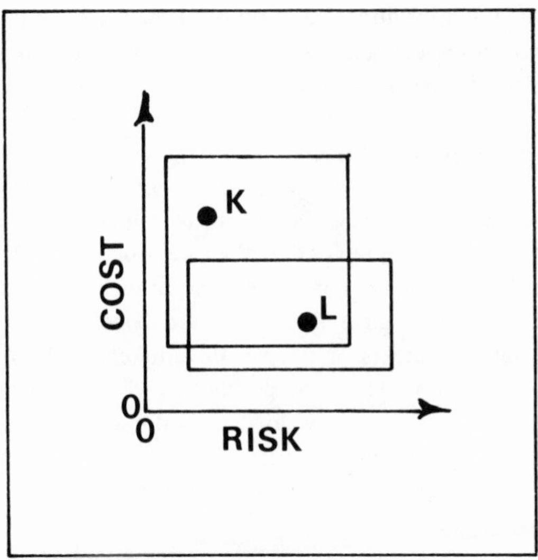

Figure 2.2. Effects of uncertainty in risk and cost estimates on the evaluation of decision options. Although the points indicate the best guess at the properties of Options K and L, each could be located anywhere in its respective rectangle. Different locations could lead to different decisions.

Difficulties in assessing the facts

Decisions emerged so readily from the schematic figures of Chapter 1 because all relevant facts were assumed to be known with precision. Our ability to *assess* what was happening allowed us to focus on *evaluating* the situation to decide what we wanted. Many acceptable-risk decisions involving familiar, recurrent hazards are similarly straightforward. For example, we may have quite accurate estimates of the costs involved and lives saved by adding a mobile trauma unit or a fire station or by mandating airbags or motorcycle helmets. Often, however, critical facts are clouded by uncertainty (as in Figure 2.2). Each point in Figure 2.2 represents a best guess at the cost and risk of an option; however, the actual levels may lie anywhere in the respective rectangles. Option K might actually be superior to option L on both dimensions or on neither.

Uncertainty about the facts should come as no surprise to any scientist involved in providing information for risk decisions. Learning the limits of data is the essence of scientific training. For the decision maker, an understanding of these limits is critical to assessing the confidence with which decisions can be made. An approach to acceptable-risk decisions can be characterized by how, if at all, it copes with such uncertainties. The full litany of relevant problems would require tutorials in the methodology of the physical, social, and biological sciences. The following sections describe a few common and critical problems.

Assessing very low probabilities

One fortunate feature of our natural environment is that the most fearsome events are quite infrequent. Major floods, disastrous plagues, and catastrophic tremors are all the exception rather than the rule. Social institutions attempt to constrain hazards of human origin so that the probability of their leading to disaster is low. However great their promised benefit, projects that might frequently kill large numbers of people are unlikely to be developed. The difficult cases are those in which the probability of a disaster is known to be low, but we do not know just how low. Unfortunately, quantitative assessment of very small probabilities is often very difficult (Fairley, 1977).

At times, one can identify a historical record that provides frequency estimates for an event related to the calamity in question. The U.S. Geological Survey has perhaps 75 years of reliable data upon which to base assessments of the likelihood of large earthquakes (Burton, Kates, & White, 1978). Iceland's copious observations of ice-pack movements over the last millennium provide a clue to the probability of an extremely cold year in the future (Ingram, Underhill, & Wigley, 1978). The absence of a full-scale meltdown in 500 to 1,000 reactor-years of nuclear power plant operation sets some bounds on the probability of future meltdowns (Weinberg, 1979). Of course, extrapolation from any of these historical records is a matter of judgment. The great depth and volume of artificial reservoirs may enhance the probability of earthquakes in some areas. Increased carbon-dioxide concentrations in the atmosphere may change climate in ways that amplify or moderate yearly temperature fluctuations. Changes in design, staffing, and regulation may render the next 1,000 reactor-years appreciably different from their predecessors. Indeed, any attempt to learn from experience and make a technology safer renders that experience less relevant for predicting future performance.

Even when experts agree on the interpretation of records, a sample of 1,000 reactor-years or calendar-years may be insufficient. If one believes the worst-case scenarios of some opponents of nuclear power, a 0.0001 chance of a meltdown (per reactor-year) might seem unconscionable. However, we will be into the next century before we will have enough on-line experience to know with reasonable confidence whether the historical probability is really that low.

Need for modeling

To the extent that historical records (or records of related systems) are unavailable, one must rely on conjecture. The more sophisticated conjectures are based upon models such as the fault-tree and event-tree analyses of a loss-of-

"IT MAY VERY WELL BRING ABOUT IMMORTALITY, BUT IT WILL TAKE FOREVER TO TEST IT."

Drawing by S. Harris. Reprinted with permission of the author. © 1976 by Sidney Harris/American Scientist Magazine.

coolant accident upon which the Reactor Safety Study was based (U.S. Nuclear Regulatory Commission, 1975). A fault tree consists of a logical structuring of what would have to happen for a meltdown to occur. If sufficiently detailed, it will reach a level of specificity for which one has direct experience (e.g., the operation of individual valves). The overall probability of system failure is determined by combining the probabilities of the necessary component failures (Green & Bourne, 1972; Jennergren & Keeney, in press).

The trustworthiness of the analysis hinges on the experts' ability to enumerate all major pathways to disaster and on the assumptions that underlie the modeling effort. Unfortunately, a modicum of systematic data and many anecdotal reports suggest that experts may be prone to certain kinds of errors

Table 2.2. Some problems in structuring risk assessments

Failure to consider the ways in which human errors can affect technological systems.
Example: Owing to inadequate training and control room design, operators at Three Mile Island repeatedly misdiagnosed the problems of the reactor and took inappropriate actions (Sheridan, 1980; U.S. Government, 1979).

Overconfidence in current scientific knowledge.
Example: DDT came into widespread and uncontrolled use before scientists had even considered the possibility of the side effects that today make it look like a mixed but irreversible blessing (Dunlap, 1978).

Failure to appreciate how technological systems function as a whole.
Example: The DC-10 failed in several early flights because its designers had not realized that decompression of the cargo compartment would destroy vital control systems (Hohenemser, 1975).

Slowness in detecting chronic, cumulative effects.
Example: Although accidents to coal miners have long been recognized as one cost of operating fossil-fueled plants, the effects of acid rains on ecosystems were slow to be discovered (Rosencranz & Wetstone, 1980).

Failure to anticipate human response to safety measures.
Example: The partial protection afforded by dams and levees gives people a false sense of security and promotes development of the floodplain. Thus, although floods are rarer, damage per flood is so much greater that the average yearly loss in dollars is larger than before the dams were built (Burton, Kates, & White, 1978).

Failure to anticipate common-mode failures, which simultaneously afflict systems that are designed to be independent.
Example: Because electrical cables controlling the multiple safety systems of the reactor at Browns Ferry, Alabama were not spatially separated, all five emergency core-cooling systems were damaged by a single fire (Jennergren & Keeney, in press; U.S. Government, 1975).

and omissions. Table 2.2 suggests some problems that might underlie the confident veneer of a formal model.

When the logical structure of a system cannot be described so as to allow computation of its failure probabilities (e.g., when there are large numbers of interacting systems), physical or computerized simulation models may be used. If one believes the inputs and the programmed interconnections, one should trust the results. What happens, however, when the results of a simulation are counterintuitive or politically awkward? There may be a strong temptation to try it again, adjusting the parameters or assumptions a bit, given that many of these are not known with certainty in the first place. Susceptibility to this temptation could lead to a systematic and subtle bias in modeling. At the extreme, models would be accepted only if they confirmed our expectations.

The lack of clear standards for the acceptability of models may have rendered inconclusive most debates arising out of Meadows, Meadows, Randers, and Behrens's *Limits to Growth* (1972) and Forrester's *World Dynamics*

Table 2.3. Lethality judgments with different response modes: geometric means

	Death rate per 100,000 afflicted				
Condition	Estimate lethality rate	Estimate number died	Estimate survival rate	Estimate number survived	Actual lethality rate
Influenza	393	6	26	511	1
Mumps	44	114	19	4	12
Asthma	155	12	14	599	33
Venereal disease	91	63	8	111	50
High blood pressure	535	89	17	538	76
Bronchitis	162	19	43	2,111	85
Pregnancy	67	24	13	787	250
Diabetes	487	101	52	5,666	800
Tuberculosis	852	1,783	188	8,520	1,535
Automobile accidents	6,195	3,272	31	6,813	2,500
Strokes	11,011	4,648	181	24,758	11,765
Heart attacks	13,011	3,666	131	27,477	16,250
Cancer	10,889	10,475	160	21,749	37,500

Note: The four experimental groups were given the following instructions: (a) Estimate lethality rate: For each 100,000 people afflicted, how many die? (b) Estimate number died: *X* people were afflicted; how many died? (c) Estimate survival rate: For each person who died, how many were afflicted but survived? (d) Estimate number survived: *Y* people died; how many were afflicted but did not die? Responses to questions (b), (c), and (d) were converted to deaths per 100,000 to facilitate comparisons.
Source: Fischhoff, Slovic, & Lichtenstein, 1981.

(1973). Everyone agreed that these examples were somewhat wrong and oversimplified, but no one could quite tell how much that threatened the conclusions.

Need for judgment

Once the system has been modeled to one's satisfaction, failure rates for the components must be assessed. Typically, some components are entirely novel or have never been used in this particular situation. Their performance parameters must be assessed by expert judgment. Thus even the components of the modeled system are not directly experienced but are revealed through the filter of educated intuition.

Two methodological issues are worth bearing in mind when deciding how much credence to attach to such intuitions. One is that experts may not have their knowledge mentally organized in the form needed by the risk assessor. A mechanic or crisis counselor may have intimate experience with many breakdowns, but still not be able to summarize this experience in bivariate frequency distributions. Second, the technical details of how one asks for quantitative judgments can greatly affect the numbers that emerge (Poulton, 1977). Table 2.3 shows the results of asking lay people about the lethality of various potential causes of death using four formally equivalent formats. Converting these judgments to a common unit revealed some dramatic differences in expressed risk perceptions. Whether expert judgments are similarly sensitive is a matter of speculation and concern (Fischhoff, Slovic, & Lichtenstein, 1981).

Need to untangle causes

Whereas some phenomena require long periods of time for an adequate sample to be accumulated, others simply take a long time to happen. For example, most carcinogens are presumed to take 15 to 30 years to exert demonstrable effects on human populations. When a substance is released into the environment, by the time we find out what we've done (or what's been done to us) it may be too late.

A concomitant of these long periods of time is that other things happen to those exposed to the substance in question. They face other carcinogens in their homes and jobs; they practice good or bad nutrition; they undergo medical tests and treatments. Epidemiological models are needed to tease out relationships. Yet there are many such models, making different simplifying assumptions and, at times, reaching different conclusions. The impossibility of collecting adequate samples of reliable data may keep epidemiological studies from ever answering such questions as, How do health effects vary with the distribution of exposure over time? Are smokers particularly susceptible? Do simple ameliorative devices, like staying indoors during smog alerts, make a difference? (Calabrese, 1978; Kozlowski, Herman, & Frecker, 1980; Marx, 1979). As suggested by Figure 2.3, even the tragic instances in which people have been exposed to roughly measurable doses of hazardous substances may not afford unambiguous answers.

An alternative to prolonged observations with humans is briefer studies of animals given large doses (relative to body weight) of suspected carcinogens. But the results are often rendered arguable by the varying cancer rates obtained with different species, modes of administration, or numbers of animals per cage; by the fact that at times the overall rate of cancer remains the same, but the pattern of tumors changes; by the use of doses much greater than would ever be contemplated for a human population; by the presence of trace carcinogens in animal feed; by the problems of drawing inferences from animals to humans; and by incompetent laboratory practices (Ames, 1979; Carter, 1979; Holden, 1979; Knapka, 1980; Smith, 1979).

Elaborating the consequences

Knowing some basic facts about the size of an effect may still leave one uncertain about the full meaning of its consequences. Assume that a millennial climate-modeling project demonstrates that the mean world temperature will change by 3 to 4 °C in the next half century, with the greatest increases in

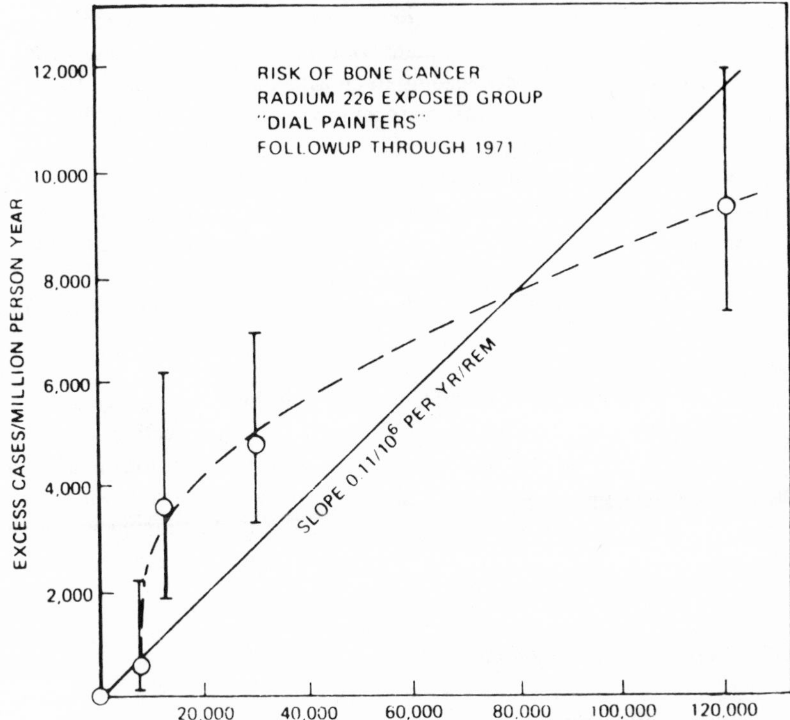

Figure 2.3. Excess cases of bone cancer observed for various levels of mean bone dose. The exposed individuals were workers who painted watches with radium during the years 1915–1935. The large error bars reflect uncertainty in the data. It is not clear whether a straight line without a threshold, or a curved line with a threshold, best fits the data. Most exposures of individuals today fall in the region below 10,000 REM mean bone dose. It is therefore critical whether the solid or dashed curve is correct. The former predicts harm at any level of exposure; the latter suggests no excess mortality below about 10,000 REM mean bone dose. By itself, the graph does not provide an answer. (The graph and its interpretation are reproduced from the Report of the Committee on the Biological Effects of Ionizing Radiation, National Academy of Sciences, 1972)

polar regions. Reduction of the temperature differential between different latitudes will, in turn, reduce atmospheric and oceanic circulation (U.S. Department of Energy, 1979; World Meteorological Organization, 1978). Although this information is much better than what can actually be obtained, it still may not be good enough to allow us to express sensible opinions about the implications of this change. Living in the world is no guarantee of being able to understand the meaning of a shift in any of its parameters (such as an increase in the median age, or the percentage of handicapped persons, or the price of fuel). We may not realize that an older population could threaten the social-security system with bankruptcy, or that a warmer climate could eliminate the hard freezes that keep pests from destroying crops in some regions, or that a near-miss at a nuclear power plant with few immediate casualties could cause an erosion of confidence leading to an acute energy shortage. The fact that such secondary or tertiary effects seem obvious once mentioned does not mean that they will be recognized at once. A National Academy of Sciences study of the effects of thermonuclear war concluded that the expected reduction of the earth's ozone shield would not imperil the survivors' food supply because many crops could survive the increased ultraviolet radiation. Only external review, however, revealed that increased radiation would make it virtually impossible to work in the fields to raise those crops (Boffey, 1975).

Summary

Understanding the facts of risk problems is complicated by a variety of complex and subtle scientific problems, of which the preceding sections offer but a sample. A comprehensive approach to acceptable-risk decisions must first acknowledge and then contend with the difficulties of knowing what risks were, are, or will be. As subsequent chapters indicate, the treatment that an approach gives to these uncertainties may prejudice its conclusions.

Difficulties in assessing values

Confronting labile values

Once we understand an effect, we must assess how desirable it is. Do we want it to happen? How badly? Such questions would seem to be the last redoubt of unaided intuition. Who knows better than an individual what he or she prefers? When one is considering simple, familiar events with which people have direct experience, it may be reasonable to assume that they have well-articulated opinions. But that may not be so in the case of the novel, global consequences potentially associated with hazards such as carbon-dioxide-induced climatic change, nuclear meltdowns, or genetic engineering. Our values may be incoherent, not sufficiently thought out. When we think about acceptable levels of risk, for example, we may be unfamiliar with the terms used in such debates (e.g., social discount rates, minuscule probabilities, megadeaths). We may have contradictory values (e.g., a strong aversion to catastrophic losses of life but an awareness that we are no more moved by a plane crash with 500 fatalities than by one with 300). We may occupy different roles in life (parents, workers, children) each of which produces clear-cut but inconsistent values. We may vacillate between incompatible but strongly held positions (e.g., freedom of speech is inviolate, but it should be denied authoritarian movements). We may not even know how to begin thinking about some issues (e.g., the appropriate tradeoff between the benefits of dyeing one's hair and a minute risk of cancer 20 years from now). Our view may change so much over time (say, as we near the hour of decision or of experiencing the consequence) that we are disoriented as to what we really think.

Competent technical analyses may tell us what primary, secondary, and tertiary consequences to expect, but not what these consequences really entail. To some extent we are all prisoners of our own experience, unable to imagine drastic changes in our world or health or relationships. What unspoken presumptions limit our ability to imagine, say, what it is like to be in a foreign culture or in prison? Such considerations move some foes of nuclear power to argue that our inability to grasp the time span during which some radioactive wastes must be stored means that we should avoid the whole business. Without basic comprehension, wise decision making is impossible.

Manipulating labile values

When people do not know, or have difficulty deciding what they want, the way a question is posed may significantly affect the values expressed, or apparently expressed, in the responses it elicits. As a result, scientists, politicians, merchants, and the media can represent issues in such a way as to induce random error (by confusing the respondent), systematic error (by hinting at what the "correct" response is), or unduly extreme judgments (by suggesting clarity and coherence of opinion that are not warranted). In such cases, the method becomes the message. If elicited values are used to guide policy, they may lead to decisions not in the decision maker's best interest, to action when caution is desirable (or the opposite), or to the obfuscation of poorly formulated views that need careful development and clarification.

An extreme but not uncommon state to be in is to have no opinion but not realize it. If we are asked a question when in that state, we may respond with the first thing that comes to mind and then commit ourselves to defending that answer while suppressing other attitudes and uncertainties. As a result, we may be stuck with impulsive or clichéd responses. The low rates of no-opinion responses reported by surveys that address diverse and obscure topics suggest that most people are capable of providing some answer to whatever question is put to them. Such responses may reflect a desire to be counted rather than deeply held opinions (Payne, 1952; Schuman & Presser, 1977).

Many of the ways in which elicitation procedures can affect responses have been known since the beginnings of experimental psychology over a century ago. Early psychologists discovered that different judgments may be attached to the same physical stimulus (e.g., How loud is this tone?) as a function of whether it is presented in the context of increasingly intense or weak alternatives, whether the set of alternatives is homogeneous or diverse, and whether the respondent makes one or many judgments. Even when the same presentation is used, different judgments might be obtained with a numerical or a comparative (ordinal) response mode, with instructions stressing speed or accuracy, with a bounded or an unbounded response set, and with verbal or numerical response labels.

Such effects seem to be as endemic to judgments of value as they are to judgments of loudness, heaviness, or taste. Although the range of these effects may suggest that the study of judgment is not just difficult but impossible, closer inspection reveals considerable underlying orderliness. Poulton (1968) discovered six "laws" of the "new psychophysics," which show how the judgmental value assigned to a physical stimulus varies systematically depending upon how the judgment is elicited. There is no reason why judgments about internal states (regarding the desirability of consequences) should be immune to these effects.

Inferring values

Judgments are sensitive to elicitation procedures because formulating a response always involves an inferential process. When confronted with an issue for which neither habit nor tradition dictates our answer, we must decide which of our basic values are relevant to that situation, how they are to be applied, and what weight each is to be given. Unless one has thought deeply about the issue, it is natural to turn to the questioner for hints as to what to say. Table 2.4 summarizes the elicitor's opportunities. The first is to decide that there is something to question. In this fundamental way, the elicitor impinges on the respondent's values. By asking about the desirability of premarital sex, interracial dating, daily prayer, freedom of expression, or the fall of capitalism, the elicitor may legitimate events that were previously viewed as unacceptable or cast doubts on events that were previously unquestioned. Opinion polls help set our national agenda by the questions they do and do not ask (Marsh, 1979). Advertising helps set our personal agendas by the questions it induces us to ask ourselves (two-door or four-door?) and those it tacitly answers (more is better).

Once the issue has been evoked, it must be given a label. In the absence of hard evaluative standards, such symbolic labels may be very important (Marks, 1977). Although the facts of abortion remain constant, individuals may vacillate in their attitude as they attach and detach the label "murder." The use of economic, psychological, or anthropocentric terminology may evoke particular modes of thought and ethical standards (Ashcraft, 1977). When asked to choose between a gamble with a 0.25 chance of losing $200 (and a 0.75 chance of losing nothing) and a sure loss of $50, most people prefer the gamble; however, when the sure loss is called an "insurance premium" most people will forgo the $50. When these two versions are presented to the same individuals, many will reverse their preferences for the two options. Table 2.5 shows a labeling effect that produced a reversal of preference with practicing physicians; most preferred program A over program B, and program D over program C, despite the formal equivalence of A and C

Table 2.4. Ways an elicitor may affect a respondent's judgments of value

Defining the issue	Changing the respondent's perspective
Is there a problem?	Altering the salience of perspectives
What options and consequences are relevant?	Altering the importance of perspectives
How should options and consequences be labeled?	Choosing the time of inquiry
How should values be measured?	Changing confidence in expressed values
Should the problem be decomposed?	Changing the apparent degree of coherence
	Changing the respondent
	Disrupting existing perspectives
	Creating perspectives
	Deepening perspectives

Source: Fischhoff, Slovic, & Lichtenstein, 1980, p. 123.

and of B and D. The labels, saving lives and losing lives, inspired very different reactions to the same problem.

People solve problems, including those that involve their own values, with what comes to mind. The more detailed, exacting, and creative their inferential process is, the more likely they are to think of all they know about a question. The briefer that process is, the more they will be influenced by what is readily accessible. Accessibility may be related to importance, but it is also related to the associations that are evoked, the order in which questions are posed, imaginability, concreteness, and other factors only loosely related to importance. For example, Turner and Krauss (1978) observed that in two simultaneous national surveys, people who had first answered six items relating to political alienation expressed less confidence in national institutions. Fischhoff, Slovic, Lichtenstein, Layman, and Combs (1978) found that people judged the risks associated with various technologies to be more acceptable following a judgment task that concerned the benefits of those technologies than following a task that concerned their risks. According to Wildavsky (1966), the very act of asking people for their own personal values may suppress their social values, as might asking them what their values are rather than what they *should be,* according to whatever ethical principles seem relevant (Tribe, 1973). Even altering the time of questioning may affect an individual's outlook. Consider people who regularly take stock of the world late at night and whose existential decisions are colored by their fatigue. Are those decisions to be trusted, or should one rely instead on the way they view their lives at high noon on a bright spring day?

Evolving values

It would be comforting to be able to say which way of phrasing value questions is the right one. Indeed, there are norms and procedures for spotting deliberately confusing or biased formulations (Payne, 1952; Zeisel, 1980). However, no procedure can guarantee a polished product when respondents

Table 2.5. Two formulations of a choice problem

Imagine that the United States is preparing for the outbreak of an unusual Asian disease, which is expected to kill 600 people. Two alternative programs to combat the disease have been proposed. Assume that the consequences of the programs are as follows:

If program A is adopted, 200 people will be saved.

If program B is adopted, there is one-third probability that 600 people will be saved, and two-third probability that no people will be saved.

Which of the two programs would you favor?

Imagine that the United States is preparing for the outbreak of an unusual Asian disease, which is expected to kill 600 people. Two alternative programs to combat the disease have been proposed. Assume that the consequences of the programs are as follows:

If program C is adopted, 400 people will die.

If program D is adopted, there is one-third probability that nobody will die, and two-third probability that 600 people will die.

Which of the two programs would you favor?

Source: Tversky & Kahneman, 1981.

start with an incoherent opinion or none at all. Different perspectives may continue to evoke opinions that refuse to converge. Indeed, life is too short and too involved for anyone to have articulated preferences on every issue that might be posed by a pollster or decision-making specialist.

When the questioner must have an answer (say, because public input is statutorily required), there may be no substitute for an elicitation procedure that educates respondents about how they might look at the question and explicates the practical implications and logical concomitants of various possible perspectives. The possibilities for manipulation in such interviews are obvious; indeed, protracted interactions with respondents are an anathema to many surveyors. However, one cannot claim to be serving respondents' best interests (i.e., letting them speak their minds) by asking a question that only touches on one facet of a complex and incomplete set of views.

Just as discussion and analysis may help to shape values, so may experience. To some extent, we come to know where we stand on complex issues by making decisions as best we can and waiting to see how well we like their consequences. Changes in attitudes toward the environment over the last decade must at least in part reflect the results of the expensive and intensive period of learning by doing that followed World War II.

Summary

The existence of a value question is no guarantee that anyone has an articulated answer. Questions must still be posed in some way and the opinions that emerge may be shaped accordingly. An approach to acceptable-risk problems must acknowledge that they inevitably involve values and that uncertainty may surround our values as well as our factual knowledge. Indeed, an approach may be designed to help us learn what we want.

Uncertainties about the human element

People create both technological hazards and the schemes for managing them. They decide what their needs are, accept technologies that address those needs, assess the risks and benefits of these technologies, use them wisely or unwisely, see or miss the need for ameliorative action when things go wrong, and so forth. As consumers, voters, legislators, regulators, operators, and promoters, people shape the world within which technologies operate and thus determine the degree of hazard that these technologies pose. Approaches to acceptable-risk decisions make assumptions about human behavior by (a) predicting lay people's perceptions of and responses to the risks they face, (b) assessing decision makers' confidence in the recommendations of the risk analysts, and (c) evaluating the quality of the technical judgments provided by experts forced to go beyond the available data.

Two contradictory assumptions can be found in discussions of human behavior. One is that people are extremely perceptive and rational (as these terms are defined by economic theory): They make the best of the marketplace, reliably operate hazardous vehicles, and respond admirably to appeals and warnings. The contrasting assumption is that people are ignorant, unreasonable, and irrational: They refuse to believe competent technical analyses, fight dirty in policy debates, and generally need to be replaced by more scientific individuals and methods. A popular hybrid assumes that people are perfect hedonists in their consumer decisions but have no understanding of broader historical, political, or economic issues.

One reason for the survival of such simplistic and contradictory positions is political convenience. People who want the lay public to participate actively in acceptable-risk deliberations need to describe the public as competent; others need an incompetent public to justify an expert or political elite. A second reason is theoretical convenience; it is hard to build models of people who are sometimes shrewd, sometimes myopic. Perhaps the need to be disciplined by systematic observation is not always felt very strongly because it is so easy to speculate about human nature and even produce a few bits of supporting evidence. Good social theory may be so rare because poor social theory is so easy (Hexter, 1971). However, speculations about human behavior, like speculations about chemical reactions, must be based on evidence. Erroneous assumptions are likely to lead to unhappy outcomes. Moreover, because such assumptions can create myths about lay people and experts and their respective roles in the decision-making process, failure to validate them may mean arrogating to oneself considerable political power.

How accurate are lay perceptions?

At first blush, assessing the public's risk perceptions would seem to be very straightforward. Just ask questions like, What is the probability of a nuclear-core meltdown? or How many people die annually from asbestos-related diseases? or How does wearing a seat belt affect your probability of living through the year? The responses can be compared with the best available technical estimates, and deviations can be interpreted as evidence of the respondents' ignorance.

Unfortunately, the elicitation effects that bedevil the study of people's values may be just as potent in affecting their judgments of risk. For example, Table 2.3 showed how choice of response mode could drastically affect lay assessments of lethality; by their choice of method, researchers could similarly affect the apparent wisdom of the respondents in observers' eyes. In addition, simply documenting gaps between the risk perceptions of experts and lay people may not produce the understanding most useful to improving societal decision making. A more insightful strategy might be to ask for each kind of risk information: (a) What are its formal properties? (b) What are its observable signs? (c) How are those signs revealed to the individual? (d) Are they contradicted, supported, or hidden by immediate experience? (e) Do people have an intuitive grasp of such information? (f) If their intuitions are faulty, what is the nature of their misunderstanding and how severe are its consequences? (g) Does natural experience highlight misunderstandings and lead to improvement?

In essence, these questions address the issue of how adequate people's cognitive skills are for coping with the information they receive. Research up to now suggests that these skills are often far from perfect. People seem to lack the intuitions and cognitive capacity for dealing with complex, probabilistic problems. As a result, they resort to rules of thumb that allow them to reduce such problems to simpler and more familiar terms. On the bright side, these strategies are quite adaptive in the sense that they always produce some answer and that answer is often moderately accurate. They are maladaptive in that they can produce erroneous judgments; furthermore, the ease with which they are applied inhibits the search for superior methods (Slovic, Fischhoff, & Lichtenstein, 1977; Tversky & Kahneman, 1974).

Figure 2.4 shows the results of a study in which educated lay people estimated the absolute frequency of 41 causes of death in the United States. These people had a pretty good idea of the relative frequency of most causes of death; moreover, quite similar orderings were revealed with different elicitation procedures, suggesting a consistent subjective scale of frequency. However, respondents underestimated the differences in the likelihoods of the

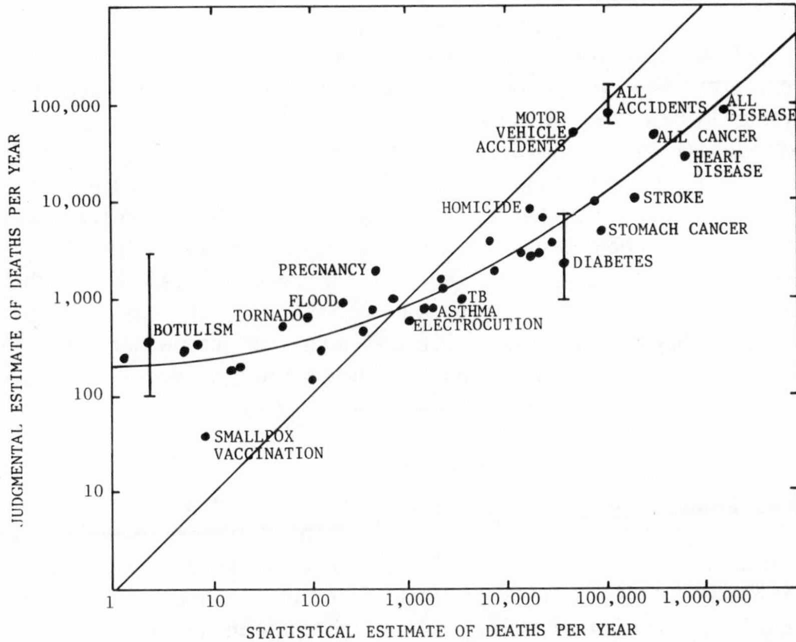

Figure 2.4. Relationship between judged frequency and statistical estimates of the number of deaths per year for 41 causes of death. If judged and actual frequencies were equal, the data would fall on the straight line. The points, and the curved line fitted to them, represent the averaged responses of a large number of lay people. Although people were approximately accurate, their judgments were systematically distorted. To give an idea of the degree of agreement among subjects, vertical bars are drawn to depict the 25th and 75th percentile of individual judgment for botulism, diabetes, and all accidents. Fifty percent of all judgments fall between these limits. The range of responses for the other 37 causes of death was similar. (Source: Slovic, Fischhoff, & Lichtenstein, 1979)

most and least frequent causes of death: Subjective estimates differed over three to four orders of magnitude, whereas the statistical estimates vary over six. In addition, respondents overestimated the relative likelihood of those causes of death that are unusually visible, sensational, and easy to imagine (e.g., homicides, accidents). In general, these hazards tend to be those that are overreported in the news media (Combs & Slovic, 1979). A similar pattern of results was found with estimates of the fatalities from various technological hazards (Slovic, Fischhoff, & Lichtenstein, 1979).

Is this performance good or bad? One possible summation is that it may be about as good as can be expected, given that these people were neither specialists in the hazards considered nor exposed to a representative sample of information. Accurate perception of misleading samples of information may also underlie another apparent judgmental bias: people's predilection to view themselves as personally immune to hazards. The great majority of individuals believe themselves to be better-than-average drivers (Svenson, 1978), more likely than average to live past 80 (Weinstein, 1979), less likely than average to be injured by tools they operate (Rethans, 1979), and so forth. Although such perceptions are obviously unrealistic, the risks look very small from the perspective of each individual's experience. Consider automobile driving: Despite driving too fast, tailgating, and so forth, poor drivers make trip after trip without mishap. This personal experience assures them of their exceptional skill and security. Moreover, the news media show them that when accidents happen, they happen to others. One could hope that people would see beyond the limits of their own minds and information; still, inability to do so need not render them incompetent to make decisions in their own behalf (Slovic, Fischhoff, & Lichtenstein, 1980).

Could the public be better informed?

If lay people have, in fact, done a good job of absorbing unrepresentative data, then it would seem that their performance might have been better had the relevant information been presented to them more adequately. The source of much technical information is, of course, the technical community. There are a number of ways in which the experts may fail to inform the public. One is by not telling the whole story about the hazards they know best because they fear that the information would make the public anxious, because dissemination is not their job, or because they have a vested interest in keeping things quiet (Hanley, 1980).

If listeners realize that the tale an expert tells is incomplete, they may discredit the expert and perhaps exaggerate the inadequacy of the presentation (If I caught that omission, how many others are there that I didn't catch?). For that to happen, however, the omission must be discovered. Some evidence suggests that typically what is out of sight is out of mind. For example, Fischhoff, Slovic, and Lichtenstein (1978) presented various versions of a diagram describing ways in which a car might fail to start. These versions differed in how much of the full diagram (shown in Figure 2.5) was left out. When asked to estimate degree of completeness, respondents were very insensitive to deletions; even omission of major, commonly known components such as the ignition and fuel systems led to only minor decreases in perceived completeness.

Experts may also exacerbate any tendency people have to deny the uncertainty associated with hazardous but beneficial technologies (Borch, 1968; Kahneman & Tversky, 1979; Kates, 1962; Lichtenstein & Slovic, 1973). In order to reduce this uncertainy, people may insist on statements of fact, not probability. Thus, just before hearing a blue-ribbon panel of scientists report being 95 percent certain that cyclamates do not cause cancer, former Food and Drug Administration Commissioner Alexander Schmidt said, ''I'm looking

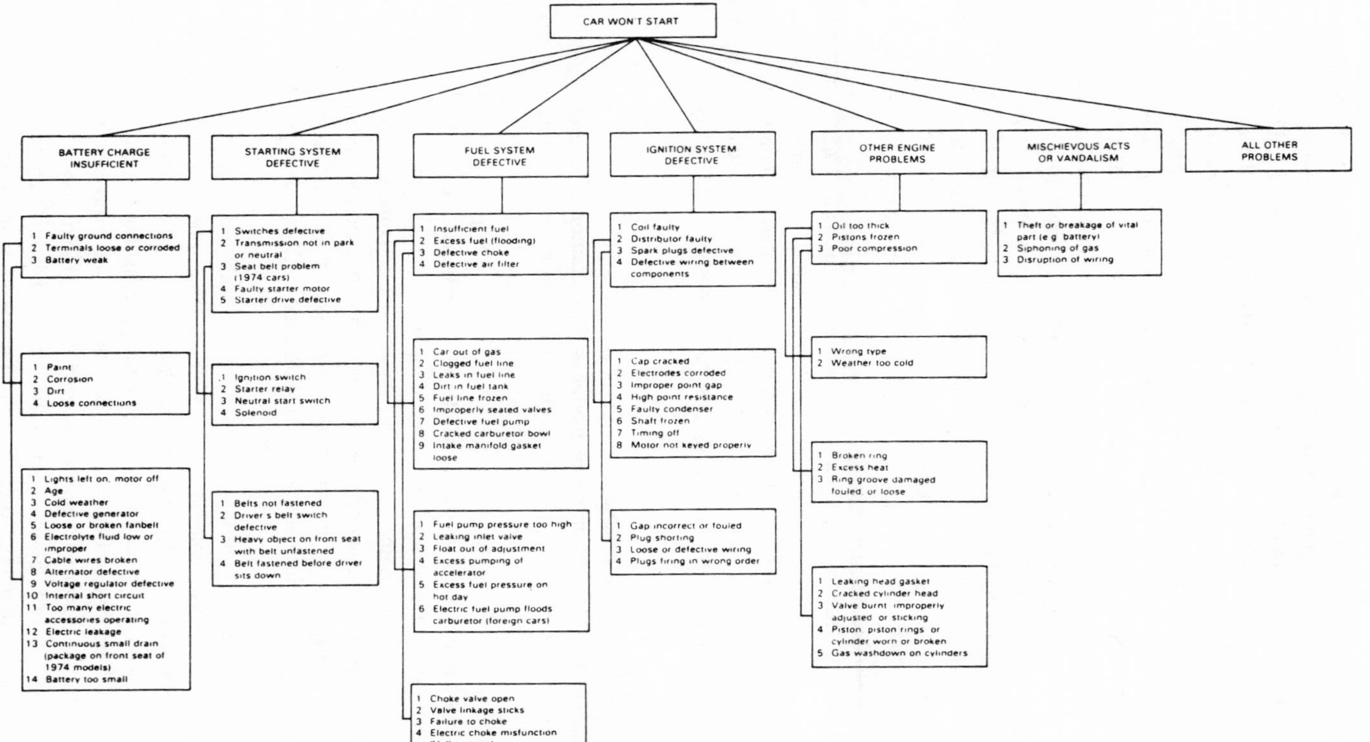

Figure 2.5. Diagram presenting reasons why a car might not start. (Source: Fischhoff, Slovic, & Lichtenstein, 1978, p. 331)

for a clean bill of health, not a wishy-washy, iffy answer on cyclamates" ("Doubts linger on cyclamate risks," 1976). Likewise, Edmund Muskie, when asked about the health effects of pollutants (David, 1975), called for "one-armed" scientists who do not respond "on the one hand, the evidence is so, but on the other hand . . ." Lord Rothschild (1978) has noted that the BBC does not like to trouble its listeners with hearing about the confidence intervals surrounding technical estimates. In this atmosphere, unduly confident, one-fisted debaters, ready to make definitive statements beyond the available data, may win the day from more evenhanded scholars. The temptation may be very great to give people the simple answers they often seem to want.

Social as well as psychological processes help to make balanced presentations an endangered genre. The constraints of legal settings (Bazelon, 1980; Piehler, Twerski, Weinstein, & Donaher, 1974), the exigencies of the political arena, and the provocations of the news media all encourage adversarial encounters that are inhospitable to properly qualified scientific evidence (Mazur, 1973). Lay people viewing such shouting matches may begin to wonder about these experts, or may feel, Since they can't agree, my guess may be as good as theirs (Handler, 1980). One positive repercussion of Three Mile Island was that for a time the public was educated in plain English about the process of nuclear-power generation and the sources of technical disputes, not just presented with conflicting assertions about overall safety.

Search for rationality

Perhaps the most reasonable assumption about people's behavior is that there is some method in any apparent madness. For example, Zentner (1979) berates the public because its rate of concern about cancer is increasing faster than the cancer rate. One rational explanation might be that people believe that too little concern has been given to cancer in the past (e.g., our concern for acute hazards such as traffic safety and infectious disease allowed cancer to creep up on us). A second is that people may realize that some forms of cancer are the only major cause of death whose rate is increasing. Just as it is counterproductive for lay people to view technology promoters as evil on the basis of insufficient or misinterpreted evidence, it is counterproductive for promoters to view lay people as misinformed and irresponsible on similar grounds.

Other apparently irrational behavior can be attributed to the rational pursuit of officially unreasonable objectives. For example, one may choose to reject the problem definition deemed reasonable by the presenting body. Consider an individual who is opposed to increased energy consumption but is asked only about which energy source to adopt or where to site proposed facilities. The answers to these narrower questions provide a de-facto answer to the broader question of growth. Such an individual may have little choice but to fight dirty, engaging in unconstructive criticism, poking holes in analyses supporting other positions, or ridiculing opponents who adhere to the more narrow definition.

Another source of apparent irrationality is opposition to reasonableness itself. The approaches to acceptable-risk decisions discussed in this book all make the political-ideological assumption that our society is cohesive enough and has enough common goals that its problems can be resolved through reason and without struggle. Although such a get-on-with-business orientation will be pleasing to many, it will not satisfy those who believe that the decision-making process should mobilize public consciousness. Their response may be a calculated attack on what they see as narrowly defined rationality.

Experts are fallible

Studies or anecdotes showing the fallibility of lay judgment are frequently cited as evidence for reducing the role of lay people in the risk-assessment process (e.g., Bradley, 1980; N. Howard & Antilla, 1979; Segnar, 1980; Starr & Whipple, 1980). This argument often presumes that experts are immune to judgmental biases. Certainly, their fund of substantive knowledge tells them where to look for information and how to recognize possible solutions (De Groot, 1965; Larkin, McDermott, Simon, & Simon, 1980). However, many risk problems force experts to go beyond the limits of the available data and convert their incomplete knowledge into judgments usable by risk assessors. In doing so, they may fall back on intuitive processes much like those of lay people. Some research evidence is presented below, mostly taken from studies in which scientists could have calculated the probabilities of events (had they been versed in statistical theory as well as their area of substantive expertise) but chose to rely on their intuitions.

Insensitivity to sample size. In an article entitled "Belief in the Law of Small Numbers," Tversky and Kahneman (1971) showed that statistically sophisticated individuals may expect small samples to represent the populations from which they were drawn to a degree that can only be assumed with much larger samples. As a result, they gamble their research hypotheses on small samples, place undue confidence in early data trends, and underestimate the role of sampling variability in causing results to deviate from expectations (offering, instead, causal explanations for discrepancies). In a survey of standard hematology texts, Berkson, Magath, and Hurn (1939–1940) found that the maximum allowable difference between two successive blood counts was so small that it would normally be exceeded by chance 66 to 85 percent of the time. They mused about why instructors often reported that their best students had the most trouble attaining the desired standard (see also Cohen, 1962, 1969).

Capitalization on chance. The ability to detect valid signals in the presence of noise is a crucial scientific intuition. Chapman and Chapman (1969; also Mahoney, 1979) have found that scientists' expectations may be so strong that they see anticipated signals even in randomly generated data. A related tendency is formulating such complicated theories that with a little creative interpretation any imaginable set of data can be viewed as being consistent with them (O'Leary, Coplin, Shapiro, & Dean, 1974). Indeed, similar problems confront attempts to validate even well-formulated theories such as fault-tree analyses. Trees and events may be so complicated that one cannot tell if an observed event actually fell into one of the categories posited by the analysis.

The converse occurs when scientists have no theory, but only a conviction that something interpretable must be happening in an observed set of important data. It is of course generally true that given a set of events (e.g., environmental calamities) and a large enough set of possible explanatory variables (antecedent conditions), one can always devise a theory for retrospectively predicting the events to any desired level of accuracy. The price one pays for such overfitting is shrinkage, that is, failure of the theory to work on a new sample of cases. The frequency and vehemence of warnings against such "correlational overkill" suggest that this bias is quite resistant to even extended professional training (Armstrong, 1975; Campbell, 1975; Crask & Perreault, 1977; Kunce, Cook, & Miller, 1975). Even when one is alert to such problems, it may be difficult to assess the degree to which one has capitalized on chance. For example, as a toxicologist, you are "certain" that exposure to a certain chemical is bad for one's health. You compare workers who do and do not work with it in a particular plant for bladder cancer, but obtain no effect. So you try intestinal cancer, emphysema, dizziness . . . until you finally get a significant difference in skin cancer. Is that difference meaningful? Of course, the way to test these explanations or theories is by replication on new samples. That step, unfortunately, is seldom taken and is often not possible for technical or ethical reasons (Tukey, 1977).

Regression to the mean. When one observes events drawn from a population with a constant mean and variance, extreme observations tend to be followed by less extreme ones. Such regression to the mean is statistically but not intuitively obvious (Kahneman & Tversky, 1973). One depressing failure by experts to appreciate this fact may be seen in Campbell and Erlebacher's (1970) article "How Regression Artifacts in Quasi-Experimental Evaluations Can Mistakenly Make Compensatory Education Look Harmful." Upon retest, the performance of the initially better students tends to be lower. Similar misinterpretations may occur whenever one asks only limited questions, such as whether environmental-management programs have weakened strong industries or reduced productivity in the healthiest sectors of the economy.

Judging the quality of evidence. Judgmental errors may be less troublesome to effective decision making than the failure to realize the possibility of such errors. As discussed in the next section, a decision-making process might get by with rather faulty inputs as long as it acknowledges that they may be fallible. But when the top experts are generating the inputs, no one else may be knowledgeable enough to correct errors or spot unwarranted assumptions. Thus the experts must judge the quality of their own judgments. An extensive body of research suggests that lay people are overconfident in assessing the quality of their own judgment, so much so that they will accept highly disadvantageous bets based on their degree of confidence. Furthermore, this bias seems to be impervious to instructions, familiarity with the task, question format, and various forms of exhortation to be modest (Fischhoff, Slovic, & Lichtenstein, 1977; Lichtenstein, Fischhoff, & Phillips, 1977). A major culprit seems to be insensitivity to the tenuousness of the assumptions upon which beliefs are based. Table 2.2 offered some anecdotal evidence of similar insensitivity among experts. Figure 2.6 shows other examples of experts' overconfidence. The problem lies not in getting the wrong answer, but in failing to realize how great the possibility for error was. Summarizing its review of the Reactor Safety Study, the Lewis Commission noted that despite the great advances made in that study "we are certain that the error bands are understated. We cannot say by how much. Reasons for this include an inadequate data base, a poor statistical treatment, [and] an inconsistent propagation of uncertainties throughout the calculation" (U.S. Nuclear Regulatory Commission, 1978, p. vi).

Summary
However mathematical their format, approaches to acceptable risk are about people; for an approach to aid the decision-making process, it must make assumptions about the behavior and, in particular, the knowledge of experts, lay people, and decision makers. When these assumptions are unrecognized or in error, they can lead to bad decisions and distortions of the political process.

Difficulties in assessing decision quality

The four preceding sections have shown how uncertainty may surround acceptable-risk decisions: their definition, the facts they use, the values they evaluate, and the behavior of the individuals whom they describe and serve. The overall quality of the decisions that are reached is a fifth area of uncertainty. An appraisal of that quality tells consumers how much confidence they should place in the approach that was used, and it tells the purveyors of the approach whether they should try again before reaching any conclusions – by

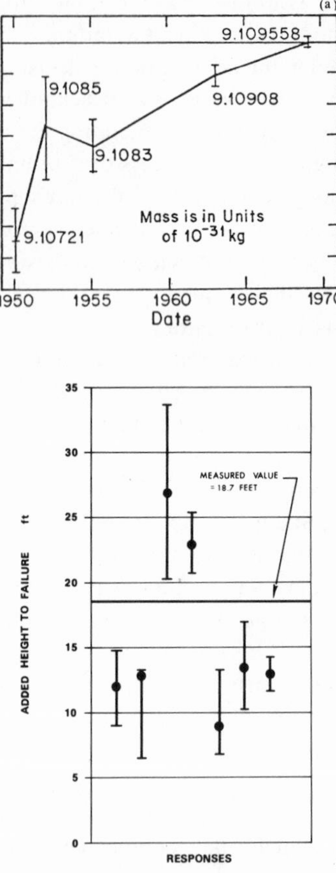

Figure 2.6. Two examples of overconfidence in expert judgment. Overconfidence is represented by the failure of error bars to contain the true value. (a) Estimates of the rest mass of the electron. (b) Estimates of the height at which an embankment would fail. Our thanks to Max Henrion for Figure a. (Sources: *a* from Taylor, 1974; *b* from Hynes & Vanmarke, 1976)

recruiting more information, assessing value issues more thoroughly, consulting additional individuals, changing the problem definition, or using an alternative method. In principle, an approach should be capable of reporting that it is not up to the task, either because the uncertainties are so great as to render its conclusions indeterminate or because crucial uncertainties remain in areas that the method does not address. When an approach fails to assess the sturdiness of its own conclusion, it implies that what it says goes, or is at least the best guess available.

The following sections survey a number of general approaches to assessing decision quality.

Sensitivity analysis

One general approach to assessing decision quality is sensitivity analysis, which has been developed by formal analysts (see Chapter 6). First, a best guess at the most acceptable option is derived from the best available estimates of the relevant facts and values. The decision-making process or computation is then repeated, using alternative estimates for uncertain components. That is, the sensitivity of the conclusions to possible errors in these estimates is tested to help determine how robust those conclusions are. In informal decision making, sensitivity analysis might take the form of such statements as, The climb may be riskier than our guide thinks, but even if it were, I'd still be willing to go.

To apply a sensitivity analysis, one must know both the locus and the possible extent of the uncertainty. For example, one would test for uncertainty arising from judgmental biases only if one were aware of and impressed by the relevant psychological findings. Judgmental biases can threaten the sensitivity analysis itself if, as suggested in previous sections, they render the analyst insensitive to omissions and overconfident about current knowledge.

A further threat arises when sensitivity analyses treat possible problems in isolation; in such cases, the analyst may have a very limited feeling for how uncertainty from different sources of error compounds. As noted by the Lewis Commission, "errors and uncertainties must be made explicit and carried through succeeding stages of the calculation to see how they affect the final conclusion" (U.S. Nuclear Regulatory Commission, 1978, p. 9). Although varying more than one parameter at a time, multivalued sensitivity analyses are complex and costly. It is too often assumed that errors in different inputs will cancel one another out rather than compound in some pernicious way (Tihansky, 1976). One situation in which this independence assumption seems doubtful is when a set of judgments is elicited with the same procedure, inducing the same perspective. By asking about preferences in a mode that uses a reference to dollar values, assessments of the importance of environmental as well as other less tangible values may be persistently deflated. Or, to take an example from the elicitation of judgments of fact, the Reactor Safety Study (U.S. Nuclear Regulatory Commission, 1975) called upon its experts to assess unknown failure rates by the "extreme-fractiles" method, choosing one number so extreme that there was only a 5 percent chance of the true rate being lower, and another so extreme that there was only a 5 percent chance of the true rate being higher. Research with a variety of other tasks and judges indicates that this technique produces particularly narrow confidence intervals, systematically exaggerating the precision of estimates (Lichtenstein et al., 1977).

Such correlated errors of recurrent biases represent a sort of analytical common-mode failure. From a technical standpoint, sensitivity analyses might be devised that could simultaneously handle the uncertainties arising from a variety of sources. Conceptually, however, it seems inappropriate to treat a persistently induced bias in subjects' responses as an error of measurement. Nor can the most sophisticated sensitivity analysis address the issue of inappropriate or incomplete problem definitions.

Error theory

An alternative to case-by-case sensitivity analyses is to develop a theory offering some general insight into how seriously the limits or uncertainties of a decision-making process imperil its conclusions. For example, Kastenberg, McKone, and Okrent (1976) found that risk assessments are as a rule extremely sensitive to how outliers (unusual observations) are treated. Thus, whether or not one takes unusual events seriously may greatly influence the decisions one reaches. On the other hand, von Winterfeldt and Edwards (1973) showed that under quite general conditions modest inaccuracy in assessing probabilities or values should not have too great an effect on decisions with continuous options (e.g., invest *X* dollars or increase production by *Y* percent). Furthermore, when one is assessing the corresponding probability for each of several alternatives on the basis of a set of common attributes (e.g., the probabilities of candidates succeeding in graduate school on the basis of attributes indicated by their scores on various tests), it often does not matter very much how one weights the different attributes (Dawes & Corrigan, 1974).

When the decision options are discrete, however (e.g., operate/don't operate), poor probability assessment can be quite costly (Lichtenstein et al., 1977). Assessment of low-probability events is particularly precarious. Modest underassessment may push the event below the threshold of concern, so that not only may nothing be done, but the event may not even be monitored in the future. Overassessment of one event may lead to the neglect of other areas that warrant vigilance. Many advocates of nuclear power believe that its risks have been exaggerated to the detriment of concern over the effects of fossil fuels, such as carbon-dioxide-induced climatic changes or acid rain.

These fragments of an error theory allow one to make some general statements as to which problems are likely to be most difficult and which conclusions are most likely to be suspect. An approach for acceptable-risk decisions could either generate its own error theory or adjust itself so that these quality-assessment techniques could be applied.

Convergent validation

Trevelyan observed that "several imperfect readings of history are better than none at all." Sometimes, when a decision-making process is known to be

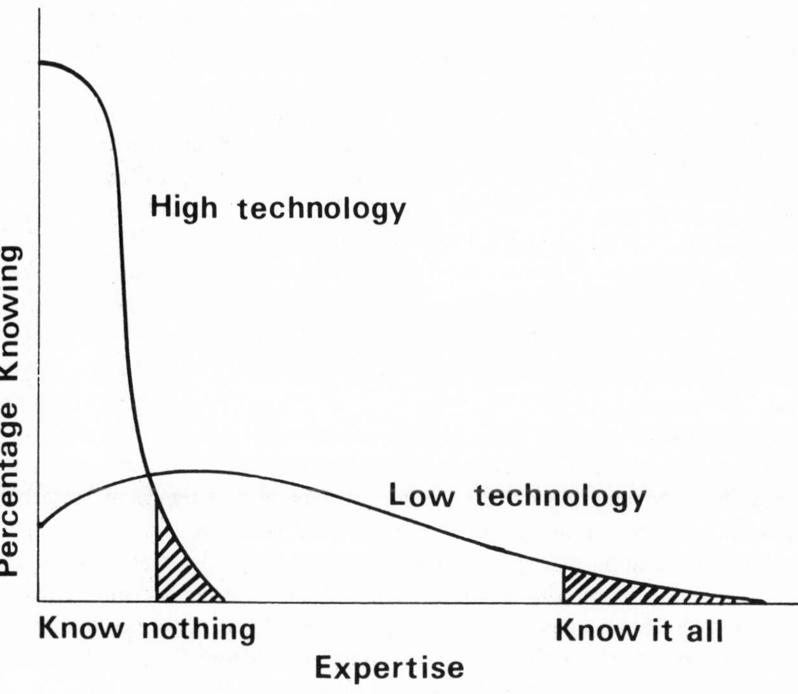

Figure 2.7. Possible distributions of expertise for simple and sophisticated technologies. The shaded area indicates the 5 percent of population who know most.

imperfect, additional methods are tried and additional experts' views are sought in the hope that they do not share common flaws. If the same conclusion is indicated, our confidence in the quality of our decisions should increase; if different results emerge, then at least we know something about the range of possibilities. Such convergent validation is akin to a sensitivity analysis in which the inputs remain the same but the method for integrating them varies.

The feasibility of this strategy hinges upon the existence of truly independent methods and opinions. A persistent threat is that conceptions and misconceptions may be widely shared within a decision-making or expert community. Studies of surprise attacks reveal that the experts, however great their number, shared the same essentially incomplete perspective (Janis, 1972; Stech, 1979). In a sense, they were all reading the situation from the same limited perspective; the better they read, the more quickly they met their demise (Lanir, 1978). Thus, even when experts or decision-making methods do agree, one must still try to determine their absolute level of wisdom. The fact that someone knows more than anyone else about a topic does not necessarily mean that the person knows very much. Figure 2.7 illustrates this point. Relative novices in automotive mechanics may understand as much about cars as "experts" understand about some sophisticated technologies. Creating a technology does not guarantee that a cadre of experts who comprehend it entirely will also be created.

Agreement may not always be desirable or reassuring. Some issues may be so complex that no one method can possibly find the right answer. In such cases, agreement may indicate that despite their exterior differences the methods share underlying assumptions and prejudices. It may seem better to adopt an interactive approach to knowledge, in which different disciplines and vested interests are encouraged to criticize one another's arguments. The emphasis would be on identifying and correcting mistakes rather than trying to produce the right answer from whole cloth. Old problems would have to be corrected until doing so stopped revealing new ones. No one would charge that the consensual positions that emerged from this process had been achieved the easy way.

But the search for disagreement can produce disagreeable situations. At times, the estimates made by a sample of experts will reveal an orderly, unimodal distribution of opinion, as represented in Figure 2.8a, which is a fictional distribution of expert assessments of a single parameter. At other times, a majority and a minority opinion will cluster around distinct means (Figure 2.8b). Such a pattern may emerge in assessments of the health effects of cigarettes (Burch, 1978), low-level ionizing radiation (Marx, 1979), or natural lead concentrations (Settle & Patterson, 1980). Whereas a measure of central tendency might serve to summarize opinions in the first case, aggregation seems more dubious in the second. The mean, for example, may represent an opinion held by no one, whereas the mode or median would obscure the disagreement.

Track record

Approaches are adopted in part because they have the reputation of producing good decisions. Yet it is hard to find systematic field studies of the efficacy of any approaches to resolving acceptable-risk questions. The absence of studies may reflect the difficulty of establishing whether a society is better off for having adopted an approach.

For example, one need not endorse an approach simply because it is widely accepted. People may favor an approach because it embodies their world outlook, produces congenial recommendations, or provides their livelihood. Nor need one reject an approach because it has produced some notably bad outcomes. The muckraker in us is drawn to stories of welfare cheaters or overregulated hazards. However, any fallible decision-making system produces errors of both kinds; for every hazard handled too harshly, there is one (or several or a fraction of a hazard) that is treated too lightly by the same imperfect system. In fact, the two error rates are tied in a somewhat counterin-

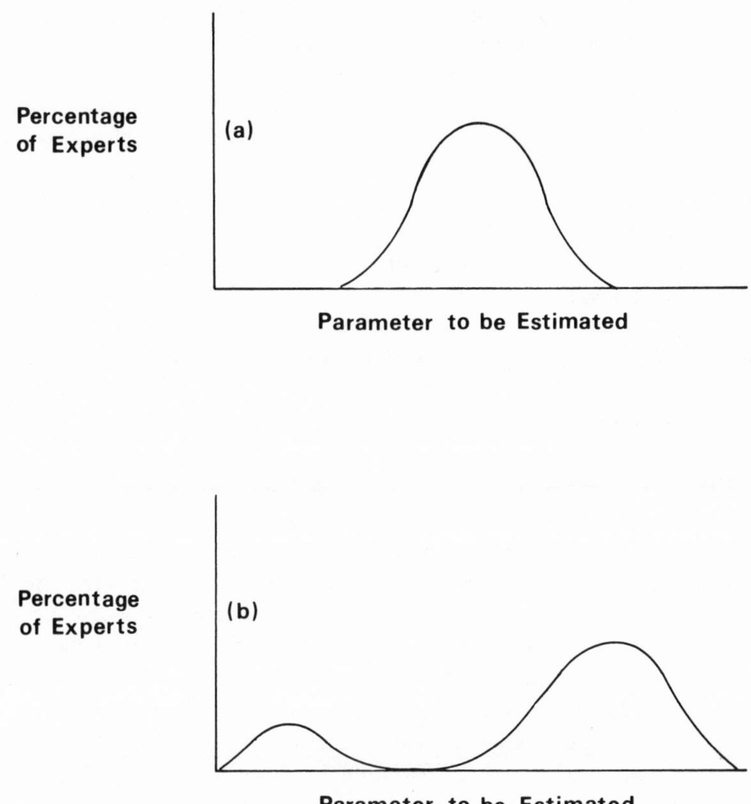

Figure 2.8. Distribution of expert opinion: (*a*) Consensual issues; (*b*) split opinions.

tuitive fashion that depends upon the quality of the decision-making process and on the available resources (Einhorn, 1978). Before criticizing the regulatory system for coming down too hard (or too easily) in a few cases, one should ask whether there are not too *few* horror stories of that type, given the ratio of errors of commission to errors of omission.

In other problems, apparently poor decisions may be the result of efficaciously solving the wrong problem. For example, the decision-making process that led Ford Motor Company to reduce costs in manufacturing the Pinto's fuel system received much criticism, especially after the company had lost a $125 million settlement. The validity of such criticism depends upon the problem to which that decision-making process was applied. If it was purely a matter of profits, then a guaranteed saving of $11 on each of 10 million Pintos would make the risk of a few large lawsuits a more reasonable gamble. Since the judgment was reduced to $6 million upon appeal, the company may have come out ahead financially in the short run (although the impact of the adverse publicity might affect that assessment). The decision must be evaluated differently if Ford was trying to decide among alternative ways to improve safety–including, for example, leaving the fuel tank unchanged and passing the saving on to consumers who might be able to use it more efficaciously to reduce other risks in their lives.

These evaluations of Ford's approach to making acceptable-risk decisions were dependent on knowing what problem Ford was trying to solve as well as how things turned out after the decision was made. Although such outcome knowledge is thought to confer the wisdom of hindsight on our judgments, its advantages may be oversold. In hindsight, people consistently exaggerate what could have been anticipated in foresight. They not only tend to view what has happened as having been inevitable, but also to view it as having appeared "relatively inevitable" before it happened. People believe that others should have been able to anticipate events much better than they actually did. They even misremember their own predictions so as to exaggerate in hindsight what they knew in foresight (Fischhoff, 1975). Although it is flattering to believe that we would have known all along what we could only know in hindsight, that belief hardly affords us a fair appraisal of the extent to which surprises and failures are inevitable. It is both unfair and self-defeating to castigate decision makers who have erred in fallible systems, rather than admitting to that fallibility and doing something to improve the system. According to Wohlstetter (1962), the lesson to be learned from Pearl Harbor is not that American intelligence was incompetent, but that we must "accept the fact of uncertainty and learn to live with it. Since no magic will provide certainty, our plans must work without it" (p. 401).

A further obstacle to evaluating decision-making methods is identifying their areas of proficiency. For example, banks are usually viewed as adroit decision makers. Yet this reputation may come primarily from their success in making highly repetitive and secure tactical decisions. Home mortgages are issued on the basis of conservative interpretations of statistical tables developed and adjusted through massive trial-and-error experience. Banks' ventures into more speculative realms (e.g., real-estate investment trusts in the 1960s, loans to Third World countries in the 1970s) suggest that the prowess of their methods may not carry over to more innovative strategic decisions.

Table 2.6 presents further complications in the evaluation of decision-making methods. The list is based on a study of the attempts of another helping profession, psychotherapy, to assess its own efficacy.

Summary

To guide social policy, an approach to acceptable-risk decisions must be able to assess its own limits and to inform us of that assessment. Because the methodology needed for this task is in a rather primitive state, we must rely

Table 2.6. Effects that complicate attempts to evaluate the efficacy of a decision-making method

1. The fact that practitioners have been trained in a method and claim to be carrying it out is no guarantee that they are. Assessing fidelity of implementation is crucial for knowing what is being evaluated.

2. A well-designed method may fail because of unanticipated and uncontrollable changes in the world. Thus "good method" does not necessarily imply "good outcome."

3. Sometimes decision-making methods look good because they were fortunate enough to be used at times when they could not fail. Almost everybody and every method made money in the stock market of the 1950s and early 1960s. Thus "good outcome" does not necessarily imply "good method."

4. In some cases, defining a "good outcome" is far from a trivial matter - for example, when one must weigh short-term and long-term well-being.

5. The apparent success of some methods may be attributable less to their substance than to the atmosphere they create. These "non-specific treatment effects" include reduced anxiety, increased self-confidence, and heightened attention to the problem.

6. Anecdotal evaluations are often skewed by tendencies to be influenced by professional folklore and to interpret random fluctuations as consistent patterns.

7. An evaluation can be distorted by looking only for the positive effects a method produces and ignoring possible negative effects - or by looking only for the negative effects.

Source: Fischhoff (1980b).

heavily on our own experience and intuitions. As elsewhere, these judgments can lead us astray, producing too much or too little confidence in the quality of decisions.

Can facts and values be separated?

Throughout this chapter it has been assumed that there is a clear-cut distinction between facts and values. As Hammond and Adelman (1976), Mazur, Marino, and Becker (1979), and others have argued, this distinction can be very useful in clearing the air in debates about risk, which otherwise tends to fill up with half truths, loaded language, and character assassinations. Even technical experts may fall prey to partisanship as they advance views on political topics beyond their fields of expertise, downplay facts they believe will worry the public, or make statements that cannot be falsified.

Although a careful distinction between values and facts can help prevent values from hiding in facts' clothing, it cannot assure that a complete separation will ever be possible (Bazelon, 1979; Callen, 1976). The "facts" of a matter are only those deemed relevant to a particular problem, whose definition forecloses some action options and effectively prejudges others. As discussed earlier, deciding what the problem is goes a long way to determining what the answer will be. Hence, the "objectivity" of the facts is always conditioned on the assumption that they are addressing the "right" problem, where "right" is defined in terms of society's best interest, not the interest of a particular party. The remainder of this section examines how our values determine what facts we produce and use, and how our facts shape our values.

Values shape facts

Without information, it may be hard to arouse concern about an issue, to allay fears, or to justify an action. But information is usually created only if someone has a use for it. That use may be pecuniary, scientific, or political. Thus we may know something only if someone in a position to decide feels that it is worth knowing. Doern (1978) proposed that lack of interest in the fate of workers is responsible for the lack of research on the risks of uranium mining; Neyman (1979) wondered whether the special concern with radiation hazards has restricted the study of chemical carcinogens; Commoner (1979) accused oil interests of preventing the research that could establish solar power as an energy option. In some situations, knowledge is so specialized that all relevant experts may be in the employ of a technology's promoters, leaving no one competent to discover troublesome facts (Gamble, 1978). As noted in the discussion of decision quality, if one looks hard enough for, say, adverse effects of a chemical, chance alone will produce an occasional positive finding. Although such spurious results are likely to vanish when studies are replicated, replications are the exception rather than the rule in many areas. Moreover, the concern raised by a faulty study may not be as readily erased from people's consciousness as from the scientific literature (Holden, 1980; Kolata, 1980; Peto, 1980). A shadow of a doubt is hard to remove.

Legal requirements are an expression of society's values that may strongly affect its view of reality. Highway-safety legislation affects accident reports in ways that are independent of its effects on accident rates (Willson, 1980). Crime-prevention programs may have similar effects, inflating the perceived problem by encouraging victims to report crimes (National Academy of Sciences, 1976). Although it is not always exploited for research purposes, an enormous legacy of medical tests has been created by the defensive medicine engendered by fear of malpractice. Legal concerns may also lead to the suppression of information, as doctors destroy "old" records that implicate them in the administration of DES to pregnant women in the 1950s, employers fail to keep "unnecessary" records on occupational hazards, or innovators protect proprietary information (Lave, 1978; Pearce, 1979; Schneiderman, 1980).

Whereas individual scientists create data, it is the community of scientists and other interpreters who create facts by integrating data (Levine, 1974). Survival in this adversarial context is determined in part by what is right (i.e., truth) and in part by the staying power of those who collect particular data or want to believe in them. Scrutiny from both sides in a dispute is a valuable safeguard, likely to improve the quality of the analysis. Each side tries to eliminate erroneous material prejudicial to its position. If only one side scrutinizes, the resulting analyses will be unbalanced. Because staying with a problem requires resources, the winners in the marketplace of ideas may tend to be the winners in the political and economic marketplace.

Facts shape values

Values are acquired by rote (e.g., in Sunday school), by imitation, and by experience (Rokeach, 1973). The world we observe tells us what issues are worth worrying about, what desires are capable of fruition, and who we are in relation to our fellows. Insofar as that world is revealed to us through the prism of science, the facts it creates shape our world outlook (Appelbaum, 1977; Henshel, 1975; Markovic, 1970; Menkes, 1978; Shroyer, 1970). The content of science's facts can make us feel like hedonistic consumers wrestling with our fellows, like passive servants of society's institutions, like beings at war with or at one with nature. The quantity of science's facts (and the coherence of their explication) may lower our self-esteem and enhance that of technical elites. The topics of science's inquiries may tell us that the important issues of life concern the mastery of others and of nature, or the building of humane relationships. Some argue that science can "anaesthetize moral feeling" (Tribe, 1972) by enticing us to think about the unthinkable. For example, setting an explicit value on human life in order to guide policy decisions may erode our social contract, even though we set such values implicitly by whatever decisions we make.

Even flawed science may shape our values. According to Wortman (1975), Westinghouse's poor evaluation of the Head Start program in the mid-sixties had a major corrosive effect on faith in social programs and the liberal ideal. Weaver (1979) argues that whatever technical problems may be found with Inhaber's (1979) comparison of the risks of different energy sources, he has succeeded in creating a new perspective that is dangerous to the opponents of nuclear power. Page (1978, 1981) has demonstrated how the low statistical power of many toxicological studies effectively represents a social policy that protects chemicals more than people. In designing such studies, one must make a tradeoff between avoiding either false alarms (e.g., erroneously calling a chemical a carcinogen) or misses (e.g., not identifying a carcinogen as such). The decision to study many chemicals with relatively small samples both increases the miss rate and decreases the false-alarm rate. The value bias of such studies is compounded when scientific caution also becomes regulatory caution.

Summary

Separating issues of fact and issues of value is fundamental to intellectual hygiene. Failure to do so may lead scientists to play pundit and politicians to play expert. However, commitment to this principle must not blind us to the subtle ways facts and values are intertwined as we define our problems, choose topics for study, interpret data, and react to nonscientific evidence. Science both reflects and forms social conditions.

Summary

Any approach to answering acceptable-risk questions must contend with a series of generic problems. These include (a) ambiguities in how to define the decision problem, (b) difficulties in ascertaining the facts of the matter, (c) uncertainty regarding whose values are to be represented and how they are to be elicited, (d) cognitive limitations in the people who apply the approach and in those who deliberate its recommendations, and (e) questions about how to evaluate the quality of the decision process. The following chapters appraise several approaches in the light of these problems. How each approach attempts to contend with them reveals its underlying logic. How well each succeeds indicates its viability as a guide to social policy.

3 Choosing an approach to acceptable risk: a metadecision problem

Unlike organized sports, hazard management has no "book" summarizing extensive trial-and-error experience into a set of rules for decision making. As a result, there may be as many methods for making acceptable-risk decisions as there are decision makers. Two people might agree on what risks to accept from one energy source and disagree on what risks to accept from another source, like opinionated fans watching (or playing) a game whose intricacies they have yet to understand. The sharp disputes about procedures for making acceptable-risk decisions between Lord Rothschild (1978) and the editors of *Nature* ("Rothchild's numerate arrogance," 1978) or between Herbert Inhaber (1979) and John Holdren (Holdren, Smith, & Morris, 1979) suggest that we are a long way from consensus even among society's better-informed citizens. Agreement is most likely to be found among groups concerned with only a segment of acceptable-risk problems with which they have had hands-on experience. These include vested interests who have confidence in simple decision rules such as, What is good for (General Motors, wilderness, etc.) is good for America, and specialists who "know" how to make components (e.g., valves, evacuation schedules) that are safe enough. Without a unifying procedure or conceptual framework, there is no way to pass from a narrow focus to more comprehensive wisdom. Even if one trusted the market or the corporations or the environmentalists or the engineers to make some decisions within their area of expertise, one might not believe that this competence extended to more global decisions such as whether coal or nuclear power is to be preferred. Nor need one assume that expertise acquired through trial and error in the past assures any advantage in complex, novel situations. Having developed effective rules of behavior does not guarantee mastery of rules of decision making.

Given the lack of consensus about methods, it is hard to say how acceptable-risk decisions are being made today. There seems to be a variety of approaches, often with poorly articulated rationales and an idiosyncratic application that reflects transitory balances of intellectual, political, and economic power. Rather than try to describe and critique the many specific approaches, we have chosen to focus on a few archetypal approaches under which we believe the rest can be subsumed.

One basic categorization is into process-oriented and strategy-oriented approaches. With the former, one creates or chooses a process that one will use to make acceptable-risk decisions. Once a process has been chosen, it needs no further justification than that it has followed its own rules of operation. Strategy-oriented approaches are more deliberative, centralized, and public and have a more explicit logic. The market might be seen as an archetypal process-oriented approach, relying on the interaction of economic actors to produce adequate risk decisions under the assumption that products and actions that are "too risky" would not be competitive with better alternatives. Cost–benefit analysis might be seen as an archetypal strategy-oriented approach. Of course, strategy-oriented approaches are embedded in society's processes and often guide activity within them.

We have chosen to concentrate on strategy-oriented approaches. Process-oriented approaches have been far more common in the past and are generally much better understood, whereas strategy-oriented approaches are a relatively recent development.

Types of approaches

Although there are many schemes for strategic decision making, we believe that they can be organized into the three families of approaches briefly summarized in Table 3.1 and the following sections. Chapters 4 to 6 evaluate how well these families of approaches deal with the five generic complexities of risk problems described in Chapter 2, as well as how likely each is to satisfy the diverse demands of society. To best understand the properties of these approaches, we focus on the prescriptive appeal of their pure forms. Some of the approaches in use today might best be described as hybrids that mingle elements of the different pure forms. In practice, one might want to deliberately design hybrids in order to integrate what is best in the separate approaches.

Formal analysis

Formal analysis assumes that intellectual technologies can help us manage the problems created by physical technologies. Cost–benefit analysis and decision analysis are the most prominent techniques for thinking our way out of whatever troublesome situations we have created for ourselves. These approaches, both of which evolve from economic and management theory, share a number of common features:

1. Conceptualizing acceptable-risk problems as decision problems, that is, requiring a choice among alternative courses of action. For example, cost–benefit analysis attempts to identify the option with the greatest preponderance of benefits over costs.
2. A divide-and-conquer methodology. Complex problems are decomposed into more manageable components that can be studied individually and then combined to provide an overall assessment.
3. A strongly prescriptive decision rule. The components are combined accord-

Table 3.1. Three archetypal approaches to acceptable-risk decisions

Approach	Decision maker	Decision-making criterion	Locus of wisdom	Description
Formal analysis	Government	Societal optimization	Formalized intellectual processes	Formal methods of decision theory specify decisions most consistent with accepted view of facts and values
Bootstrapping	Government	Preservation of historical balance	Societal processes	Implicit standards derived from description of past or present policies are used as prescription for future action
Professional judgment	Technical experts	Professional judgment	Intuitive intellectual processes	Selected options emerge from decisions of qualified experts conforming to professional code; they may be formulated in terms of practices, performance standards, or good judgment

ing to a formalized procedure; if one accepts the assumptions underlying the analysis and its implementation, then one should follow its recommendations.

4. Explicit use of a common metric. Decisions are difficult when one must make value tradeoffs between conflicting objectives. In order to compare different consequences, formal methods reduce them to a common unit (e.g., dollar value).
5. Official neutrality regarding problem definition. These techniques are intended to be applicable to all problems with clearly delineated conquences, measurable options, and identifiable decision makers.

Purveyors of formal analysis tout its rigor, comprehensiveness, and scrutability. Skeptics wonder how often this potential is realized. Are analyses accessible to interested observers? Can all relevant consequences and options be accommodated? Don't actual applications have a more ad-hoc flavor than the theory would suggest? Critics also worry about power being concentrated in an intellectual elite, analysts failing to appreciate the organizational obstacles to implementing recommendations, and ideological biases lurking in the ostensibly neutral assumptions underlying the methods.

Bootstrapping approaches

Whatever theoretical appeal formal analysis may have, the technical difficulties of conducting an analysis have led some observers to despair of ever devising a comprehensive formula for acceptable-risk decisions. One alternative approach produces a quantitative answer without recourse to a complicated formula by first identifying and then continuing policies that have evolved over time. Proponents of this family of approaches argue that society achieves a reasonable balance between risks and benefits only through a protracted period of hands-on experience. The safety levels achieved with old risks provide the best guide as to how to manage new risks. Assuming that one has identified such an equilibrium state, the balance between costs and benefits that was achieved there should be enshrined in future decisions so that we can short-circuit the learning-and-adjustment process and, in effect, lift ourselves up by our own bootstraps.

One member of this family, the revealed-preferences approach, uses the cost–benefit tradeoffs effected by our market, social, and political institutions in the recent past as prescriptions for future balances. Another member, the natural-standards approach, looks to the geologic past; it argues that the ambient level of pollution that existed during the development of a species is the level to which that species is best suited and the level to be sought when setting future tolerances. In either case, a description of past policies is taken as a prescription for the future. The resulting policy should be consistent with existing decisions and sensitive to complex tradeoffs that are hard to accommodate in formal computations. One conceptual limitation of bootstrapping is that for new hazards, which are often the most troublesome, there may be no relevant experience to refer to. Another is that these methods pass judgment on the acceptability of individual options without explicitly considering the alternatives. One possible political limitation is bootstrapping's strong bias toward the status quo; it assumes, in effect, that whatever is (or was), is right for the future.

Professional judgment

Another response to the possibility that there is no one formula for determining "how safe is safe enough?" is to rely on the judgment of the technical experts most knowledgeable in a field. Professional judgment is exercised whenever a physician decides that a bypass operation or immunization program is worth the risk, a civil engineer decides that soil porosity has been adequately accounted for in the design of a dam, or a boilermaker decides not to further reinforce a potentially leaky joint. In making their decisions professionals may avail themselves of whatever formal analyses exist, but they are not bound by the conclusions of those analyses nor need they articulate the reasons for their decision. Their own "best judgment" is the final arbiter of whether to accept the risks associated with an option.

Although one might balk at even the suggestion of letting technical experts make decisions about value issues, technicians are trained to be servants responsive to their clients' needs. If society as a whole is defined as the client, professional judgment may be the best way to determine what is desirable, feasible, and practical. When professionals deliberate, they may not only incorporate existing knowledge but also create new knowledge in the form of new and better options. A physician may finesse the question of whether a drug is safe enough for a careless patient by devising a therapeutic regimen that circumvents the problem; a safety engineer may alter traffic patterns so as to increase the effective safety of an aging bridge with fixed load-bearing capacity.

Professionals may stumble in some areas where formal methods are much stronger. An inarticulable rule frustrates critics and colleagues attempting to assess the professional's performance. Under the cloak of professional wisdom may lie only a vague notion of what options are available, or even an inability to consider more than one traditional solution. Finally, there is no necessary link between expertise in a substantive area and expertise in decision making.

Similarities and contrasts

These three approaches are not as conceptually distinct as they might appear to be. Formal analyses require a large element of professional judgment, whereas professionals can (and at times do) base their judgments on formal analyses. Bootstrapping requires risk and benefit measurements that resemble those of formal analysis; for their part, formal analyses often turn to the historical record for critical measure and make assumptions that resemble those of bootstrapping. Professions are often tradition oriented, relying on previous policy making; the past that bootstrapping studies has largely been created by the actions of professionals.

The approaches also face similar difficulties. Comparing a proposed technology with a historically derived standard entails many of the same technical problems as comparing it with alternative courses of action in a formal analysis. Both bootstrapping and professional judgment may falter by failing to consider alternatives. Furthermore, the prescriptive validity of each is contingent upon its descriptive validity. Professionals should be allowed to make acceptable-risk decisions only if they do know more; evolutionary processes should be consulted only if they properly accommodate social pressures and realities. These correlated weaknesses may decrease the possibilities for hybridizing approaches to compensate for one another's vulnerabilities.

In succeeding chapters, these approaches are treated as ideal types in two senses. First, each is discussed as though it were in itself a complete approach to making acceptable-risk decisions. By taking each very seriously, perhaps even more seriously then its strongest proponent, the most light is shed on inherent strengths and weaknesses. Second, each approach is looked at not only as it is practiced today, but as it might be practiced if applied as conscientiously and deliberately as possible. From this ideal standpoint it can be determined how much potential each approach holds, how far the state of the art lags behind the state of knowledge, and how things could be done better.

Other approaches

Common to all these strategic approaches is the assumption of identifiable decision makers applying a deliberative scheme. Once we abandon that assumption, we enter the realm of process-oriented approaches, within which two other families of approaches can be identified. These might be described as embodying *market* and *procedural* logic.

A pure market approach would eliminate all centralized acceptable-risk decision making, allowing risk levels to evolve through the action of unrestrained market forces. A pure procedural approach would entail sophisticated muddling through, allowing political, economic, and intellectual pressures to shape decisions. Although the actors in either of these processes might refer to analytic, bootstrapping, or professional arguments, they would not be bound to them. Rather, these approaches rely upon the wisdom of the participants, their interaction with one another, and the feedback provided by their environment to produce relatively satisfactory results.

Although a detailed consideration of these approaches is beyond the scope of the present analysis, some mention is inevitable to the extent that the strategy-oriented approaches draw on them. For example, the conceptual adequacy of some bootstrapping and analytic approaches depends in part upon the efficacy of market processes, whereas questions of procedural logic emerge in assessing both professional and bootstrapping approaches.

Seven criteria for evaluating the acceptability of approaches to acceptable risk

In deciding which approach to use, the options include the pure-form methods described above, deliberate hybrids, and the poorly articulated, mixed methods by which decisions are being made today. In this context the do-nothing option probably translates into "do as we've been doing."

This metadecision problem of deciding how to decide is made difficult in part by the fact that the options are not directly comparable. Each approach embodies an alternative concept of how rational decisions should be made. If applied competently, each does best what it sets out to do. Rather than posing the metaphysical question, What is the best form of rationality? we have chosen to ask, Which technique best serves our interests in dealing with acceptable-risk problems? To answer that question, we have developed a set of seven evaluative criteria, representing what a society might want out of an approach. These criteria appear in Figure 3.1 and are elaborated in the remainder of this chapter. They make provision both for benign, cooperative, and responsive social environments and for highly charged controversies and hidebound institutions.

Chapters 4 to 6 analyze the three approaches in terms of how well each could, in principle, satisfy these seven criteria and how well each currently does in practice. Although such an analysis evaluates the decision options from various perspectives, it does not tell us which to choose. Unless one option surpasses the others in all respects, society must judge which criteria are most important. Such judgments may reflect personal values, legislative mandates, or the exigencies of particular situations. The approach preferred for one problem might be rejected in another situation for which its particular strengths (e.g., political acceptability) are not essential.

Comprehensive

Chapter 1 described the basic elements of acceptable-risk problems and Chapter 2 indicated the complexities these elements present to the decision maker. An effective approach should address these elements explicitly and persuasively. Failure to do so means that an approach is at best solving only part of the problem. Thus, an approach should accommodate a comprehensive problem definition, reflect the uncertainty surrounding technical issues, acknowledge the labile or conflicted nature of social values, realistically appraise the human failings confronting the decision-making and -implementing processes, and assess the quality of its own conclusions. Moreover, it should

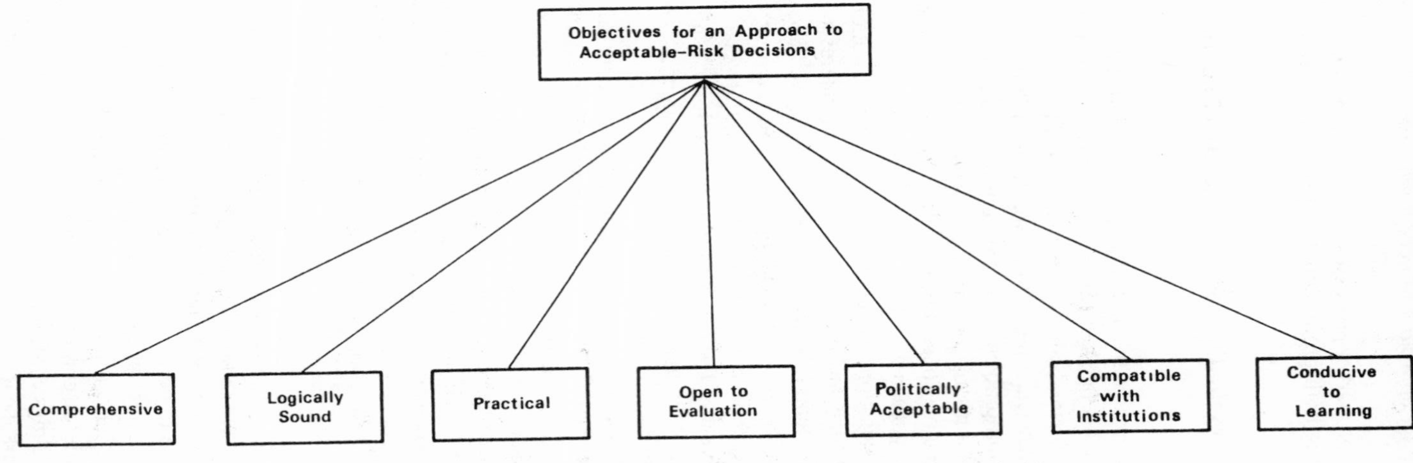

Figure 3.1. Qualities desired of an approach to making acceptable-risk decisions.

be flexible enough to accommodate new information, particularly such insights as are generated by the analysis itself.

Logically sound

Delineating the problem is not the same thing as providing guidance. Indeed, comprehensiveness alone can lead to confusion and frustration. For example, a 17-volume, 9,000-page Department of the Interior study of the environmental impacts of an Alaskan gas pipeline has been called "a monument to irrelevancy. Nowhere in it can one find a succinct analysis of the choice that must be made" (Carter, 1975, p. 363). To be useful, an approach must provide a timely and logically defensible summary of all that it encompasses. Without such summaries, "analyses" can unnecessarily discourage projects by inducing such feelings as, We shouldn't mess with anything that's so poorly understood; breed mistrust by making observers think, They must be hiding something in that morass; or encourage capricious action by seeming to suggest, We might as well go ahead with this project since there's no convincing evidence against it. Thus, a viable approach must produce some conclusion, if only, Collect more data; we don't know enough to decide at the moment.

Moreover, that conclusion must be derived via a defensible decision rule. Such a rule must be:

1. *Sensitive* to the various aspects of a decision problem; it should be possible for changes in available options, information, values, or degrees of uncertainty to lead to different recommendations;
2. *Reliable* (or reproducible) in the sense that repeated application to the same problem should produce the same result;
3. *Justifiable* in terms of either theoretical arguments demonstrating why it should lead to good decisions or empirical evidence showing that it has worked in the past;
4. *Suitable* to societal-risk problems and not uncritically imported from other realms (e.g., corporate decision making or problems not involving potential loss of life); and
5. *Unbiased* in its recommendations, not giving undue weight to any interest or type of consideration.

Practical

Like the technologies they are meant to manage, decision-making methods must not only look good on the drawing board but work in reality. It must be possible to implement the approach with real problems, real people, and real resource constraints.

Real problems. To apply an approach, one must establish a reasonable correspondence between its terms and their equivalents in reality. Cost-benefit analysis, for example, will have limited usefulness if one has no operational definition of cost. Any approach can fail if it uses one statistical summary of risk (e.g., expected annual fatalities) when policy makers are interested in others (e.g., catastrophic potential), or if it is able to consider only a fixed set of alteratives in a reality that persists in creating new ones. Like box cameras, an approach may capture a situation only when the subject is at a great distance, in the sun, and immobile (Zuniga, 1975).

Real people. Weighing strategies for the management of a technological hazard is a labor-intensive enterprise that draws upon a select pool of skilled individuals, including substantive experts (those who know most about a particular hazard) and normative experts, who specialize in decision making per se. Can enough of these special people be recruited to implement a reasonable facsimile of the approach? If experts can be found, does their task use them to best advantage? Is it too novel and complicated to be comprehended as posed? Do its questions fit the cognitive structure of their knowledge? Finally, one must ask if the experts can be trusted. In the contract-research age, problems breed putative experts. When the stakes are high enough, substantive experts are often employed by vested interests who may restrict their freedom to study certain questions and report certain answers. All of these questions become more acute as the scientific data base shrinks and experts are asked to create instant knowledge in the form of educated intuitions rather than draw upon the fund of knowledge that has undergone peer review (Fischhoff & Whipple, 1980).

Resource constraints. When decision makers admit to needing help, they typically want it immediately in order to respond to a crisis in which their traditional decision-making procedures have obviously failed. There are likely to be not only time constraints but monetary constraints as well. Decision makers may be reluctant to spend hard cash for the probabilistic benefits of good advice, which at best increases one's chances of making the right choice. When the resources needed to adequately implement an approach are lacking, one must ask whether the result is close enough to the ideal to be worth the effort.

Open to evaluation

As discussed in Chapter 2, it is hard to assess the quality of a decision or method even under the best of circumstances. An approach should not make matters worse by obscuring its internal functioning. All those whose fate it may affect have a right to ask: What are its underlying assumptions? What are its political and philosophical roots? What options does it foreclose or prejudge? Where are fact and value issues mixed? What inputs were used? What computational procedures were followed? How much uncertainty surrounds the entire enterprise?

To be valid an approach must provide answers to these questions. Many acceptable-risk questions are so complex and multidisciplinary that no one can expect to get the right answer on the first try. In such cases, an approach should indicate that it provides only an approximate answer. It should invite constructive criticism designed to spot omissions, errors, and hidden assumptions that can be treated in a subsequent iteration. But even destructive criticism may be better than none at all if it catches some problems and adds some new perspectives.

Evaluation is particularly frustrated by poorly defined procedures and lack of conceptual clarity. The unexamined approach is hardly worth using. An approach that fails to test its effectiveness and clarify its prejudices is not to be trusted.

Politically acceptable

In the harsh, politicized world within which hazards are managed, an approach can fail because it works too poorly, works too well, or works in a vacuum.

If an approach is palpably invalid (e.g., because it misdefines the problem or has no defensible integration rule), critics will readily impeach any displeasing recommendations. For example, the fuzzy logic of some environmental-impact statements exposed them to interminable litigation by dissatisfied parties (Fairfax, 1978). At the other extreme, an approach may encounter little resistance because all interested parties see how they can manipulate it to their own purposes. In time, combatants may learn to conduct their debates in, say, the nomenclature of cost–benefit analysis, transforming the technique into a rhetorical device and voiding its impact.

Conceptual strength can also bring about political complications. If an approach produces a clear, persistent, and unwanted signal, the offended parties may choose to discredit the whole approach rather than just contest one particular conclusion. Similarly, an approach that redresses an existing imbalance of power between, say, producers and consumers, employers and employees, or laborers and the general public may be attacked by the side whose advantage is jeopardized.

Finally, an approach can fail by disregarding means in its quest for the optimal end. In any participatory system, recommendations must be sold as well as generated. One aspect of that selling job is assuring people that their views have been accommodated. Usually that means asking them early and sincerely enough to affect even the problem definition. Attention to the process of decision making may also facilitate creative solutions, such as negotiated settlements between opposing parties. Moreover, a good process may itself have positive consequences, such as helping participants live and work together, reducing social alienation, and enabling participants to monitor a decision's implementation by educating them in its rationale and technical details. With a successful approach, process may be the most important product.

Compatible with institutions

For better or worse, hazards are being managed today. To accommodate this fact, a complex of social institutions has evolved. An approach's chances of survival drop as it departs from the standard operating procedures of the institutions. Even a method that satisfies the six other criteria may not get very far if no one is empowered or ordered to heed its recommendations, if legal precedents bind the hands of crucial actors, if it fails to produce the paperwork required for documentation, or if the personnel it requires are neither found nor wanted in the relevant halls of power.

On the other hand, an approach may fit too well. Institutions have their own agendas, which need not coincide with those of the people they represent. Decision makers in institutions may prefer an approach that cloaks their decisions in ambiguity, reduces their accountability, establishes a position for them in hazard management, defers difficult value questions to external "experts," or studies complex issues forever. On the other hand, they may feel uncomfortable with many of the elements of a good approach, such as extended time horizons, explicitly acknowledged uncertainty, or extensive reliance on outsiders.

Hence it may be the institution rather than the approach that needs adapting. The ability to handle an acceptable approach to acceptable-risk decisions may be a valid test of an institution's fitness for the challenges of the late twentieth century.

Conducive to learning

The attempt to satisfy these criteria encounters a fundamental conflict: the need to respect political and institutional realities without being overwhelmed by them. A final objective is to change those realities. An approach should educate its participants, eliminate opportunities for obstructionism, and build up its own record of precedents. Somehow society should become better or wiser for its adoption. Achieving that objective might even lead one to sacrifice short-term benefits, such as efficiently solving a particular problem, for the sake of long-term goals such as developing generic standards.

Several features "make" an approach conducive to learning: (a) leaving a clear record of deliberations and assumptions in order to facilitate evaluation and the accumulation of knowledge; (b) affording two-way communication between scientists and decision makers in order to improve understanding of one another's problems and uncertainties; (c) educating lay observers in order to enhance their ability to follow the process and develop expertise in the substantive issue at hand as well as the subtleties of acceptable-risk questions in general; and (d) having enough scope to be used on many problems so that users can acquire an in-depth understanding of one technique rather than a superficial grasp of various methods.

An approach can also play the more active role of recruiting talented scientists and lay people to a problem. It may alert users to recurrent oversights. Or, it may point to a set of hazards that can be managed consistently by drawing on the same decision-making effort. Yet another role is to increase the credibility of society's decision-making bodies by offering them more trustworthy tools. Perhaps the most general criterion for judging the contribution of an approach to long-term effective management is whether it raises the level of debate.

Contrasts

Like the approaches they are designed to evaluate, these criteria are not entirely independent. Weaknesses in some may preclude strengths in others. An approach is unlikely to be comprehensive if it does not get competent criticism from several perspectives. Without openness to evaluation, there is little chance of learning from experience and increasing understanding over the long term. An approach with obvious logical flaws is unlikely to fare well politically. As a result, an approach that stumbles in one respect is likely to encounter other difficulties as well.

On the other hand, some of these goals may be in conflict. It may be easier to find a logically sound integration rule by leaving out certain awkward issues and thereby sacrificing comprehensiveness. Political acceptability may require involving so many parties in the decision-making process that the responsible institutions are overwhelmed. Openness to evaluation may mean vulnerability to cheap shots and unfair criticism that damage political acceptability.

If no approach does, or even can, satisfy all of these criteria and if their respective strengths and weaknesses lie in different realms, then we must decide what we really want. The choice of an approach is inevitably a value-laden and political act that reflects our preferences for how society should look and function.

Summary

Through a review of current acceptable-risk decision making we identified three generic methods: (a) formal analysis, which decomposes complex problems into simpler ones and then combines the results into an overall recommendation; (b) bootstrapping, which uses history as a guide for setting safety standards; and (c) professional judgment, which relies on the wisdom of the best available technical experts.

Since these methods have rather different strengths and weaknesses, choosing among them requires some notion of what is important in an approach to acceptable risk. Seven evaluative criteria were described, including (a) comprehensiveness, (b) logical soundness, (c) practicality, (d) openness to evaluation, (e) political acceptability, (f) compatibility with institutions, and (g) conduciveness to learning. Determining the relative importance of these criteria is a political matter that underlies the choice of a method.

4 Professional judgment

Until they attract public attention, most hazards are managed by the technical experts most familiar with them. Engineers are responsible for designing dams, chemists for developing new solvents, and doctors for prescribing drugs. In balancing risks and benefits, these professionals rely on personal experience, accepted professional practice, and their clients' desires. *Professional judgment* is the method for integrating this assortment of facts and values.

As a hazard gains notoriety, other actors enter the decision-making arena. These newcomers depend upon the professionals for guidance as to the existence, practicality, and effectiveness of possible actions. These factors are often so ambiguous, esoteric, or complex that it is hard for a nonprofessional to deal with them independently. Once decisions have been made, professionals guide their implementation and improvise solutions to problems that arise. Thus even in politicized decisions professional judgment plays a major role, making technical experts the arbiters of acceptable risk for most hazards.

How do professionals determine acceptable risk?

A variety of codes govern the behavior of professionals in their role of hazard managers. These codes may be characterized according to two dimensions: (a) their source, and (b) their type.

Sources of standards

Perhaps the most important codes are unstated; they represent implicit standards of professionalism inculcated during training and apprenticeship. One learns what a physician, engineer, or chemist does and does not do; what are the right and wrong ways to do things; what risks one does and does not take with others' lives; when to defer to higher authorities; when to admit defeat; when to take a colleague to task; what is "good enough for government work"; what shortcuts and cost-cuts are legitimate; when one's job is done and a problem can be entrusted to others. These implicit standards are general enough to give the professional a feel for what might be acceptable actions in all of the varied problems that arise. Because they are oriented to reality and compromise, such codes may lead to different solutions to the same technical problem in different economic and political contexts.

Professionals produce explicit as well as implicit standards. For example, the American Society of Mechanical Engineers' (ASME) Boiler and Pressure Vessel Code gives technical specifics for that subsystem of nuclear-power-generating facilities. Such standards reflect a profession's collective trial-and-error experience in designing systems that work reasonably well. However, explicit balancing of costs and benefits is the exception in professional organizations.

A third source of rules is governmental agencies. Although such rules are not issued by professional societies, their technical content ensures that they are developed with the help of professionals and hence reflect their philosophy. For example, the federal code known as 10CFR50 specifies the criteria for a minimally acceptable nuclear-power-generating reactor design. Some parts were created specifically for the code; in other instances, the code defers to standards like those published by ASME.

Types of standards

The most general rules might be called *ethical standards*. Typically adopted by professional organizations, they appeal to members to adhere to some vaguely stated "principles of sound practice" and to consider the health and safety of those affected by their decisions. Although the sanctions a profession can impose on its members give these standards some teeth, they are probably too general to provide much guidance in specific situations. Because they rarely prescribe or proscribe particular behaviors, their primary function may be to legitimate fixing blame on professionals whose work has been proven to be inadequate by the occurrence of a mishap.

Quality standards are a fairly recent development. They specify the kind and intensity of effort that should go into solving a particular problem. For example, the Canadian Standards Association (1978) recommends looking at the following factors: How difficult is the design to execute? How much of the design is proven or known? How many different processes are required? How complex is the product? What are the probability and consequences of failure? Through this analysis a project is classified as requiring one of four increasingly stringent levels of quality. Each level is defined by requirements specifying the degree of detail required in the inspection, monitoring, development, design, and documentation of a project. Although loosely defined, these procedures are an important attempt to systematize a previously unarticulated area of professional judgment.

A third kind of rule, *technical (or design) standards,* specifies the nuts and bolts of how a system is to be designed. For example, 10CFR50 offers the following design parameter: "materials for bolting and other fasteners with nominal diameters exceeding 1 inch shall meet the minimum requirements of 20 mils lateral expansion and 45 ft. lbs. in terms of Charpy V-notch tests conducted at the preload temperature or at the lowest service temperature, whichever temperature is lower'' (Appendix G, Part IV, para. A4). Less explicit technical standards can be found in terms such as ''best available technology.''

Whereas technical standards specify hardware, *performance standards* specify immediate output and, in doing so, address issues that are more closely related to our real concerns (e.g., health). For example, an explication of the Clean Air Act might state that ''emissions of 1.5 ppm are permissible and we don't care how you achieve that goal'' (see Moreau, 1980). Vaguer expressions include ''with an adequate margin of safety,'' ''affording adequate protection,'' or ''avoiding adverse health effects in sensitive groups.'' Performance standards are popular because they stimulate professional creativity in the search for the most efficient way to achieve a fixed goal. Technical standards, on the other hand, may be seen as overemphasizing quality control and as too inflexible to accommodate new designs.

Preview

The following discussion characterizes professional judgment by how it addresses the five generic problems that face any approach to acceptable risk. Like the analogous discussions in Chapters 5 and 6, it accentuates the negative. Examining the failings of professional judgment seems to be the best way to clarify how it can be improved and where it is good enough to be left alone. A critical look will also help identify the reasons for the apparently increasing mistrust of our scientific and technical elites. When as venerable and valuable an organization as the American Society of Civil Engineers feels pressed to launch an advertising campaign attesting to its social worth (Florman, 1979), something is happening that should be understood. Do the problems lie in the codes that guide professional judgment, in the minds of those who implement the codes, or in the political-social-economic world within which professionals function? Unless professionals receive usable public or legislative guidance, it may be disingenuous to criticize too harshly the risk-benefit balances they strike.

Generic problems

Technical experts are an invaluable social resource, displaying knowledge, integrity, and devotion to service. The present task is to determine to what extent their competence extends to resolving societal safety issues and to what extent the constraints of their jobs allow them to exercise that expertise. Professionals answer many questions for us; can they also tell us ''How safe is safe enough?'' If they cannot provide a complete answer, how can we best exploit the partial answers they can give us?

Defining the problem

Professional socialization emphasizes service – that is, satisfying a client's perceived needs within resource limitations. Thus professionals depend upon their clients for defining the problem they are to solve. If their client's perspective is overly narrow or misconceived, whatever creativity they muster may be misapplied, and they may adroitly solve the wrong problem. For example, when the client asks for technical standards specifying the details of the official solution to a problem, alternative solutions may be ignored. When the nature of a product is specified but not who will use it, professionals may be trapped into designing systems that are prone to operator failure. Unless told about a project's social setting, professionals cannot even consider such possibilities as, This is not an engineering, but a social problem. Let's find out what aspects of current risks upset people before worrying about design issues; or, People want this project to be safer because they mistrust its promoters. Those feelings are so deep that no level of safety may be acceptable to them.

Tom Lehrer struck a responsive chord in many lay people's image of professionals with his caricature,

> Once the rockets go up, who knows where they come down?
> That's not my department, says Werner von Braun.

When professionals communicate only with technology promoters or regulators or environmentalists, they are unlikely to be responsive to the way other sectors of society would define a problem. On the other hand, balanced interaction may be easier to advocate than to achieve. Often physical isolation, professional ethics, or conditions of employment constrain professionals to a technician's role. Narrow solutions are to be expected when professionals have a limited perspective on their own role and little influence on higher-level policy making.

Some professionals may find these restrictions not so onerous. They may be more comfortable with solving problems than with defining them; they may like working within constraints rather than having to worry about delineating society's goals; they may be content with what they contribute to society by successfully managing a well-defined component problem (e.g., composing an unbiased package insert describing a drug or designing a safety valve); or they may fear the manipulative potential in helping to define one's client's problems.

In some ways, though, professionals shape the problem definition they receive by shaping the world within which they and their clients live. Their research activities establish what options can be considered. For example, some feminist groups have claimed that male control of contraception research has led to a predominance of solutions whose risks are borne by women. In this light, the recent push for better warnings about the side effects of oral contraceptives is an attempt to ameliorate the consequences of an improper problem definition. Professionals' standard practices also determine which options become readily available alternatives. For example, the low status afforded safety engineers in many work groups reduces the centrality of safety considerations and effectively forecloses consideration of safety options other than last-minute tack-ons and warning labels (Hammer, 1980).

Like other large and reasonably affluent social groups, professionals influence the diffuse debate that shapes a society's view of problems. For example, the central role of technology and technologists in American society has been linked to a deep-seated faith in *technique,* in engineered solutions to problems ranging from front-end collisions to shyness and loving (Ellul, 1969; Riesman, 1961). Professionals express their world outlook in the course of such daily activities as talking to neighbors, teaching in colleges, and serving on advisory boards. In addition, major professional organizations have lobbyists in Washington who urge that certain issues be raised, certain alternatives be considered, and certain kinds of expertise be deemed important. Not only is this a legitimate activity in a democratic society, but elected representatives rely on these lobbyists for technical information needed in formulating political opinions. Because lobbyists who get caught lying lose their audiences, there is a strong incentive for candor in these meetings. Nonetheless, it may be hard for all concerned to know when experts' assertions about the proper problem definition arise from political or pecuniary interest rather than technical expertise.

Knowing the facts

By definition, professionals know more than anyone else about the substantive issues raised by technological hazards. But the facts do not always speak for themselves. Some interpretation is required, and in providing it professionals are often caught between conflicting pressures.

Book learning versus experience. Every aspiring professional is taught a "book" of standard solutions that comprises the corpus of externally validated knowledge upon which the profession bases its claim to expertise. However, few professions allow full status to an individual who has merely been schooled. An apprenticeship is demanded in which the novice learns tricks of the trade that are not and perhaps cannot be explicitly expressed (Polanyi, 1962). These are not so much professional secrets as judgmental subtleties to which one is gradually socialized. One learns, for example, how to identify real-life problems with the recognized set of ideal types around which knowledge is organized, how much credence to give to various researchers' published work, and what deviations from approved research methods are tolerable. To the extent that expertise begins where the book leaves off, questions of validity become matters of judgment; the definitive judgments are those of a field's most experienced members.

Experience may be particularly important when conflicting versions or interpretations of the facts must be reconciled. If the authorities tend to have outmoded information or undue commitment to their own pet interpretations, the profession may reach a biased view of the facts of the matter. If the authorities are intellectually active and situated at communications crossroads, the profession may have remarkable synthetic abilities.

Clinicians versus scientists. As applied scientists, professionals are trapped between the norms of experimenters and of practitioners, between the desire to learn and innovate and the pressures of apprenticeship and licensure. This conflict can produce both healthy intellectual tensions and unbalanced beliefs. For example, because of its need to have some response to every presenting problem, the medical profession has at times adopted clinical opinions and practices supported by little research. Once practices have been adopted, however, clinicians may be legally and ethically prohibited from withholding them in order to create the comparison groups necessary to test their validity (Bunker, Barnes, & Mosteller, 1977). Fear of malpractice suits may also distort the evidence coming from the field by encouraging unnecessary clinical tests that swamp clinicians with information, thereby obscuring signals. Another systematic bias may arise from the fact that practitioners are more likely to learn that a safety margin is inadequate (through observing a failure) than that it is more than adequate.

The interaction between theory and practice also affects a clinical scientist's view of the facts by shaping the abstract models that professionals use to describe the world. Blueprints, disease models, and computerized simulations of nuclear reactors are all theoretical formulations whose relation to reality varies across situations. They represent some compromise between the scientist worried about abstracting the essential elements from complex realities and the practitioner concerned about what aspects of reality escape the model. The consummate professional understands both perspectives, being able both to devise a model of a situation and to improvise solutions to problems arising in its application. The ideal civil engineer, for example, can calculate structural tolerances by the book yet anticipate mistakes in the pouring of cement.

The apparent success of civil aviation in managing hazards might be traced to the way the insights of both field and design personnel are exploited. Pilots and aeronautical engineers typically work together to develop systems and procedures (planes, navigational aids, etc.). Even here, however, practical and theoretical knowledge are not always optimally integrated. Some "classic" aviation tragedies can be traced to the earnest efforts of designers unfamiliar with how flight really works. For example, some World War II planes used identical handles on adjacent levers serving different functions; although the levers were easy to operate, they were also easy to confuse, particularly in emergency situations requiring quick responses and offering little opportunity to correct mistakes (Fitts and Posner, 1965).

Parts versus whole. Knowledge is also shaped by the breadth of the problem one chooses to or is allowed to address. Doctors may treat only physiological symptoms of problems that are rooted in marital stress, poverty, or working conditions. Some professions, such as architecture, have specialists whose job it is to know about the broader context within which a project is set (e.g., neighborhoods, traffic patterns) and about the interactions among the parts into which it is decomposed (e.g., construction, financing, materials supply). In other professions, scant credit accrues to individuals who leave their own discipline in order to understand such interrelationships (White, 1979). When isolated, professionals may naturally come to see their piece of the puzzle as its centerpiece and denigrate the knowledge held by other fields. In the ensuing conflict, disciplines that boast the hardest facts may gain undue prominence when it comes to resolving conflicts or dividing resources. One symptom of this bias may be the preponderance of gadget-oriented solutions to safety problems as opposed to soft solutions designed to change unsafe behavior (Knoll, 1979; Sheridan, 1980).

Determinism versus uncertainty. Professionals typically manage hazards without directly expressing uncertainty about facts (M. G. Morgan, Rish, Morris, & Meier, 1978). Professionals' problem-solving orientation leads to asking first, What could go wrong? and then, How can we prevent it? Thus, uncertainty about future traffic patterns may be disregarded if one builds a bridge "strong enough to withstand any conceivable load"; precise diagnoses become less important when physicians can prescribe all-purpose antibiotics, good for whatever ails one. "Overdesign" and "large margins of safety" are other signs of coping with uncertainty without directly acknowledging it. A dam that is twice as safe as need be should not fail.

One can only speculate whether professions tend to exaggerate or underestimate these unspoken risks. In either case, the lack of explicit expression may cause problems for both science and society. Scientists lose respect for practitioners who seem to act without a word of uncertainty; practitioners lose respect for scientists who fail to produce the research they need. For nonscientists, plans that are presented without qualifications may assume the subjective status of unquestioned fact. The result may be reduced alertness to warning signs or to critics. The design and collapse of the Teton Dam revealed both of these consequences of failing to acknowledge uncertainty (U.S. Government, 1976).

Simply by virtue of its premise that even the best-designed technical system should not be presumed safe, the Reactor Safety Study (U.S. Nuclear Regulatory Commission, 1975) represented a significant step toward professional recognition of the need for treating uncertainty explicitly. The Lewis review (U.S. Nuclear Regulatory Commission, 1978) pushed professional consciousness forward by stressing that not only are there risks, but their magnitude is unknown and perhaps unknowable to the desired degree of precision. Public acknowledgment of uncertainty in one industry may encourage greater candor in other realms (e.g., Elstein, 1979; Green & Bourne, 1972; T. H. Schneider, 1979; Vanmarcke, 1977).

Assessing Values

In determining safety levels, professionals should represent the best interest of society as a whole. However, that interest is typically nebulous, conflicted, or expressed in imprecise legislative directives or legal opinions (Hoffman, 1976; B. B. Johnson, 1980). Its meaning for any particular problem must be defined, negotiated, and interpreted by the active participants, usually a mix of bureaucrats, promoters, professionals, and intervenors. To the extent that professionals must guess at society's values, they may tend to interpret ambiguities in ways that are consistent with their own values (Brown, 1965). Imputing a common set of values to any group is an exercise in stereotyping that cannot be correct in detail and is likely to be incorrect in the aggregate. The remainder of this section offers a discussion of the values that might come into play when professionals consider acceptable-risk problems.

Professional values. Like other socializing agencies, professions inculcate values as well as substantive knowledge. This process is enhanced by individuals selecting like-valued professions and professions weeding out those who see things differently. One finds few campus radicals majoring in petroleum technology and even fewer surviving (values intact) to executive rank; a similar fate may befall libertarians in the welfare system.

Although the ambience of various professions differs, a common theme is confidence in professionals' competence to handle society's technical problems and perhaps a stout faith in technological progress in general. One value that results is loyalty to colleagues, as seen in physicians' reluctance to testify against one another; a second is distrust of nonprofessional involvement, as seen in disparaging remarks about the public's ignorance and irrationality; a third is a preference for self-regulation over external supervision, as seen in battles to control state licensing. Belief that the system works may encourage deference to tradition and avoidance of innovative solutions. Professionals try to improve through modest reforms, rather than sweeping changes. One example of the power of these values to shape work practices is the intelligence community's response to charges that the like-mindedness of analysts was hampering their decision-making ability. A call for pluralism was not taken to mean that fresh perspectives were needed but that duplicate groups of like-minded analysts should be convened (Lanir, 1978).

Pecuniary interests. In order to stay in business, professionals may be motivated to err in the direction of affirmation when asked, Can you manage this hazard? The current jockeying by professions to establish a position on risk must reflect desires both to help and to have a piece of the action. It may be hard for an engineer to believe or admit that money devoted to tech-fix research could be ill spent. One constraint on optimism is legal liability. Unlike bureaucrats and analysts, professionals are often monetarily responsible for their actions. Defensive medicine and overengineering protect society's safety in order to protect professionals' finances, perhaps at the price of buying more safety than is needed.

If professionals are not to impose their own perspectives on ambiguous value issues, they need explicit guidance. Pecuniary interest would lead them to seek that guidance from those whose satisfaction is most important; if that client typically comes from one sector of the hazard-management community, that sector's values will naturally be overrepresented in the professionals' work. Since decisions must be interpreted in response to all the little problems that arise in the course of a project, influence also accrues to those with the resources to hang around the professionals as they do their work.

Conflicting values. Whether professionals' values create conflicts of interest depends upon their ability to set aside their own values and act in the best interest of society's more poorly informed citizens. Measuring that ability is difficult because the imposition of any particular set of values is often hard to detect. Not only are society's "official" values rarely explicated, but professionals' implicit values are seldom communicated as such. In many cases only the resulting design decisions or safety margins are visible, making it hard for either professionals or their critics to tell just how risks and benefits were traded off against one another. Indeed, professionals, like other people, may not really know what motivated their decisions (Nisbett & Wilson, 1977). A further complication is the tendency for value conflicts to surface in the form of debates about facts (Sjöberg, 1980). Instead of arguing about how safe nuclear plants should be (about which everyone is entitled to his or her own opinion), people argue about how safe they are (focusing on those issues that are most moot). Thus professionals' values express themselves in terms that are diverse and hard to characterize.

Uncertainties about the human element

Problem solving is easiest when one deals with components that are well understood and joined by orderly cause-and-effect relationships. Professionals, aware of that fact, are wont to concentrate on the known and knowable.

Since human behavior is seldom as predictable as mechanical or chemical reactions, humans (operators, intervenors, sponsors) may be given little thought in the problem-solving process, except perhaps to recognize their nuisance value (Norman, 1980; Sheridan, 1980). Even physicians may worry most about physiology and ignore the whole patient, who may have home and work pressures, poor nutritional habits, or lapses in taking medication.

Design. Knoll (1979) describes the consequences of focusing on hard components in engineering:

> In construction, there is a tendency to forget . . . such humans as the owner or tenant who overloads or alters the structure or the executive of a utility company who decides to assign insufficient personnel to the checking of gas and water lines which may eventually cause accidents [or] people who are only accidentally or indirectly interrelating with the structure, such as the truck driver ramming a column with his vehicle, or a Code Committee who leaves gaps or erroneous statements in the building regulations, or merely complains that a code cannot be used because it is too complicated or lacks clarity [or] the owner or promoter with a tight budget or a schedule who forces designers and builders to deliver skimpy or shoddy work, with insufficient supervision or the like. Although these individuals cannot always be reached by the legal system, structural safety is related to them and if the frequency of accidents ought to be controlled or reduced, their contribution must be dealt with, which means: designed for. (pp. 249–250).

According to Bøe (1979), overemphasizing technical issues in system design may eliminate the cues and feedback needed to give operators the "personal qualities of knowledge which are necessary to detect and control an unforeseen situation where the technical system has broken down, or more important, is about to break down" (p. 242). In the extreme case, "an installation may have reached such huge dimensions and the technical and physical chain reactions may have become so fast that life-saving equipment and contingency plans no longer are in balance with the rest of the technology creating the risks" (p. 243).

One result of technical overdesign and human underdesign is that humans are held responsible for failures over which they had no real control. For example, children or cyclists are blamed for becoming casualties in traffic accidents that occur in a world designed for adult motorists (P. Howard, 1978). Table 4.1 details some design flaws likely to lead to a misattribution of operator error should anything go wrong.

The failure of flood-control projects to appreciably reduce flood damages is another case in point (Burton et al., 1978). By eliminating frequent minor flooding, dams deny residents an appreciation of their own vulnerability and promote development of the floodplain. When a rare flood does exceed containment capacity, the damage is catastrophic. Thus, a failure of social engineering limits the value of a civil-engineering success. The National Flood

Table 4.1. Examples of design flaws observed at a nuclear power plant

1. A selection switch for boration (adding borated water, which moderates the fission reaction) has four positions: 0 to 550, 500 to 1,050, 1,550, and 2,050. The last two indications really mean "1,000 to 1,050" and "1,500 and 2,050." But that's not what they say.

2. Two digital borating controllers are side by side and look exactly the same. But the left one is for concentrating and the right one is for diluting. The operator has to remember that the decimal point is one digit *before* the end on the left controller and *after* the last digit on the right controller.

3. Water flows through seven feedwater heaters in succession. Each heater has numbered controls on the panel. The controls are numbered in inverse order to the direction of the water flow.

4. After heater 3 (above) there are three pumps, A, B, C, and after heater 7 there are two pumps. The switches for these are arranged in two rows: 3A and 3B in one row and 7A, 7B, and 3C in the other row.

5. Four meters on the left are for neutron flux, and four meters on the right are for the rate of change of neutron flux. The two on the far left correspond to the two on the far right, i.e., they are for intermediate range, and the two which are just left of center go with the two just to the right of center for source range.

6. The auxiliary feedwater meters are labeled A (on left) and B (on right). The corresponding switches are also labeled A and B, but B is on the left and A on the right.

7. There are four steam generators in this plant. There are four pen recorders to indicate temperature in the hot and cold legs of each steam generator. Each pen recorder has two pens, red and green. The first recorder on the left has red for hot 1, green for hot 2. The next one has red for cold 1, green for cold 2. The third recorder from the left has red for hot 3, green for hot 4. The right-hand recorder has red for cold 3, green for cold 4.

8. General procedures during a loss-of-coolant accident call for the operator to check whether all of the lights are lit in a matrix of check indicators. But some of the lights (which do not have lettering on them) are not supposed to be lit.

9. The valves for safety injection of coolant are all nicely arranged in a cluster. The cluster is 60 identical switches arranged 3 high by 20 wide, with only small engraved alphanumeric tags underneath to indicate which valve is which. Mostly the alphanumerics are in order—except for one lost soul which is completely out of order and a long distance away from any other switches it corresponds to functionally.

Source: Sheridan, 1980, p. 29.

Insurance Program (not without its own problems arising from unsubstantiated assumptions about behavior) was designed to overcome these difficulties by mandating sound land-use planning (Kunreuther, Ginsberg, Miller, Sagi, Slovic, Borkin, & Katz, 1978).

Lack of awareness about the human element may also prevent professionals from recognizing their own role as human operators. The growing awareness that substantive experts may not be experts in managing the risks they create has led to enhanced roles for health physicists, human-subjects review panels, and pathogen advisory groups.

Public relations. The increasing intrusion of outsiders into the professionals' realm has evoked some strong opinions about the intruders' competence. Two conflicting themes may emerge from the professional community. When the discussion concerns the need for regulation, one hears about consumer competence and how people know enough about hazards to fend for themselves in the marketplace. When the topic is public participation in hazard management, charges of ignorance and emotionalism are heard.

As discussed in Chapter 2, uncertainty about human capabilities is what makes such politically motivated interpretations possible. One can find at least anecdotal evidence for almost any assertion one would like to make about people. To take a responsible approach to the problem of apparent disagreements with lay people, the professional should ask: Is there systematic research to which I can refer? Are people acting strangely because they are solving a different problem from the one I am focusing on? Has their experience been misleading or inadequate, and might better information help to mend our disagreements? Might they see something that I haven't noticed? Might my own experience be misleading? What are the consequences of forcing people to accept solutions that they distrust, however invalid the basis of that distrust?

Professionals, like everyone else, are entitled to opinions about the behavior of society and its citizens. But these opinions, like everyone else's, should be taken with a grain of salt. In explaining why physicists seem particularly prone to the guile of parapsychology charlatans, Hyman (1980) suggested that they fail to define the limits of their professional competence. Their training gives them an extraordinary ability to discern signals in certain kinds of random error, but not in the systematic error generated by masters of deception. Scientists' judgments about people and society in general may suffer from a similar malady.

Assessing decision quality

When and how professionals evaluate the quality of their own decisions depend largely on how they resolve the various uncertainties discussed in the preceding sections. These uncertainties are the source of two major difficulties.

Characterizing solutions. If professionals did everything by the book, evaluation would be relatively easy. Not only would solutions be well characterized and well documented, but there would be some, even many replicates whose consequences could be compared and aggregated. Often, though, professionals begin with a well-defined option and then adjust it to accommodate local conditions, producing a unique, hard-to-assess design. For example, calculated load factors only approximate those in the actual dam, which evolves in response to the porosity, seismicity, esthetic, and construction constraints encountered on-site. Similarly, a physician who knows the documented rate of side effects from a drug still does not know their likelihood for a particular patient, whose ailment may be misdiagnosed, who may be taking other drugs, or who may not follow the therapeutic regimen. Indeed, the physician may choose a second-best treatment program whose risks are more predictable because it is less vulnerable to these factors. Such real-life compromises, particularly those made at the last minute, may not be well documented.

The nature of a solution and its degree of safety tend to be unclear, not only because conditions force changes in the standard solution, but because the safety of those solutions, even when adopted in toto, depends on context. A familiar coefficient, resistor, or drug may perform differently under new conditions. If knowledge about performance is like other kinds of human knowledge, those who hold it may be only vaguely aware of the untested and unexplicated assumptions upon which it rests. Successful experience with a component in some contexts may confer unjustified confidence that its performance can be predicted in other contexts. Summarizing attempts to assess the overall safety of existing or proposed systems, Knoll (1979) found that "no absolute calibration [of safety margins] has been found possible, based on rational scientific fact. The overall magnitude of the combined [safety margin] is still entirely a matter of the consolidated judgment of the code committee" (p. 254).

If every project is unique and hard to characterize and if the deliberations of professionals are hard to explicate, it is tempting to evaluate their work by the consequences of individual decisions. The complexity of many projects, however, makes it difficult to know just what has happened. When a living system responds to a treatment, one cannot always tell whether it would have recovered spontaneously. When a physical system works, one cannot always tell whether cheaper alternatives would have worked as well or even which components were overdesigned and which were being pushed to their limits. In the case of failure, this focus on concrete instances will encourage asking, What went wrong here? rather than, Are we taking reasonable gambles (or ones with reasonable failure rates)? The search for causes may become a search for a single cause (or culprit) as people try to minimize their cognitive load and to derive suggestions for future changes. Unfortunately, "to take one simple cause-effect relationship out of a complicated pattern may just as well serve to hide what actually happened as to tell the truth" (Bøe, 1979, p. 243).

Underlying such fault finding is the assumption that all problems are identifiable and correctable. Seldom is the possibility raised that the system may be so complex as to be somewhat unknowable and unmanageable; that is, at some point complexity may place an asymptote on reliability, with further safety measures as likely to introduce new problems as solve old ones. Thus the assessment of decision quality may be biased by the assumption that the problems posed are eventually solvable.

Characterizing evaluators. Among professionals' strongest values is the need for a powerful professional organization, responsible both for protecting its members' interests and for assuring the quality of their work. As the theory goes, society's loss through this restraint of trade is more than compensated for by the stringent control of technical performance that lay people could not independently monitor. Professionals bear a sort of collective responsibility that makes meaningful self-evaluation less improbable. If they do not police and occasionally punish the worst of their members, all members will suffer. If, for example, all physicians resolutely refused to testify against one another, society would take matters in its own hands, producing different, if not necessarily wiser, evaluations.

The need to protect both members as well as society is perhaps the essential contradiction that faces guilds. The financial incentives for denying past failures are so great that in structural engineering, for example, "failures are most of the time not clearly reported, a fact which relates quite closely to the practicalities of restitution and the workings of the legal system which in most cases sets the incentives against comprehensive and public reporting" (Knoll, 1979, p. 253). When a failure is admitted, it is defined as narrowly as possible (one bad actor, bad mistake, or bad beam) lest confidence in the profession as a whole be eroded. Defenses are often based upon the existence of standards that diffuse responsibility for errant acts through a profession, industry, or government. The decomposition of complex projects may leave no one directly in charge of problems that arise from the interfaces between components.

These pecuniary pressures on the evaluation process may be compounded by psychological ones. Professionals often assume enormous responsibility for other people's lives and safety. They may have to daily give others such assurance as, This pill won't kill you, or, That structural member will hold until the other ones are in place. Bearing this responsibility may require a special ability to deny or tolerate uncertainty. The multiple roles that professionals play by designing, approving, and implementing risky programs make them highly visible targets for criticism, some of it unfair (as when the hindsight bias of others works against them, or when they have been left with responsibility for making decisions that others have shirked). In reassuring others about the quality of their decisions, they may also be reassuring themselves. Doctors' frequent claims that patients do not want to know the risks they face do not seem to be supported by empirical evidence (Weinstein, 1979); but belief in these claims may help doctors cope with their own anxiety. In cost-plus enterprises, practices like overdesign and defensive medicine to some extent finesse these conflicts by making the consumer pay for the professionals' protection.

How adequate is professional judgment for resolving acceptable-risk questions?

Comprehensive

Professionals' actions embody de-facto answers to acceptable-risk questions. But these answers are no guarantee that the questions have been addressed in their full complexity (T. H. Schneider, 1979). Whether because of legal-ethical constraints or personal preference, professionals often accept a fairly narrow problem definition. They do so whenever they restrict themselves to the consequences that interest their immediate client (perhaps ignoring broader societal concerns), or to solutions within their areas of professional competence (rather than pointing the client elsewhere), or to alternate versions of the proposed technology (without seriously considering the no-go option). Indeed, judicious choice of experts is one of the best indirect ways to influence problem definition (and, hence, problem resolution).

Within these constraints, the professional is likely to invoke a comprehensive view of the technical facts and their incumbent uncertainties. Indeed, the design process may create as well as utilize knowledge. On the other hand, professionals may have only a rough idea of some of the political and economic aspects of the problems they are confronting. Thus, professional judgment is likely to afford a very comprehensive view of a restrictively defined problem.

Logically sound

It is difficult to assess the soundness of the procedures used by professionals to integrate those aspects of acceptable-risk problems that they have chosen to address. Many of their decisions are reached by judgmental processes that are inarticulate and perhaps inarticulable. In the absence of empirical studies, one can only speculate whether these processes are prone to the same problems studies have shown lay people to have in integrating diverse kinds of information. Do professionals, for example, give undue weight to considerations that are known with certainty (Kahneman & Tversky, 1979), or do their training and experience confer some special immunity from this bias?

Other decisions are reached through reliance on explicitly formulated public standards. Such standards also assure consistent decisions across the contexts in which they are applied. To the extent that standards have been evolved through trial-and-error experience with systems that provide useful feedback and an opportunity for the input of varied groups, they may reflect a balanced consideration of all relevant factors. To the extent that they merely represent the application of judgment to general cases, the logic of general standards may be as unspecified as that of specific decisions.

Practical

Professional judgment works. Except when thwarted by intervenors, professionals produce answers, the best answers they can arrive at given their training and resource constraints. Professional judgment is also practical in that its decisions are formulated in terms concrete enough to allow implementation. Moreover, when problems in implementation arise, professionals are often near enough and informed enough to improvise variations that preserve the spirit of the original decisions. By minimizing outside involvement, professional judgment reduces operating costs. Costs are further reduced to the extent that professionals have access to the cumulative wisdom (and canned solutions) of their colleagues. The relatively low status of safety specialists in most professions, however, suggests that the decisions that are being made so practically and efficaciously may not always be primarily acceptable-risk decisions; that is, safety issues may not be given all that much emphasis.

Open to evaluation

As Polanyi (1962) describes, the ways of the professional can only be understood by another who has gone through the same extended apprenticeship, learning those subtle tricks of the trade which embellish the fundamentals that can be acquired from public sources like books and blueprints. As a result, professional decisions are made not only in nonpublic settings (e.g., on-site, at the drafting table, by the patient's bedside) but also in a nonpublic manner. Because the processes and rationale of their decisions are inaccessible, professionals, from Hammurabi to product-liability suits, have been judged on the outcomes of their decisions. If a bridge fails or a patient dies, claims about the soundness of the logic underlying a decision may pale in hindsight. Experts' intolerance for lay criticism may reflect both a feeling that they know more than their critics (and that substantive knowledge is the best guarantee of wisdom) and a realization that professional judgment is in some senses indefensible. The defense of having adhered to accepted practice only transfers the responsibility to the judgments of others.

Politically acceptable

The increasing encroachment of regulators, lawyers, and intervenors on decisions previously left to professionals' unfettered management suggests dissatisfaction with their acceptable-risk decisions. To some extent professionals serve as scapegoats for unfortunate outcomes of decisions left to them by default. Other criticism is politically motivated; one way to influence acceptable-risk decisions is to wrest power from the professionals. Still other critics view professionals as pawns in a larger struggle; they comment on professionals' work only insofar as it produces decisions that they dislike. Much environmental politics can be interpreted as an attempt to control the context that most immediately influences professionals' decisions.

Finally, some people view professionalism as the enemy itself. Agreeing with G. B. Shaw that professions are conspiracies against the laity, they see any concession of power to professionals as fostering a technocracy in which undue deference is given to professionals' social and pecuniary values. In this view, reliance on professional judgment not only surrenders control but legitimates one's subjection.

Compatible with institutions

Professional judgment fits current institutional arrangements well because in many situations, it is the institution. Unless someone intervenes, professionals manage by default (within the constraints provided by their clients or employers). Even when alternative decision-making methods are tried, professionals may be relied on because of their knowledge and experience.

For their part, professionals accommodate themselves to the bureaucracies within which many decisions are made. They are team players, used to interacting with varied clients. Unlike scientists whose cautionary norms may keep them from making statements definitive enough to allow the bureaucrats to do their jobs, professionals are willing to venture a best guess at most topics. It is unclear how professionals would fit into innovative decision-making forums that emphasize more public participation.

Conducive to learning

Professions are organized for long-term effectiveness. Indeed, they exist to ensure the orderly accumulation and transmission of knowledge. Unlike some sectors of the public, they are not fickle in their commitment to particular substantive problems. Unlike many elected and administrative officials, they do not come and go in 2-, 4-, or 6-year cycles. Their connections with corporate, government, and university research laboratories allow them to stimulate intensive study of the problems that confound them in the field. Just as their research and training produce general solutions to technical problems, so do their standard-setting efforts produce general solutions to social problems.

The inward focus of these activities may mean, however, that the professions are strengthened at the expense of other sectors of society. Some of their activities may be interpreted as erecting bigger and better barriers to lay involvement and to the development of an informed and effective citizenry. Other activities may be seen as part of a careful, cumulative imposition of professionals' values and standards on society. Any persistent contentment with narrow problem definitions may be interpreted as a long-term contribution toward digging society into a hole.

Summary

Professional approaches for acceptable-risk decision making rely on the experience and educated intuitions of professionals. By definition, technical experts do their job better than anyone else could. That job, however, may not yet include a viable approach to acceptable-risk decisions. Professionals' training, personal values, work practices, and relations with various client groups may leave them without the rich and balanced view that one would want before conferring sole responsibility for such decisions. Professional judgment may be most trustworthy in routine problems of relatively limited scope that offer an opportunity for feedback from both the world and clients, and that help to show how the systems they design work and how well people like them.

5 Bootstrapping

Both the professional-judgment and formal-analysis approaches assume that we can think our way to sensible acceptable-risk decisions. With a little computational help, one can accommodate all relevant points of view and achieve a balance that acknowledges political and technical realities. Proponents of the bootstrapping approach reject this assumption, arguing that risks cannot be analyzed adequately in any short period of time. Rather, society achieves an acceptable tradeoff between risks and benefits only through a protracted period of hands-on experience that allows for trial-and-error learning.

Methods of bootstrapping

What are decision makers to do when they cannot wait for these slow processes to evolve, but must immediately make lasting decisions about acceptable-risk issues? The bootstrapping approach proposes using the level of risk that has been tolerated in the past as a basis for evaluating the acceptability of proposed risks. For example, if one believes that our market, social, and political institutions have been able to effect a nearly optimal balance of risks and benefits for familiar technologies, that experience can be codified into historical standards that can then be applied to future decisions. By short-circuiting history's cumbersome balancing process, we can move immediately to that nearly ideal balance. In effect, we can lift ourselves up by our own bootstraps, adopting standards that are consistent with current social policy and sensitive to the realities that frustrate the implementation of utopian solutions.

Although bootstrapping methods resemble formal analysis in that they use explicit calculations and an articulated decision rule, their logic is very different. Formal approaches assume that policies that have evolved without the benefit of careful quantitative analysis may be inappropriate; hence, most existing policies have no prescriptive weight. Bootstrappers' faith in adjustive processes leads them to believe that descriptions of past policies may afford prescriptions for future ones. Four bootstrapping methods are discussed below. They differ with regard to the past that each describes and in the biological, cybernetic, or economic mechanisms they invoke to argue that an acceptable equilibrium was achieved in that past.

Risk compendiums

Believing that many people have a poor grasp of the risks of modern life, some bootstrappers have tried to quantify many risks in common terms. These estimates are aggregated into compendiums designed to aid decisions makers' intuitions and eventually produce more consistent standards for different hazards. For example, R. Wilson (1979) argued that we should "try to measure our risks quantitatively . . . Then we could compare risks and decide which to accept or reject" (p. 43). Likewise, Sowby (1965) observed that we need to pay more attention to "some of the other risks of life" when deciding whether or not we are properly regulating radiation hazards, and Lord Rothschild (1978) added, "There is no point in getting into a panic about the risks of life until you have *compared* the risks which worry you with those that don't, but perhaps should" (emphasis in original).

Typically, such exhortations are followed by elaborate tables, or even "catalogs of risks" (B. Cohen & Lee, 1979), in which diverse indices of death or disability are displayed for a broad spectrum of life's hazards. Thus Sowby (1965) provided extensive data on risks per hour of exposure, showing, for example, that an hour riding a motorcycle is as risky as an hour of being 75 years old. R. Wilson (1979) developed Table 5.1, which displays a set of varied activities, each of which he estimated to increase one's chances of death in any year by 1 in 1 million. Wilson explained that "these comparisons help me evaluate risks and I imagine that they may help others to do so, as well. But the most important use of these comparisons must be to help the decisions we make, as a nation, to improve our health and reduce our accident rate" (p. 45). In similar fashion, Cohen and Lee (1979) ordered a large set of hazards in terms of expected reduction in life expectancy (Table 5.2) on the assumption that "to some approximation, the ordering in [this table] should be society's order of priorities. However, we see several very major problems that have received very little attention . . . whereas some other items near the bottom of the list, especially those involving radiation, receive a great deal of attention" (p. 720). Since current risk levels are viewed as a valid basis for comparison, such risk compendiums imply bootstrapping on the present. A proponent might paraphrase Lincoln Steffens and claim, I have seen the present and it works, or at least that it works well enough to single out the few outliers that are receiving too much or too little attention.

Properly speaking, however, comparing existing hazards is not a decision-making procedure but merely an aid to intuition. The logic of such calculations does not require any particular conclusion to be drawn, say, from the contrast between the risks of motorcycling and of advanced age.

Revealed preferences

The revealed-preferences method, as discussed by Starr (1969, 1972), improves upon simple comparisons of risk both by considering benefits and by

Table 5.1. Risks estimated to increase chance of death in any year by 0.000001 (1 part in 1 million)

Activity	Cause of death
Smoking 1.4 cigarettes	Cancer, heart disease
Drinking 0.5 liter of wine	Cirrhosis of the liver
Spending 1 hour in a coal mine	Black lung disease
Spending 3 hours in a coal mine	Accident
Living 2 days in New York or Boston	Air pollution
Traveling 6 minutes by canoe	Accident
Traveling 10 miles by bicycle	Accident
Traveling 150 miles by car	Accident
Flying 1,000 miles by jet	Accident
Flying 6,000 miles by jet	Cancer caused by cosmic radiation
Living 2 months in Denver on vacation from New York	Cancer caused by cosmic radiation
Living 2 months in average stone or brick building	Cancer caused by natural radioactivity
One chest x-ray taken in a good hospital	Cancer caused by radiation
Living 2 months with a cigarette smoker	Cancer, heart disease
Eating 40 tablespooons of peanut butter	Liver cancer caused by aflatoxin B
Drinking Miami drinking water for 1 year	Cancer caused by chloroform
Drinking 30 12-oz. cans of diet soda	Cancer caused by saccharin
Living 5 years at site boundary of a typical nuclear power plant in the open	Cancer caused by radiation
Drinking 1,000 24-oz. soft drinks from recently banned plastic bottles	Cancer from acrylonitrile monomer
Living 20 years near PVC plant	Cancer caused by vinyl chloride (1976 standard)
Living 150 years within 20 miles of a nuclear power plant	Cancer caused by radiation
Eating 100 charcoal-broiled steaks	Cancer from benzopyrene
Risk of accident by living within 5 miles of a nuclear reactor for 50 years	Cancer caused by radiation

Source: R. Wilson, 1979.

providing a decision rule. It assumes that our society has already reached an essentially optimal balance between the risks and benefits of any existing technology and that this preferred balance is revealed in contemporary risk and benefit data. A new technology's risks are deemed acceptable if they do not exceed the level of risk associated with ongoing technologies that have similar benefit to society.

Starr tried to demonstrate the usefulness of revealed preferences by examining the relationship between risk of death and economic benefit for a number of common technologies (see Figure 5.1a). He derived several hypotheses about the nature of acceptable risk:

1. The acceptable level of risk is roughly proportional to the third power (cube) of the benefits.
2. The public is willing to accept risks from voluntary activities, such as skiing, that are roughly a thousand times greater than those it will tolerate from involuntary activities that provide the same level of benefit.

Table 5.2. Estimated loss of life expectancy due to various causes

Cause	Days
Being unmarried (male)	3,500
Cigarette smoking (male)	2,250
Heart disease	2,100
Being unmarried (female)	1,600
Being 30% overweight	1,300
Being a coal miner	1,100
Cancer	980
Being 20% overweight	900
<8th-grade education	850
Cigarette smoking (female)	800
Low socioeconomic status	700
Stroke	520
Living in unfavorable state	500
Army in Vietnam	400
Cigar smoking	330
Dangerous jobs, accidents	300
Pipe smoking	220
Increasing food intake 100 cal/day	210
Motor vehicle accidents	207
Pneumonia, influenza	141
Alcohol (U.S. average)	130
Accidents in home	95
Suicide	95
Diabetes	95
Being murdered (homicide)	90
Legal drug misuse	90
Average job, accidents	74

3. The acceptable level of risk decreases as the number of persons exposed to a hazard increases.

Although its logic has some intuitive appeal, the revealed-preferences method has several drawbacks. For example, it is hard to produce convincing measures of the risks and benefits of such diverse technologies. Otway and Cohen (1975) reanalyzed Starr's data and reached somewhat different conclusions (Figure 5.1b), as did Fischhoff, Slovic, and Lichtenstein (1979), who performed an alternative analysis using the same underlying logic (Figure 5.2). These technical problems pale before the political difficulties raised by the basic assumption that current risk–benefit tradeoffs are satisfactory.

A variant of revealed-preferences analysis has been used to answer the question, What is a life worth? by rephrasing it as, What is the value placed on a particular change in survival probability? Thaler and Rosen (1976) observed the "market behavior" of people trading occupational risks for economic benefits and found that a premium of about $200 a year was required to induce workers in risky occupations (e.g., coal mining) to accept an increase of 0.001 in their annual probability of accidental death. Assuming that this

Table 5.2 (*cont.*)

Cause	Days
Drowning	41
Job with radiation exposure	40
Falls	39
Accidents to pedestrians	37
Safest jobs, accidents	30
Fire, burns	27
Generation of energy	24
Illicit drugs (U.S. average)	18
Poison (solid, liquid)	17
Suffocation	13
Firearms accidents	11
Natural radiation (BEIR)	8
Medical X rays	6
Poisonous gases	7
Coffee	6
Oral contraceptives	5
Accidents to pedalcycles	5
All catastrophes combined	3.5
Diet drinks	2
Reactor accidents (UCS)	2[a]
Reactor accidents—Rasmussen	0.02[a]
Radiation from nuclear industry	0.02[a]
PAP test	−4
Smoke alarm in home	−10
Airbags in car	−50
Mobile coronary-care units	−125
Safety improvements 1066–76	−110

[a] These items assume that all U.S. power is nuclear. UCS is Union of Concerned Scientists, the most prominent group of critics of nuclear energy.
Source: B. Cohen and Lee, 1979.

tradeoff was acceptable to all concerned, they inferred that society should be willing to pay about $200,000 to prevent a death. Here, too, technical difficulties may be considerable; a replication by Rappaport (1981) using somewhat different data and procedures derived a value of $2 million.

Implied preferences

Belief in society's ability to manage hazards might lead one to examine its legal records rather than its statistical traces. The legacy of laws, tort precedents, and regulatory actions can be interpreted as reflecting the compromise between what people want and what current economic and political arrangements allow them to have. One could attempt to shorten these sometimes tortuous processes by identifying their implicit risk–benefit tradeoff and applying it as a standard for the acceptability of other hazards.

The logic of implied preferences can be seen in the following proposal by

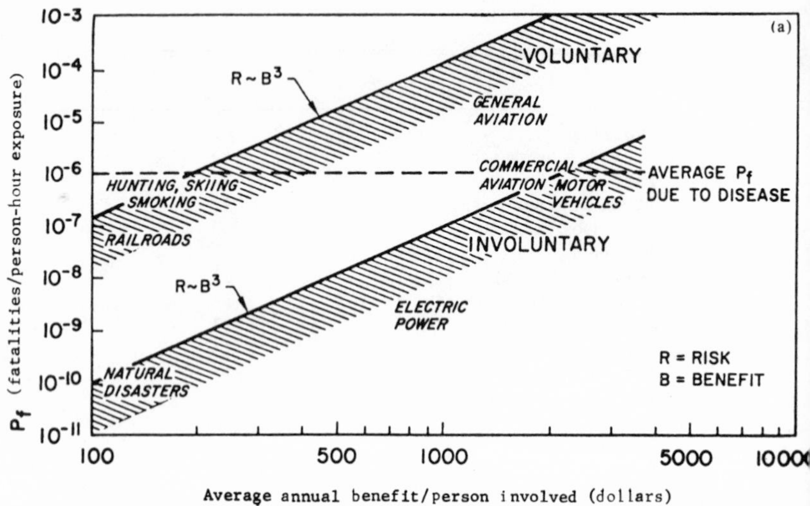

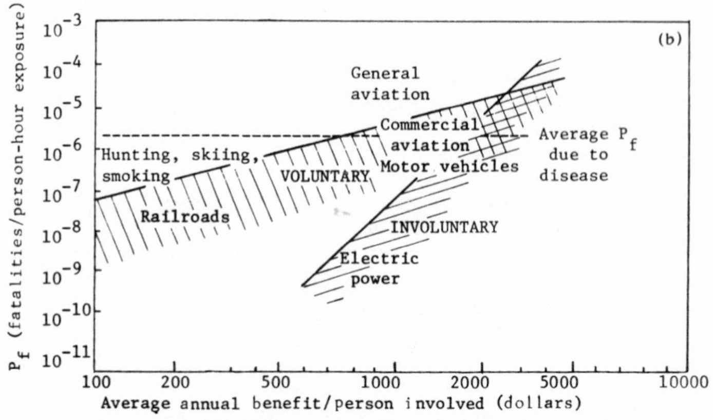

Figure 5.1. Relationship between statistically measured risk of death and economic benefit, (a) as studied by Starr (1972) and (b) as reanalyzed by Otway and Cohen (1975). In both figures, risk is measured by fatalities per person per hour of exposure. Benefit reflects either the average amount of money spent on an activity by an individual participant or the average contribution an activity makes to a participant's annual income. In (a), the best-fitting lines were drawn by eye with error bands to indicate their approximate nature. In (b), regression procedures were used after deleting natural disasters from the category of involuntary risks.

the Atomic Industrial Forum (1976) to adopt the risk levels then tolerated in nuclear power plants as a guide to setting tolerable levels in the future.

The Nuclear Regulatory Commission has recognized an acceptable level of risk, at least for regulatory purposes, in granting permits and licenses. While this level of risk has not been specifically quantified, the Reactor Safety Study now provides a bench-

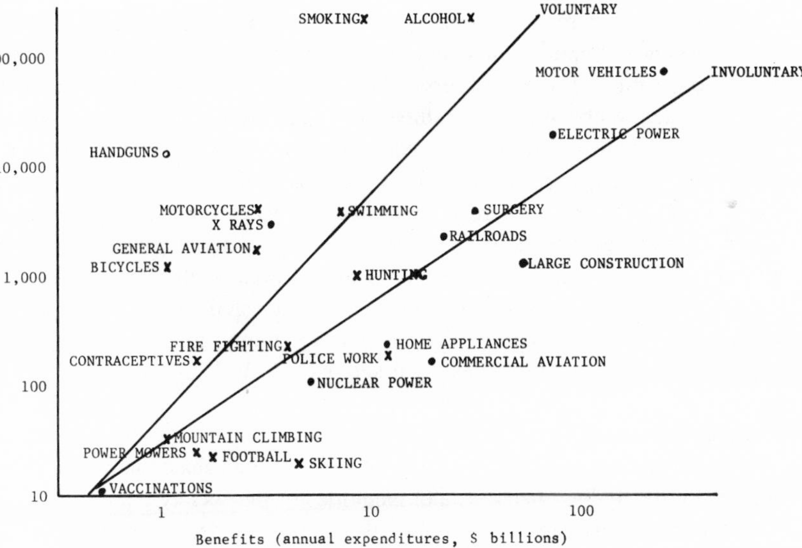

Figure 5.2. One possible assessment of current risks and benefits from 25 activities and technologies. Items are marked with an X if voluntary; with a closed circle if involuntary. Handguns and large construction could not be classified as primarily voluntary or involuntary. They are marked here with open circles and are not included in the calculation of the two regression lines shown in the figure. (Source: Fischhoff, Slovic, & Lichtenstein, 1979, p. 20)

mark for comparison. With this background, new issues can be assessed by judging whether these issues impact significantly on the plant risk envelope as determined in the Reactor Safety Study. If an issue can be shown not to affect significantly this risk, then design alterations additional to the vintage plant design analyzed in the Reactor Safety Study could not be justified.

The Reactor Safety Study [has shown] the probability of exceeding 10CFR100 guidelines to be approximately 1×10^{-5} per reactor per year. In this regard, an event with a probability of 1×10^{-6} per reactor per year of exceeding 10CFR100 guidelines would not significantly affect the plant risk characterized in the Reactor Safety Study. (p. 6)

Proponents of implied preferences, like proponents of the democratic process (Lindblom, 1965), make no claims that existing rulings are perfect. Rather, such rulings are thought to represent society's best attempt so far to accommodate people's desires and the facts of life in a hazardous world. Their weaknesses are the weaknesses of democracy itself: Laws are sometimes hastily conceived and poorly written; they are often extended to situations undreamed of when they were written; their precise formulation may reflect fleeting political coalitions and public concerns.

As a result, despite the respect it gives to precedence, this legal legacy may lack coherence. Simultaneous actions at federal, state, and local levels may defy coordination. The varied forms these actions take may defy comparison and consistency checks; they include laws (and their rhetorical preambles), regulations (expressed in performance, technical, or vague standards), court cases (and appeals), federally subsidized risk-reduction programs, and so forth. In addition, this record is incomplete. Successfully managed hazards may be absent because their risks were acceptable without legal intervention; unsuccessfully managed hazards may be absent because their promoters were strong, their victims weak, or their risks underrated. To the best of our knowledge, there has been no comprehensive attempt to determine what, if any, consistent policy underlies legal actions (B. B. Johnson, 1980).

Natural standards

The bootstrapping methods we have looked at so far all share the flaw of being subject to the myths, mistakes, and inequities of the society whose decisions they depend on. Perhaps safety standards should be independent of a particular society, especially for risks that have collective, cumulative, or irreversible effects. Rather than examining historical time for guideline periods that reveal social wisdom, one might want to look to geological time for biological wisdom. Tolerable exposure levels would then be considered those that were characteristic of the conditions in which a species evolved. Such "natural" standards need not constitute outright bans, as traces of many hazardous chemicals are needed for survival and some level of radiation- or chemical-induced mutation may be good for a species (if not for individual members). Because exposure has varied from epoch to epoch and from place to place, one could establish ranges of tolerable exposure.

The philosophy of nondegradation of the environment expressed by Agricola (1556) in *De Re Metallica* was one of the earliest natural standards. He advocated prohibiting human activities that would impose risks greater than those experienced in some "pre-existing natural state." In this spirit, Settle and Patterson (1980) suggest restricting lead levels in food to those found in archeological remains; the Natural Resources Defense Council has proposed that the risk to future generations from the entire nuclear-fuel cycle be limited to the risk presented by the ore bodies used in these operations before they are mined (Rotow, Cochran, & Tamplin, 1979). A related approach, analogous to the Atomic Industrial Forum's proposal to ignore risks that are small relative to those already accepted by society, would deem those events acceptable that contribute only a small increment over natural exposures (International Commission on Radiological Protection, 1973; Maxey, 1979). Figure 5.3 shows how the U.S. Atomic Energy Commission standards compared with natural background levels of radiation. It also compares then current levels of sulfur

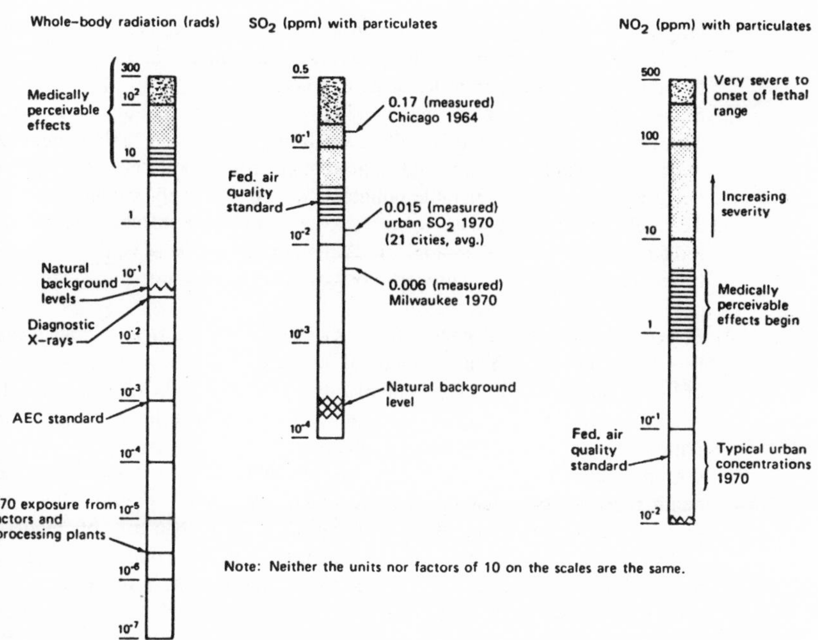

Figure 5.3. Comparison of pollutant standards, background levels, exposures of human origin, and health effects for radiation, SO_2, and NO_2. (Source: WASH-1224, U.S. Atomic Energy Commission)

dioxide and nitrogen dioxide with background levels, and in doing so suggests the implications of invoking natural standards in this manner.

Adler (see Weinberg, 1979) proposes shifting the focus of natural standards from the average level of background radiation to the (apparently harmless) variations in that level to which the species may be accustomed:

> Rather than trying to determine the actual damage caused by very low radiation insult, and then setting an allowable dose, one instead compares the man-made standard with the background. Since man has evolved in the midst of a pervasive radiation background, the presumption is that an increment of radiation ''small'' compared to that background is tolerable and ought to be set as the standard. [Adler] suggests that small, in the case of gamma radiation, be taken as the standard deviation of the natural background - about 20 millirads per year. (Weinberg, 1979, p. 10)

One attractive feature of natural standards is that they can be set without knowing precise dose-response relationships; another is that they avoid the problems of converting consequences into a common unit (like dollars per life lost). Nonetheless, as a guide to policy the natural-standards method has several logical flaws that lack obvious remedies:

1. Unless natural exposures have diminished, any new exposure adds to nature's dose and thereby constitutes excess and "unnatural" exposure (although conceivably within the range of toleration).
2. Some technologies, such as steel making, produce many pollutants. In principle, each effluent may constitute a small and hence acceptable increment over background exposure. But natural standards provide no criterion for deciding when singly tolerable pollutants are cumulatively intolerable.
3. Technologies may increase some exposures and reduce others (e.g., by replacing "dirtier" technologies). Although it seems sensible to make tradeoffs between such gains and losses, natural standards pass judgment only on individual increases.
4. For completely new substances (e.g., saccharin) no historical tolerance can be established. In such cases, a natural-standards policy would tolerate none of the substance at all, unless it involved no risk. The Delaney Amendment, which outlaws the addition of any known carcinogen to food, reflects this philosophy and encounters its limitations.
5. One possible interpretation of the natural-standards idea is that historical death rates set the tolerable limit to death rates in the present. Because present rates are lower than past rates, in part because of modern technologies, the standard would indicate that no further controls are needed and that indeed life might be allowed to become riskier - conclusions that few observers would accept.

Generic problems

Defining the problem

The first step in bootstrapping is deciding which past constitutes the lode of wisdom. Are the nearly optimal tradeoffs to be sought in the present (risk compendiums), the recent past (revealed and implied preferences), or the distant past (natural standards)? When these tradeoffs fluctuate over time, should we rely on the most recent values, on those from particularly stable periods, or on extreme values? These alternatives might be interpreted as representing, respectively, the results of the balancing process, some local equilibrium, or stress limits.

One must then decide which hazards to look at in that ideal past. One reasonable criterion for including a hazard is that riskiness should be a limiting factor. That is, it should be possible either to save money by making the activity riskier (e.g., by skimping on design, production, or regulation) or to save lives by spending money on safety measures. The revealed-preferences analyses in Figures 5.1 and 5.2 adhered to this criterion, yet produced somewhat different conclusions, suggesting that the method needs more complete specification before it can produce robust results.

The next problem is defining the contemporary hazard that is to be compared with this historical set, in particular the breadth of the hazard category.

Making general reference to the magnitude of risks currently "tolerated," Comar (1979b) argued for ignoring any hazard bearing less than 10^{-5} per year risk of death (unless it provides no benefit or can be easily reduced). Okrent and Whipple (1977) advocated a similar threshold for beneficial technologies (such as manufactured goods). Implementing either of these bootstrapping schemes means deciding what a technology is. Are asbestos brake linings and asbestos-lined hairdryers to be treated as one or two technologies? Aggregation or disaggregation could mean the difference between having two technologies under the threshold or one above it. Kletz's (1977) rule of removing any activity that causes more than one fatal accident per 2,500 workers spending their careers in the chemical industry encounters a similar problem, as do proposals to ignore events whose risks are only slightly above natural or implied standards. Without clear guidelines to the contrary, a consequential event could be redefined as a set of inconsequential events each of which poses a small and hence negligible threat.

Once the hazards have been selected, one must decide which of their consequences to measure (deaths, accidents, etc.). An important lacuna in both the natural-standards and risk-compendiums methods is that benefits are not included among the consequences. For those consequences that are considered, a unit of observation is needed (per capita, per mile traveled, per vehicle). Starr chose to look at deaths and measure them per hour of exposure, both because of the availability of statistics and a personal speculation regarding how people think about hazards. This scheme founders when an hour of exposure is hard to define (e.g., with handguns, vaccinations, or smoking), just as other indices (e.g., deaths per mile traveled) fail because they cannot be applied to all relevant hazards. The choice of index is important because different indices may cast the acceptable-risk problem in different perspectives. For example, reducing the risk per ton of coal mined may increase the risk per miner's hour of work; a project that extracted a certain quantity of coal at minimal cost in lives might be unacceptable to miners unless their hourly risk or workweek was also reduced (Crouch & Wilson, 1979).

The final step in defining a problem for bootstrapping is choosing moderator variables, such as voluntariness, which are allowed to establish double standards for acceptability of a risk. The importance of moderators emerges clearly when one notes the weak overall correlation between risk and benefit in Figure 5.1. The hypothesis (or assumption) that society manages hazards so as to get more benefit from more risky ones was only supported when voluntariness was introduced as a moderator. A skeptic might ask, How many other moderators were tried before one was found that created a double standard? If many were tried, the "historic" risk–benefit tradeoff may be a statistical artifact.

To take an analogous example from revealed-preferences studies of the value of life, in some industries (e.g., logging) the riskiest jobs are generally the most poorly paid. That is, the regression equation predicting wages from risk has a negative coefficient for risk. The bootstrapper's response may be, Let's control, statistically, for experience or agility or job security or . . . whatever it will take to produce a (multiple) regression equation with a positive coefficient on the risk variable. Although that equation will show workers being reimbursed rather than being charged for taking risks, one must wonder whether the agile analyst can always find some moderators showing that risk taking is rewarded. What if a different set of moderators were needed for every profession? What does it mean that the workers who are ostensibly being reimbursed for the risks they take are but statistical constructions, living in that nonexistent world where the relevant moderators are partialed out (Meehl, 1970)?

Logical criteria for selecting moderators might require them to (a) be readily assessable for all hazards, (b) make some sense as a basis for social policy, and (c) not represent surrogates for other considerations. For example, involuntariness is often invoked as a sufficient condition for society to demand more stringent standards. Yet for some hazards it is poorly defined (e.g., handguns, motor vehicles). Empirically, it seems important only when associated with catastrophic potential (i.e., when many people are simultaneously threatened by a hazard they could not avoid), a fact that suggests that voluntariness may not be the key variable (Slovic et al., 1980).

Bootstrapping analyses offer an incomplete problem definition. Although they consider some fact and value issues in great detail, they ignore the question of what options are available. Judgments are rendered on the absolute acceptability of individual options, regardless of the superiority or inferiority of the alternatives or whether there indeed are any. Bootstrapping provides guidance in choosing between two options only when one passes its threshold of tolerance and the other does not.

Knowing the facts

Although bootstrapping methods are all strongly data based, they have rather different concepts of what facts are important. Risk compendiums can take whatever statistics are available; no ordering is made in terms of relevance, and no input is considered indispensible. Revealed preferences makes similarly minimal demands; if suitable risk and benefit statistics are not available, a hazard is dropped from the analysis.

Implied preferences occupies a middle position; the corpus of law is moderately well defined, but it is unclear how broadly or deeply it must be worked. Although these attitudes toward sampling render the procedures somewhat indeterminate, the effect of sampling bias on the validity of their conclusions is seldom discussed.

Natural standards is the most explicit about what quantities to look for. This orientation creates somewhat different problems. Although one may hope to assess natural exposure to chemicals that leave traces in bones or rock, appraising the natural incidence of accidents and infectious disease is probably impossible. Furthermore, should such an analysis be completed, it would likely show that the ecology of hazards in which humans live has changed drastically over the eons - mostly for the better, as in the case of the reduced incidence of infectious disease. The biological wisdom (or importance) of restoring one component of the mix to its prehistoric values would need to be carefully questioned.

The bootstrapping analyses cited earlier in the chapter all relied on average death rates to characterize risk. However, society may be more concerned with setting standards on the catastrophic potential of activities (Ferreira & Slesin, 1976; Rowe, 1977a; Slovic et al., 1980). Although it is considerably more difficult to assess the small (or minute) probability of catastrophic events than annual fatality rates, Farmer (1967) and others have described recent experience with some hazards in a two-dimensional space defined by probability of occurrence and magnitude of consequence (see Figure 5.4). Assuming that one had confidence in the assessments made in this figure and accepted the time period in question as representing a relevant optimum, the risks of nuclear power would be acceptable by virtue of lying below the envelope circumscribing the risks of the other hazards. The fate of a technology whose curve crossed those of the other curves would be moot (e.g., dams). For that technology, one would have to decide which part of the curve is most relevant. In doing so, one would be judging, in effect, whether a society adapts primarily to the average or to the variance of its yearly accident experience.

Another popular index that might be applied to varied hazards is reduced life expectancy (see Table 5.2). However, it too has problems. Although some people feel enlightened upon learning that a single takeoff or landing in a commercial airliner takes an average of 16 minutes off one's life expectancy, others find themselves completely bewildered by such information. Once one takes off in an airplane, they reason, one will either die prematurely (almost certainly by more than 16 minutes) or one will not, and such averages seem to them to capture the essence of the risks very poorly. Indeed, McNeil, Weichselbaum, and Pauker (1978) found that patients facing the prospect of surgery for lung cancer were as concerned about its threat of immediate death as with its contribution to their life expectancy.

Assessing values

To rely on descriptions of the past for guidance for the future is to presume that whatever was, is right. With natural standards, one might be able to derive a scientific rationale for this claim - for example, by arguing on the basis of evolutionary theory that there is an optimal level of environmental stress. Substantiating this empirical claim would not absolve one from having

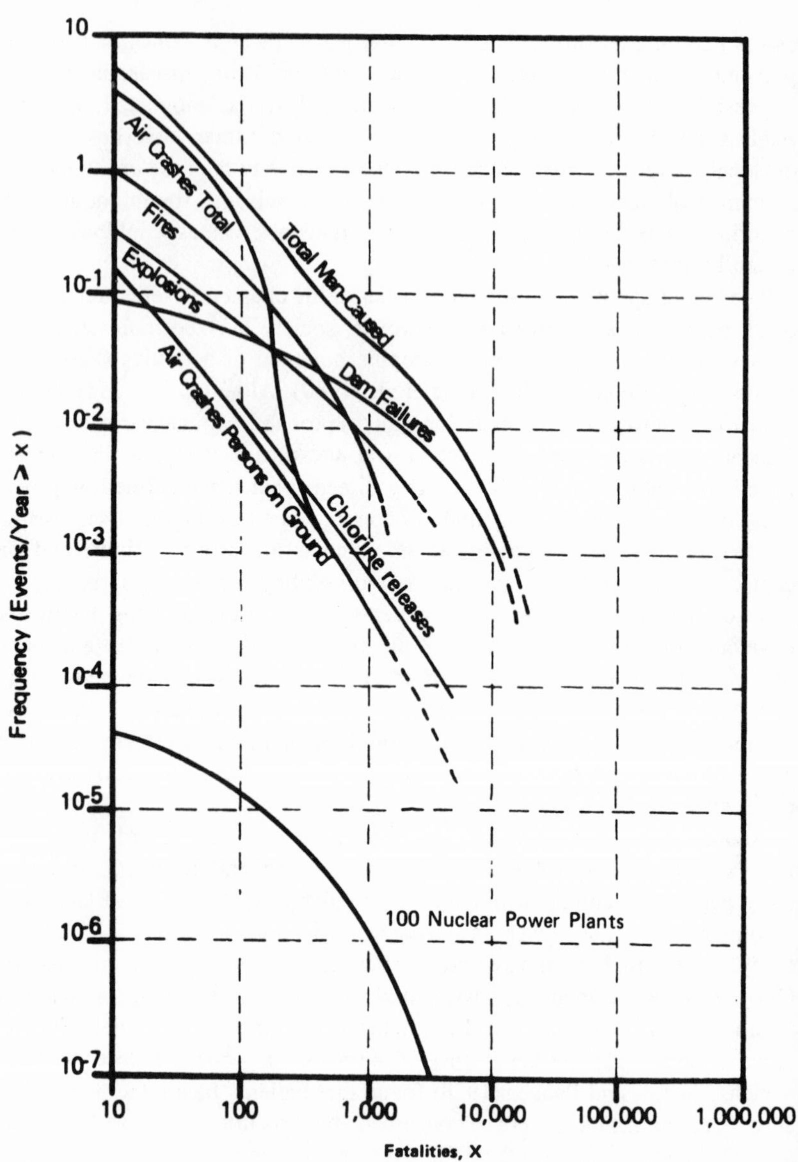

Figure 5.4. Frequency of events involving different numbers of fatalities. (Source: U.S. Nuclear Regulatory Commission, 1975)

to justify the value-laden claim that stresses imposed on individuals are to be tolerated for the good of the species and the robustness of future generations.

With revealed and implied preferences, one is clearly enshrining those economic, social, and political relations that have generated the tradeoffs described by the analysis. Thus, one asserts not only that society has reached an equilibrium, but also that it has reached an acceptable one. Neither environmentalists nor their opponents in the "regulatory-reform" movement are likely to accept this latter claim. If either group has its way, our current situation would prove to represent a very local equilibrium.

Aggregate revealed-preferences analyses like those shown in Figures 5.1 and 5.2 invite further charges of bias. Like cost–benefit analysis (see Chapter 6), such analyses fail to consider who is bearing the costs and benefits. Because they neglect equity issues, these methods offer no guidelines for selecting among options with different distributional effects, and may just as easily perpetuate current inequities as foster radical changes.

As always, technical aspects of implementing an approach prejudge certain value issues. For example, using a measure of benefits like total expenditures or total output as Starr did means taking several controversial positions. Because such measures include bads as well as goods, money spent on reducing the pollution that an industry causes is positively weighted as heavily as the value of the product that the industry manufactures. In addition, one ignores any ways in which market prices fail to reflect the full social costs of an activity. One assumes, for example, that cigarette prices take account of the smoker's higher probability of heart disease or cancer and that prices of pesticide fully reflect both their deleterious side effects and the increased yield of foodstuffs. Depending upon one's perspective, the benefits of pesticides may be undervalued or overvalued by "total expenditures." The revealed-preferences method is most prone to these criticisms because it makes the most conspicuous effort to quantify benefits.

To conclude where we began, even if a method could capture the preferences of the period it chose to study, these would indicate only what risks were *accepted,* not what risks were *acceptable*. In keeping with Hume's dictum that no ought can ever follow from an is, Tribe (1973) and others have argued that prescriptive guidelines must reflect not just what a society does want, but what it should want. Using as an example a community conflict over whether to build a dam, Tribe notes that bootstrapping analysis could help the community infer how much its inhabitants do in fact value the birds and other wildlife that would be lost if the dam were built, as compared with how much they value the boating and other activities that the dam would provide. However, it could not shed light on "*what those values ought to be* – about the extent to which theirs should be a wildlife-valuing community, with all that this might entail for how its members view and value both nature and one another" (p. 656, emphasis in original).

Coping with the human element

Except perhaps for natural standards, all these bootstrapping methods make strong behavioral assumptions. It is only by empirically validating these assumptions that bootstrappers can claim prescriptive weight for their descriptive results. One such assumption is that the state described by an analysis was the final stage in a balancing process, not just an intermediate point. Thus, for example, the recent past could not be regarded as a guide if one believed that social and market institutions were just beginning to achieve reasonable compromises with the myriad new technologies that have recently emerged. One symptom of disequilibrium might be rapidly increasing risks (reflecting, say, a cancer time bomb that has yet to be recognized and managed); or, by the same token, rapidly decreasing risks (reflecting, say, the gradual impact of recently enacted regulations).

Once the existence of an equilibrium was established, one would want evidence that it was brought about by some underlying optimizing process. The advocate of natural standards would want to show that there is some ideal level of environmental stress (or insult) for human evolution or survival. The revealed-preferences or risk-compendiums positions would be strengthened by evidence that people make decisions informed and "rational" enough that their behavior can be said to reflect their own best interests (Viscusi, 1979). The research cited in Chapter 2 does not support this assumption. Consumers often fail to inquire about the riskiness of different alternatives; when they do, advertising and marketing strategies may deny them that information. For example, unless automobile buyers know from a design standpoint what degree of safety is possible and at what price, and unless the industry provides varied alternatives, market behavior may not reflect the personal cost–benefit tradeoffs an individual might make after thoughtful inquiry.

One doubtful assumption of any method that relies on market mechanisms to achieve an acceptable equilibrium is that those mechanisms are sufficiently responsive when a long time gap separates exposure and consequence (e.g., carcinogens). Technologies whose carcinogenic potential is unknown when they are first introduced may be unduly dangerous, particularly when subsequent control is difficult (either because no other options exist or because the industry is heavily capitalized). Consumers and workers could not negotiate fair deals for such hazards. Even with known hazards, our societal institutions free many polluters from paying for long-term effects, if only by allowing them to go bankrupt.

One option open to bootstrappers who look to contemporary social institutions to produce nearly optimal balances is to improve the functioning of those institutions. Bootstrappers could press for more research on the properties of new technologies, better programs for informing consumers about risks, and innovative legal institutions for fairly distributing the costs and benefits of risky technologies. If they were to be successful, we would have a society that managed hazards so that our experience in the near future would create a balance that could be exploited by the bootstrappers of more distant futures.

Finally, the behavioral assumptions of some bootstrapping methods seem to contain internal contradictions. For example, reliance on risk compendiums assumes both that people are informed and astute enough to manage most hazards consistently and effectively, and that they are incapable of getting along without simplistic decision aids. All methods except natural standards assume that society manages hazards well; yet some hazards are so mismanaged that they must be taken out of the political-social-economic arena and have "consistent" standards forced on them. With new technologies, this segregation may be justified as a way to avoid time-consuming processes. But when bootstrapping is applied to veteran hazards, the analyst has some explaining to do: How is it that society manages so well in general, but not here? Finally, if society does adjust hazards by trial and error, is it fair to subject a new hazard as proposed on the drawing board to the standards achieved by old hazards? A new technology may be judged too harshly if it is not given the opportunity to reduce costs through economies of scale, increase productivity as experience is gained by its work force, or evolve superior configurations by responding to competitive pressures.

Assessing decision quality

The absence of any qualification of the estimates provided is a striking feature of Tables 5.1 and 5.2. This omission might be defended on the ground that, given the weak logical underpinnings of risk compendiums as a decision rule, further specification (e.g., through the use of confidence intervals) might represent misplaced imprecision. A rough list provides all the information that such analyses can supply. However, this argument belies the contention that risk compendiums are aids to intuition. Those who need such aids most would also be most poorly equipped to guess what qualifications should accompany these risk estimates or to understand how qualification would weaken whatever conclusions such lists suggest.

The hash marks in Starr's revealed-preferences analysis (Figure 5.1a) acknowledge imprecision in at least one aspect of the analysis - the fact that he roughed in the best-fit lines in the figure. However, when one compares the divergent pictures created by Otway and Cohen's (Figure 5.1b) reanalysis of Starr's data and the comparable analysis of Figure 5.2, the tidy hash marks in Figure 5.1a seem to generate too much confidence in the quality of the conclusions drawn from it. These figures might become indecipherable blurs if one added vertical and horizontal error bars to the points, along with confidence intervals around the best-fit lines. The order-of-magnitude disagreement between the value-of-a-life estimates produced by the conceptually similar efforts of Thaler and Rosen and of Rappaport affords a quantitative assessment of the robustness of revealed-preferences procedures. An error theory is needed for deciding how much analysis-to-analysis variation renders the results too unstable to provide a basis for public policy.

Although these examples refer to revealed preferences, all bootstrapping methods seem to be quite sensitive to the precise way the problem and its components are defined. In the absence of established guidelines for resolving definitional issues, the procedures become ill defined and hardly an assurance of quality decisions.

These analyses are made additionally uncertain by the uncertain status of their underlying behavioral assumptions. For example, we know that people are not the "compleat" decision makers postulated by the revealed-preferences method, and that completely unrestrained markets are unachievable particularly with technologies that have only a few producers or are vital to national defense. What we do not know, and what is critical to assessing the quality of the conclusions generated by these analyses, is the extent to which these failings negate the claim that such analyses reveal people's preferences. A final source of ambiguity is that revealed-preference theory was originally developed by economists to handle private goods with monetary consequences; it is unclear to what extent it can be extended to decisions about public goods with life-and-death consequences (McNown, 1978).

How adequate are bootstrapping methods for resolving acceptable-risk questions?

Comprehensive

The deficiencies of three of these bootstrapping methods are quite straightforward. Risk compendiums and natural standards consider risks in great detail, but entirely ignore the benefits accruing from technologies. Revealed preferences accommodates one expression of benefits, but includes no consideration of how those benefits (and the risks) are distributed. At the other extreme, analysis of implied preferences reflects whatever factors happened to influence the political processes it chooses to describe; its comprehensiveness cannot be assessed.

All of the methods ignore the question of what alternatives are available. Indeed, because they pass judgment on the acceptability of particular technologies, none of them provides guidance for choosing between two alternatives when they both pass or both fail the acceptability test. In that sense the methods fail to address the decision makers' problem of choosing between options.

Logically sound

The strength of the bootstrapping methods is their breadth. More than other methods, they attempt to look at a full spectrum of hazards so as to impose consistent safety standards. The summary measures they use are interpreted, with some justification, as reflecting society's or nature's empirical (i.e., nonanalytic) integration of a wide range of factors (e.g., economic pressures, political negotiations, public preferences, engineering ingenuity).

The weakness of bootstrapping methods is their lack of depth. The logic of exactly how these societal or natural processes perform their integrative magic is neither made very explicit nor empirically validated. The details of how such analyses are to be conducted are left equally inexplicit. Conclusions are highly sensitive to problem definition, yet there seems to be no theoretical basis for choosing among alternative definitions.

One purpose of revealed preferences is to avoid the logical thickets of trying to reduce risks and benefits to a common unit. This problem is finessed by comparing the risks and benefits of a test case with the pattern of risk–benefit tradeoffs currently accepted. One purpose of the analysis in Figure 5.4 was to avoid the similar difficulties of reducing probability-of-risk and magnitude-of-risk statistics to a common measure. Each of these strategies works only if a clear pattern emerges and the standing of the test case vis-à-vis that pattern is unambiguous. Such clarity becomes increasingly unlikely as the number of relevant dimensions increases - for example, when one wants to consider benefits, probability of fatal accidents, magnitude of fatal accidents, expected number of cases of disability, and so forth. When clarity is lacking, the bootstrapping methods offer no decision rule.

Practical

The weakly specified conditions for an adequate bootstrapping analysis usually make these methods eminently implementable. At times, any set of data that can be expressed in a common unit will do. When stricter requirements are imposed, these methods can quickly become quite impractical. For example, with natural standards, there is no cheap way to assess ambient levels of many chemicals in geological time; there is no feasible way to derive rates of disease or accident; and there is no conceivable way of looking for geological effluents of newly created chemicals. With revealed preferences or risk compendiums, there might be no way of expressing the set of relevant hazards in a common unit. Even if a common unit exists in theory, it might not be the unit in terms of which the hazards were managed; within a set, various hazards may be thought of in terms of risk per hour of exposure, risk per unit of production, total annual casualities, or consequences of their maximum credible accident. Finally, it may be hard to define some of the terms needed for such an analysis. For example, what constitutes an hour of exposure to handguns? How voluntary are risks from prescription antibiotics or motor vehicles? Are traffic accidents that occur on the way to the airport (or that are caused by the congestion near airports) to be included as risks of aviation?

Open to evaluation

Like other computational methods, bootstrapping analyses are, in principle, highly scrutable. As with those other methods, however, this potential is somewhat frustrated by problems in both theory and practice. Problems of practice arise whenever inadequate attention is given to making the substance, assumptions, and limitations of analyses comprehensible to the recipients whose intuitions they are intended to educate. For example, the pioneering analyses of Tables 5.1 and 5.2 gave little attention to how lay people interpret very small probabilities, what degree of precision they impute to point estimates like those presented, or whether they think to question the scientific validity of the statistics. Statements such as, The risk from nuclear power is equal to the risk of riding an extra three miles in an automobile may confuse rather than enlighten many people. Without a better understanding of cognitive processes, attempts to aid intuition may only confound it, or even deliberately exploit its weaknesses for rhetorical purposes.

In the original presentation of his results, Starr (1969) carefully detailed the limitations he saw in his analysis. Although his list included several points not mentioned here, it still omitted many of the conceptual or political limitations of the revealed-preferences method that were discussed earlier in this chapter. We are just beginning to develop a full understanding of these limitations. Even if a full set of qualifications were to accompany any of these analyses, the recipient would probably still be hard pressed to know how to deal with it. Whenever a method has such fundamental problems, it is hard to determine whether even the best of all possible applications is good enough to guide societal decision making.

Politically acceptable

At the heart of the bootstrapping approach lie two strong political presumptions. One is that the past worked, in the sense that its denizens were able to achieve their legitimate goals. The second is that the future should work in the same way; that is, the goals of the past should be our goals. If made explicit, these presumptions would not sit very well with many people, particularly those who feel that society has not done right by them or those who feel that the notion of a smooth, efficient, responsive society is a myth promulgated by those interested in preserving the status quo.

Other ethical presumptions emerge when the bootstrapping methods are implemented. The lack of distributional or equity considerations is one. The precise way that benefits are measured is another. Natural standards, for example, ignores immediate benefits (e.g., income, innovation, employment) in favor of vaguely specified, long-term goals such as survival of the species or the integrity of ecological systems. For better or worse, such abstract and absolute standards are likely to fare poorly in political battles. On the other hand, without such standards there is often no one around to negotiate for future generations (or "minor" animal species, or vegetation without recognized economic value). In choosing a relevant past and the set of relevant hazards, the analyst may prejudge other value questions and invite trouble from knowledgeable observers.

Compatible with institutions

Although widely invoked in recent risk discussions, bootstrapping analyses have little legal standing in present-day institutions. The Delaney Amendment imposed natural standards on the Food and Drug Administration; but the fact that the amendment is rarely invoked and even more rarely upheld suggests that it was a misfit even there. Perhaps the bootstrappers have made their greatest inroads with the International Committee on Radiation Protection, a collegial body that has constantly referred to background exposures in its deliberations (e.g., K. Z. Morgan, 1969), and whose recommendations have been adopted for many purposes. Otherwise, bootstrapping analyses are more likely to be found on the pages of *Science* or *Technology Review* than on those of the *Federal Register* or the *Code of Federal Regulations*.

Because it offers specific directives, requires no involvement with the public, and adopts a simple, narrow problem definition (by ignoring alternatives), bootstrapping should lend itself well to the procedures of bureaucratic regulatory agencies. Because it mandates performance standards, bootstrapping should also find a home in professional organizations, whose members can search for creative solutions to problems unshackled by the constraints of design standards. Although poorly developed, the implied-preferences method would seem to fit easily into existing institutions, as it assumes that those institutions are doing such a good job that they only need to be helped to do faster what they do naturally. Implied preferences may fit too well in that it may reinforce bad practices as well as good ones.

We suspect, however, that ambiguities in problem definition will render bootstrapped rulings vulnerable to court (or other) challenges. In any specific application the details will make all the difference, and the choice of details may be hard to defend. For example, the problems of implementing the Delaney Amendment largely reflect the unresolved debate over what zero risk means, a debate that arises from the vast improvement over the last 20 years in science's ability to detect deleterious effects of chemicals (Bradley, 1980).

Conducive to learning

Because they aggregate experiences over time, bootstrapping analyses embody a long-term perspective. Because they provide a systematic way to accommodate new scientific information, they facilitate the integration of knowledge about diverse hazards. Because they look to the past, they promise consistent standards that will codify existing wisdom.

They may be somewhat less successful, however, in providing for the future. Although bootstrapping takes into account the standards adopted for other hazards in the past, it does not consider the cumulative impact of the decisions it derives. Accepting many tolerable hazards may lead to an overall risk burden that is intolerable. In addition, bootstrapping is most likely to be applied to decisions about the acceptability of new technologies. New hazards are required to pass a test that many familiar technologies have failed. This double standard may be seen as an obstacle to innovation or as a response to society's overall risk burden. From the public's perspective, one way to reduce a currently intolerable risk level is to forbid any new technologies unless they reduce dependence on more hazardous ones already in use.

Summary

Bootstrapping assumes that an adjustive process has produced a nearly optimal balance of risks and benefits in our social or natural environment, and that descriptions of past or present policies therefore provide reasonable prescriptive guides. If our society has managed hazards well, that experience can be codified and applied to future decisions. By circumventing the need for costly trial and error, we can, in effect, lift ourselves up by our own bootstraps.

What seems at first glance to be a simple and compelling approach looks less viable under careful examination. Risk compendiums are superficial and misleading in that they ignore benefits, equity, catastrophic potential, and uncertainty. The revealed-preferences method takes benefits into account, but relies on strong and unsubstantiated assumptions about human behavior and the validity of market data. Although implied preferences may be the most inclusive, this method makes less sense if one considers the tumultuous way in which government often makes decisions. Even if these methods could ascertain what people have wanted in some ideal past, they fail to consider what people *should* want. The natural-standards method is less susceptible to the flaws of society, but its insensitivity to economic issues is politically unrealistic.

Finally, all four methods leave critical details of their implementation unspecified, making them too imprecise as decision rules. Bootstrapping analyses appear at first glance to be a natural way to edify our intuitions. Yet the facts do not speak for themselves – unless listeners already know what they want to hear. When the facts must be interpreted, the weakness of the logic underlying bootstrapping analyses makes their conclusions problematic.

6 Formal analysis

Formal analyses attempt to clarify the issues in acceptable-risk decisions through the application of analytical schemes based upon formally defined principles of rationality. Cost–benefit analysis and decision analysis are the two most prominent representatives of this genre and the ones that will receive the greatest attention here. All versions of formal analysis attempt to evaluate and compare the advantages and disadvantages of proposed actions. They do so in four steps:

1. The decision problem is defined by listing alternative courses of action and the set of all possible consequences. The scope of these lists is a critical determinant of the adequacy and acceptability of the analysis.
2. The relationships between these alternatives and their consequences are described. Sophisticated mathematical or structural models may be used in this step. These reflect a divide-and-conquer strategy, decomposing complex problems into more manageable parts; they include models of physical processes, market behavior, dose–response relationships, and so forth. Probabilistic aspects of the alternative–consequence relationships are quantitatively expressed in most decision analyses and in some cost–benefit analyses.
3. All consequences are evaluated in a common unit. In cost–benefit analysis, money is the measure of value; decision analysis uses subjective value judgments of worth or utility.
4. The components of the analysis are integrated to produce a bottom-line number evaluating each alternative. In cost–benefit analysis, this number represents the difference between the benefits and costs to be expected if that alternative is selected; in decision analysis, it represents the option's expected utility. Often, review procedures (e.g., sensitivity analysis) are applied to assess the robustness of these numbers.

If these analytic tools are interpreted as constituting *methods* for acceptable-risk decisions, then the alternative that fares best on the bottom line should be adopted. Anyone who accepts a technique's underlying assumptions and its implementation should follow its recommendations. A more moderate view holds that the simplifying assumptions and deficiencies of even the best analyses render them only an *aid* to decision making. In this view, the goal of analysis is to clarify a problem's facts, values, and uncertainties, thereby making it easier for decision makers to rely on their own intuitions in choosing an alternative.

Cost–benefit analysis

Cost–benefit analysis goes by many different names, including benefit–cost analysis, risk–benefit analysis and other permutations. Techniques whose label includes the word *risk* always focus on threats to life and limb, but so do some cost–benefit analyses. In addition, many different techniques go by the name cost–benefit analysis. The label has been used for almost any explicit consideration of the monetary advantages and disadvantages of one or more decision options. For convenience, however, the term cost–benefit analysis will be used here and will refer to those analyses most firmly grounded in economic theory.

Drawing by S. Harris. Reprinted with permission of The New Yorker Magazine, Inc.

Conceptual basis

Cost–benefit analysis first gained prominence in the 1930s when the U.S. Army Corps of Engineers adopted it for evaluating water-resource projects. Its origins lie in economic theory, particularly in the economics of social welfare and resource allocation. Somewhat in the spirit of accounting, it attempts to add up the values of all of the good and bad consequences of a project. These values are defined as individuals' preferences (or subjective valuations). The tools of economic theory are used to assess these preferences, particularly as they are revealed in market behavior, in order to study the economic efficiency of proposed projects. That project is selected that best fulfills the utilitarian criterion of the greatest good for the greatest number (i.e., it has the greatest preponderance of benefits over costs summed over all affected individuals). Elementary expositions may be found in Layard (1974) and Stokey and Zeckhauser (1978); Mishan (1976) offers a more complete discussion.

Simply adding costs and benefits ignores who gets what. The Pareto optimality criterion is designed to accommodate equity concerns: An action is considered acceptable (indeed preferable) if it improves the subjective economic status of at least one member of society without making any other member worse off. Many social policies benefit some people and harm others, thereby violating the Pareto criterion. In such cases, the criterion can be met only by having those who gain compensate those who would otherwise lose, either directly (e.g., through negotiated payments) or indirectly (e.g., through tax relief to the losers). The difficulty of creating viable compensation schemes has led to development of the less stringent criterion of *potential* Pareto improvement (also called the Kaldor–Hicks criterion). According to this criterion, an action is acceptable if the gainers *could* compensate the losers; the requirement that they actually do so is dropped. This criterion legitimates choosing the alternative that maximizes the difference between total benefits and total costs, regardless of their distribution.

In its pursuit of economic efficiency, cost–benefit analysis aims to include all consequences amenable to economic valuation and to exclude all others (Parish, 1976). The phrase "amenable to economic valuation" is subject to different interpretations, particularly when one is deciding whether to include "soft" values such as scenic beauty or national honor. Many practitioners evaluate only those commodities and services that have readily measurable market values (e.g., construction costs, sales, and wages). Indirect economic-evaluation methods using demand principles, shadow prices, and the like may extend the range of considerations to which a dollar value may be attached. There is, however, some disagreement as to how far these methods should be pushed to allow inclusion of social and political consequences. Some analysts argue that the introduction of noneconomic consequences would confuse the analysis, obscure the purely economic facts, and prevent a ''clear interpretation and social rationale'' (Mishan, 1974, p. 91). According to Parish (1976), ''we should render unto Caesar those things that are Caesar's; *our* primary expertise and responsibility lies in explicating the workings of Mammon. And we certainly should not attempt to play God'' (p. 314, emphasis in original).

Although the idea of listing, calculating, and summing monetary consequences is straightforward, its execution may be very difficult. Some economic effects must be ignored for want of credible assessment techniques. Other problems have generated enough conflicting techniques to fill the professional literature with critiques and rebuttals. With some problems, such as establishing the monetary value of life, those conflicts seem far from resolution.

Variants of cost-benefit analysis

Cost-effectiveness analysis. In some problems, all alternatives have the *same benefits*. For example, a chemical firm may have several ways to reduce workers' inhalation of a toxic substance by a fixed amount. Since the benefits of the methods are equal, cost becomes the only issue. In other problems, all alternatives have the *same cost*. For example, the chemical plant may allocate a fixed sum of money for protecting workers. The problem then becomes choosing the alternative that achieves the greatest reduction in toxic inhalation for that amount of money.

In neither case is there any need to reduce costs and benefits to a common metric. Cost-effectiveness analysis is designed to reveal which alternative produces the greatest effect for the amount of money one has to spend or which produces the desired effect with the smallest expenditure. As a result, it avoids the sticky task of directly assessing the economic value of a given reduction in exposure. Of course, the value placed on workers' health affects the analysis indirectly through the decision about how much to reduce exposure or how much to spend.

One danger of cost-effectiveness analysis is that the opportunity to avoid comparing costs and benefits may tempt one to oversimplify the problem. For example, one may fail to ask (a) whether the budgeted amount is too large or too small given the severity of the problem; (b) whether the firm might use those funds better in other ways (e.g., on alternative safety options whose benefits might be difficult to compare or on increased compensation to workers); or (c) whether there are subtle differences in the options that render their costs or benefits less equivalent than they seem (e.g., a filter that costs more may also remove other pollutants). Although all techniques may define problems too narrowly or omit subtle costs and benefits, the temptation may be particularly great with cost-effectiveness analysis.

Using cost-benefit analysis to set acceptable risks

Like other formal decision-making tools, cost–benefit analysis may be regarded as either a method or an aid. That is, one can use it to determine which option has the greatest preponderance of benefits over risks, or merely as a guide to be supplemented by other considerations. Rowe (1977b) offers a four-stage process for accommodating such considerations. Stage 1 analyzes direct economic benefits and costs. If the former are greater than the latter, indirect and nonquantitative effects are analyzed (Stage 2), followed by examination of the cost of additional reductions in risk (Stage 3). Rowe notes that "the central question in this risk-reduction analysis is determining the point at which risk has been sufficiently reduced" (p. 962), and acknowledges the difficulty of specifying what "sufficiently" means. Stage 4 reconciles inequities, using society's current practices as a reference point. Thus, this final stage uses bootstrapping to elaborate a formal analysis.

Rowe's proposal raises questions omitted in cost–benefit analysis more than it resolves them. For example, it leaves unanswered: How are the nonquantitative consequences of Stage 2 to be integrated with the formal analysis? What is the criterion for deciding how much risk reduction to buy? What bootstrapping approach to risk inequities avoids the problems discussed in Chapter 5?

Decision analysis

Decision analysis has its origins in the theory of individual decision making developed by von Neumann and Morgenstern (1947) and Savage (1954). Decision theory is an axiomatic theory for making choices in uncertain conditions. It is also a prescriptive theory; if you accept the axioms and their interpretation in practice, you *ought* to make the recommended choices. Decision analysis implements decision theory with the aid of techniques drawn from economics, operations research, and management science. The details of this marriage of axiomatic theory and applied methodology may be found in R. A. Howard (1968), R. A. Howard, Matheson, and Miller (1976), Keeney and Raiffa (1976), Raiffa (1968), and Schlaifer (1969).

A thorough decision analysis has five main steps:

1. Structuring the problem. The analyst defines the decision problem by identifying the relevant alternatives, consequences, and sources of uncertainty. Structural models are used to express the interrelationships among these elements; the construction and application of such models require both technical expertise and good judgment.

2. Assessing probabilities. Uncertainties about the present and future states of the world are quantified as probabilities. Decision analysts view probabilities as expressions of individuals' beliefs, not characteristics of things. As a result, probabilities are elicited as judgments from the decision maker or from experts (Spetzler & Staël von Holstein, 1975).

3. Assessing preferences. Unlike cost–benefit analysis, which quantifies preferences by analysis of market data, decision analysis uses subjective value judgments, that is, utilities. Thus, decision analysis can in principle accommodate any consideration that the decision maker deems appropriate. Values for such soft considerations as esthetics or satisfying Senator X can be judged and included as easily as for hard considerations like monetary cost.

In this process, attitudes toward risk are also accommodated. For example, an analysis could reflect the decision maker's feeling that a safety device having a 0.5 chance of saving 100 lives is less desirable than one that will surely save 50 lives. Such an attitude, called *risk aversion,* is defined as the feeling that the desirability of an alternative with uncertain outcomes (or consequences) is less than the desirability of its expected outcome (i.e., its outcomes weighted by their probability of occurrence). *Risk proneness* is the reverse, representing a preference for a gamble with uncertain outcomes over the expected outcome of that gamble.

When a particular outcome has several kinds of values associated with it (e.g., a successful operation can lead to both reduced pain and prolonged life), cost–benefit analysis simply adds together the various costs and benefits. In decision analysis, other combination rules are also available (e.g., a multiplicative rule when the utility of one aspect of value depends on the level of another [Keeney & Raiffa, 1976]).

4. Evaluating alternatives. The attractiveness of each alternative is summarized by its expected utility, which is equal to the sum of the utilities of each possible outcome, weighted by their respective probabilities of occurrence. The alternative with the greatest expected utility is the indicated choice.

5. Sensitivity analysis and value of information. The analysis is reexamined from two perspectives: (a) Can it be simplified by omitting components that do not affect the final decision? For example, an alternative that was inferior to another in all aspects could be dropped. (b) Are there places where a reasonable change in the structure, a utility, or a probability could lead to the selection of a different alternative? Two tools are used for this reexamination. In *sensitivity analysis,* the calculations are repeated, each time dropping or adding one or more components or using a different assessment of one or more utilities or probabilities. When a critical component is found, *value-of-information* analysis is used to assess the value of gathering further information that might change the recommended decision. For example, calculating the value of receiving perfect information sets an upper limit on how much one should pay for partial information.

Using decision analysis to set acceptable risks

As the key elements in a decision analysis (probabilities, utilities, problem structure) are subjective, they must come from someone. However, in societal decisions, there is rarely one entity (i.e., individual, organization) that is the final arbiter of these questions. When more than one set of utility or probability judgments must be considered, decision analysis may be used in one of several ways to guide acceptable-risk decisions.

For a start the analyst can prepare several complete analyses, each of which reflects the perspective of one party. Gardiner and Edwards (1975) found that when two opposing groups, realtors and conservationists, used only their own intuitions for ranking alternative solutions to a coastal-zoning problem, they were in strong disagreement. However, when their rankings were generated by a simplified form of decision analysis, much of the disagreement disappeared.

Another approach is to try to generate agreement on the judgments needed to produce a consensual analysis. Such agreement could reflect compromises (I'll give up here if you give up there; put it to a vote; let's take an average) or genuine consensus. That consensus could be seen as representing the views of a hypothetical Supra–Decision Maker.

Keeney and Raiffa (1976) recommend using a Supra–Decision Maker even when the various parties cannot agree. That entity could incorporate the probabilistic judgments of various experts into its own beliefs using theoretically justified techniques (e.g., Morris, 1974). Integrating different values would require the assumption, often made by makers of public policy, that they can accurately reflect an entire society's values. A less presumptuous technique would be to elicit the values of various stakeholders (environmentalists, politicians, manufacturers, impactees, etc.) and then have the Supra–Decision Maker determine the relative importance of each (von Winterfeldt, 1978).

Although formal analysis can help produce agreement, it may also lead to polarization of views. The act of publicly specifying one's views may harden one's commitment to them and discourage compromise. Leaders may assume extreme positions to ensure followers' allegiance. Finally, as constituent groups gain experience with formal analysis, they may exaggerate their positions in order to bias the analysis in their favor. When the parties cannot agree on the relative attractiveness of the alternatives, other procedures are needed to augment decision analysis.

Generic problems

Defining the problem

Competent formal analyses begin with a careful definition of the problem. Uncertainties and values are then addressed within that framework. An open and explicit problem definition both reduces the possibility of omitting key issues and increases the opportunities for incorporating new concerns, options, and information as they arise. In a problem definition, cost–benefit analysis can accommodate any economic consequences; decision analysis can accommodate any consequences that the decision maker can judge. Although both can incorporate any options, they may treat the set of available options somewhat differently. Decision analysis considers the entire set simultaneously, whereas cost–benefit analysis often focuses on one proposal; other options arise only in the analysis of opportunity costs, other ways that money invested in the focal option could be spent.

A corollary of having no bounds on problem definition is providing no guidance. A model can include everything (if the resources are provided), but need not include anything. Because of resource constraints, a formal model cannot include everything; it must simplify and omit. It may start as a small, back-of-an-envelope sketch and be elaborated with more details, components, and submodels in successive iterations. Cost–benefit analysis offers no guideline as to when the model is complete. Decision analysts stop when they believe that further changes in the model would not significantly alter the desirability of the selected alternative. To the extent that they are generalists, formal analysts are not able to provide an independent perspective for a client who is satisfied with an impoverished problem definition. By contrast, the professional who makes acceptable-risk decisions (Chapter 4) has substantive knowledge with which to challenge clients. To allay this problem, the analyst must either specialize in a particular topic or possess the personal skills to induce clients and experts to think more broadly. Another antidote to narrowness is to involve parties capable of providing a variety of perspectives (although this step could complicate the process of producing a single, convergent, consensual analysis).

Although critics have typically complained about overly narrow analyses, breadth may also hold dangers. An analysis may become so large as to be unwieldy and unworkable, its structure so complex as to obscure the interrelationships of its parts, the needed inputs too numerous to measure carefully. Indeed, some analysts might argue that they are most effective in fast, limited analyses designed to afford some systematic understanding of a narrowly defined problem. In some situations, full-blown analyses may promise more definitiveness than they can hope to deliver. In others, time pressures may justify deliberate omissions. For example, a flurry of complaints about severe side effects from a recently licensed drug might lead a regulatory agency to do a quick analysis that ignores considerations that would be important in more leisurely circumstances (e.g., the effect of a recall on pharmaceutical innovation). Of course, persistent narrowing of focus, as typically happens in agencies that always function under crisis conditions, will lead to the long-term neglect of larger issues.

Knowing the facts

Formal analysis holds out the promise that the facts of a matter can be organized effectively and explicitly. Analyses can, in principle, accommodate any fact or estimate compatible with their problem definition. The uncertainties surrounding these facts are commonly addressed in decision analysis, but less frequently in cost–benefit analysis. Uncertainties may be reflected in sensitivity analyses: Once the best-guess analysis has been completed using the most likely version of each component, it is repeated using alternative versions of what those components might be. Uncertainties may also be incorporated directly into an analysis in the form of probabilities used to calculate the utilities of options.

Although both cost–benefit analysis and decision analysis use probabilities, they interpret them in different ways. Decision analysts hold the subjectivist view, according to which probabilities represent an individual's degree of belief about the world, not a property of the world (Kyburg & Smokler, 1964; Savage, 1954). Hence, they feel free to elicit probabilities of unique events (e.g., a major international conflict in the next six months, an untested new drug being teratogenic) as well as probabilities of recurrent events for which frequency information is available (e.g., a valve failing in the course of 10,000 operations). Indeed, they would hold that extrapolating from frequency counts to predictions requires the exercise of judgment and is therefore inherently subjective (e.g., to rely on past failure rates, one must believe that the valve will be subject to essentially identical conditions in the future).

Although there is no conceptual requirement that they do so, most cost–benefit analysts who address probabilities appear to hold a frequentistic view in which they are seen as characteristics of events or processes. This view makes it difficult to combine frequency data with subjective judgments or to deal with uncertainties for which there are no relative frequencies.

Reliance on judgment allows decision analysts to widen the range of factual issues that can be represented in their work. It also makes them particularly dependent upon the quality of those judgments, and therefore vulnerable to the vagaries of judgment discussed in Chapter 2 and particularly the difficulties in assessing uncertainty. Although some analysts have devoted considerable thought and care to the problems of probability elicitation (e.g., Staël von Holstein & Matheson, 1978), one may still wonder how much judgmental skill the decision maker or expert can acquire in the midst of an analysis.

Assessing values

One strength of formal analysis is that many value issues are given the explicit, quantitative expression that befits their central role in societal decision making. Disagreements are brought out into the open so that it can be established which are most critical to the final decision. These processes have helped to spotlight a number of troublesome value issues.

Unstable values. People's preferences will often undergo marked changes over time. By inferring preferences from historical market data, cost–benefit analysis assumes unchanging values. Decision analysis can, in principle, ask people what they want today and what they expect to want in the future (when the consequences of today's decisions will be experienced). But values need not be well articulated. Neither cost–benefit nor decision analysis is very well suited to situations in which people do not really know what they want. Indeed, decision analysts often ask unfamiliar questions such as, How many days of uncomfortable hospitalization would you endure to lower your probability of dying this year by 10 percent? Even with far more familiar questions, subtle variations in elicitation techniques can produce quite different answers (see Chapter 2). Reliance on economic data in no way renders cost–benefit analysis immune; the essence of marketing is to manipulate people's uncertain values, altering their preferences and creating desires that they never had.

Nonmonetary consequences. Because it evaluates consequences relative to one another rather than by translation to dollar terms, decision analysis is relatively free to address noneconomic consequences (e.g., local pride, beauty, species preservation). But cost–benefit analysis can treat only economic consequences and typically does treat only those that are readily quantified in dollar terms. For example, Walker and Bayley (1977–1978) tentatively proposed evaluating the yearly "environmental" costs of building a highway across a marsh as (a) educational value: $5 for each of 50,000 student visitors, and (b) recreational value: $24 for each of 500 fishing trips, $24 for each of 100 boating trips, and $55 for each of 50 bird-watching trips. Such a procedure ignores any intrinsic value that preserving the marsh and its wildlife might have or any value that people attribute to the marsh that is not reflected by what they spend to visit it. It would logically follow that those who live close by value it less than those who travel from afar (and spend more) to visit it.

Value of a life. In placing a value on the loss of human life, as elsewhere, cost–benefit analysis must find a monetary equivalent. Unfortunately, "there is no universal agreement on how to value lives; indeed, more surprisingly, no one has even claimed to have found an unequivocal procedure for life evaluation'' (Zeckhauser & Shepard, 1976, p. 419; see also Jones-Lee, 1976; Linnerooth, 1976; Schelling, 1968).

According to one traditional economic approach, the value of a person's lost life equals the amount of money one would need to invest today to earn the income that he or she would have earned. By this view, those in society who are underpaid are also undervalued. Those who have no income (e.g., homemakers) have no value and those who ''take from society'' (e.g., retirees) have a negative value. This approach also ignores the effect on society's fabric of accepting various potentially lethal gambles, not to mention the noneconomic effects of a death on loved ones or dependents (Schelling, 1968). A second economic approach, in which the value of life is equated with court awards, may recognize pain and suffering, but is hardly more satisfactory on other counts (Holmes, 1970). Yet another economic approach focuses on the financial compensation needed to induce workers to accept increased occupational risks. As discussed in Chapter 5, this revealed-preferences approach founders on technical difficulties and overly strong behavioral assumptions regarding how much workers know about the risks to which they are exposed and how free they are to bargain effectively with their employers.

Frustration with the limits of these market-based approaches has led some cost–benefit analysts to advocate a method in the decision–analysis tradition: asking people directly what they would be willing to pay for some marginal change in their probability of survival (Acton, 1973; Linnerooth, 1975). In these efforts, an important theoretical distinction would be made as to the difference between how much people will pay to avoid a risk and how much they demand as compensation when a risk is imposed upon them. The latter value is appropriate for hazard problems that involve involuntary risks. Since it is also likely to be larger, confusing the two would underestimate the value of a life.

Within the context of decision analysis, R. A. Howard (1978) has argued that the appropriate concern is one's value to oneself, not one's value to others or to the economy. He further notes that it is not irrational to place an infinite value on one's life when the chances of dying are large (e.g., refusing a gamble involving a 0.8 chance of death for any amount of money) and yet accept a finite amount of money in return for a small increase in the risk of death. He proposed asking such questions as, How much money would I have to pay you to take a black pill that has a 0.001 probability of causing instant painless death? (see also Greene, 1980). Postulating reasonable answers to this question, Howard calculated a ''small-risk value of life'' in the range of $1 million to $4 million. Similar techniques might be developed for evaluating loss of limb or health assuming that people can imagine such states (Calabresi, 1970). Unfortunately, however, novel questions on a difficult topic may produce poorly informed and labile responses.

Despite their flaws, these various methods for determining the value of a life have produced estimates varying by a factor of only 20 (between $200,000 and about $4 million). These extreme values could be used in a sensitivity analysis and might lead to the same decision - although, of course, they might share a common bias.

Future costs and benefits. In cost–benefit analysis, future consequences are evaluated by first computing their future economic value (in today's dollars) and then applying a discount rate to find a (lower) value that represents their *present discounted value*. The rationale for assuming that a future outcome is worth less than an equivalent one today is that instead of setting aside today the total future value, K, we could invest a lesser amount, K_0, which would grow to K by the time it is needed. The rate of return on investment that takes K_0 to K in N years is called the *discount rate*. K_0, the present discounted value of K, represents an opportunity cost, the amount one could spend on something else now if one did not have to have K on hand N years hence.

Technically, discounting is hampered by the great sensitivity of decisions to the particular rate used and the absence of a consensus on the right rate. For example, Schulze (1974) argues that if we want to minimize future generations' regret about our present decisions, we should use a rate of zero. Failing to find a generally accepted rate, a National Academy of Sciences panel (1975) suggested a sensitivity analysis using a variety of rates (hoping that they would lead to similar recommendations).

Conceptually, discounting is limited whenever costs and benefits cannot be converted into interest-yielding investments. According to Lovins (1977):

> Until recently risk discounting made it attractive to jerry-build British bridges and buildings that could fall on someone's head in twenty years, as a twenty-year risk discounted at the 10 percent annual rate recommended by Her Majesty's Treasury was valued at 15 percent of an equivalent present risk. British authorities slowly realized, however, that safety and lives cannot be banked at interest as money can and that discounting risks is neither morally nor theoretically sound. (p. 918)

The fact that British civil engineers are typically accused of being overly cautious (A. Cohen, 1980) suggests that professional judgment has supplemented this economic reasoning.

The speed at which even small discount rates compound can produce absurd results over long time periods. Mishan and Page (1979) showed that conventional discounting methods would assess the cost in 100 years of banning a hypothetical chemical today at almost 10 times the GNP calculated for that future date.

Decision analysis copes with future consequences by eliciting decision makers' preferences for different streams of costs and benefits over time, which could reflect discount rates or anything else that seems relevant. Owen (1978) has developed an elegant decision-analytic model for treating transgenerational equity issues, using as inputs the answers to such questions as, How much would you pay now to raise the standard of living in the year 2080 by 5 percent?

Equity. The criterion of potential Pareto improvement, which guides cost–benefit analysis, explicitly disregards equity considerations. Although some analysts have proposed weighting schemes for avoiding unfair distributional effects, other analysts claim that equity issues have no place in an analysis, arguing that (a) the distributional inequities for different technologies tend to balance one another (I have a garbage dump in my backyard; you have an electrical plant in yours), (b) equity issues should be resolved independently of hazard management (e.g., through tax credits or progressive income taxes), or (c) cost–benefit analysis cannot do the job adequately. A compromise solution is to calculate the distributional effects of the different options and report them alongside the analysis.

Equity issues have received little attention in decision analysis. Although it would seem simple enough to include an equity dimension in the value model, Keeney (1980a) raises a perplexing issue. He shows that it is inconsistent for an individual who follows the axioms of decision theory both (a) to prefer more equitable distributions of risks over society's members, and (b) to be risk averse regarding number of fatalities. Tversky and Kahneman's (1981) finding that people may be risk prone for losses (including losses of life) suggests that, when pressed for consistency in Keeney's dilemma, people may give up risk aversion first (if they do not choose to give up the axioms).

Attitudes toward risk. Decision analysts routinely ask decision makers whether they are risk prone or risk averse regarding the problem at hand. But risk attitudes have little place in the theory or practice of cost–benefit analysis. An ad-hoc way to incorporate people's presumed risk aversion when human lives are at stake is to raise the number of lives lost in a single accident to some power (e.g., N^2) to reflect the gravity of catastrophic accidents (R. Wilson, 1975). An alternative response is to argue that no explicit consideration of risk attitudes is needed because they are automatically incorporated into the market data used in cost–benefit analyses. If people are risk averse, they will pay more for safer goods, making those prices rise. The validity of that argument depends, of course, on the extent to which a free market exists and takes risk issues into account.

One might argue on two grounds that those who make acceptable-risk decisions on behalf of others have a moral duty to be risk neutral even when the people affected by their decisions are risk averse or risk prone: The expected number of lives that will be lost by taking risky decisions using either a risk-averse or risk-prone attitude is never less than for a risk-neutral one; and one's right to be risk prone or risk averse regarding one's own life implies no right to make such value judgments when deciding others' fate.

Coping with the human element

All formal analysis relies on strong behavioral assumptions whose common element is that decision makers are highly rational, sensitive to the limits of their own knowledge, and ready to ask for help when it is needed. Cost-benefit analysts rely on rationality when they use market data to reveal people's preferences; decision analysts do so when they trust decision makers' judgments.

As mentioned in several previous contexts, the interpretation of market data is rendered ambiguous to the extent that freedom of choice is restricted (e.g., by restraint of trade, regulation) and wisdom of choice is limited (e.g., by cognitive overload, overconfidence). Problems of interpretation also arise when social values are in flux. According to Mishan and Page (1979):

> Inasmuch as the untoward consequences of consumer innovations tend to unfold slowly over time, their valuations at any point of time . . . as determined by market prices . . . may bear no relation whatever to the net utilities conferred over time. Indeed, the very pace of change today . . . is such that it is no longer possible for the buying public to learn from its own experience to assess the relative merits of a large proportion of the goods coming onto the market. In consequence, society can have no confidence that the valuations of such goods have any ex post correspondence with people's subjective wants . . .
>
> Within a modern growth economy . . . in which there is ample evidence for the allegation that the "Jones effect" is growing, or that personal attire is increasingly exhibitionist, or that norms of taste are declining, or that much of the economy's output for mass consumption is increasingly trivial if not regrettable, the task of the allocation economist is not an enviable one. In such circumstances, it can reasonably be contended that the ethical consensus to which the normative economist has to defer is itself breaking up. Wherever the consumption of some goods, or the indulgence of some commercially provided activities, are believed by some proportion of the population to be unworthy or degrading and, at the same time, are believed by others to be innocuous if not liberating, the task of the welfare economist becomes impossible. (pp. 21–24)

Decision analysis avoids at least some of these problems by being inherently au courant; it asks decision makers what they believe and want at the moment of decision. There is, however, no guarantee that the respondents will have understood, for example, how their values are changing or how they have been manipulated by others. When society's values are in conflict, few decision makers may be ready to establish by fiat an "ethical consensus"; those who are may not be trusted or empowered to do so. Observers also worry about the possibility that people's expressed opinions will be inconsistent with their behavior. Research (e.g., Fishbein & Ajzen, 1975; Schuman &

Johnson, 1976) suggests that attitudes often predict behavior quite well if several conditions are met: (a) attitude questions are formulated so as to make their logical links to behavior clear, (b) the respondent has an articulated position on the question, and (c) the respondent is not strongly motivated to lie. Even when decision analyses violate these conditions, they still offer a clear record of what was done, allowing reviewers to assess the credibility of the judgments used.

Assessing decision quality

Realizing the fallibility of the inputs they use, good analysts perform sensitivity analyses as a matter of course. The final calculations are repeated using alternative levels for questionable inputs. The robustness of the conclusion is determined by the extent to which these reanalyses produce similar results.

The discussion in Chapter 2 of the potential and limitations of sensitivity analysis was drawn from the work of the analysts. Among the issues that were cited as key determinants of the value of sensitivity analysis were (a) the extent to which it is necessary to exercise fallible judgment to identify troublesome inputs and choose the range of possible values, (b) the threat of intellectual common-mode failure, by which an analytic procedure repeatedly introduces the same bias (e.g., an elicitation method persistently evokes only one perspective, or a costing technique consistently shortchanges health or productivity concerns), and (c) the difficulty of compounding uncertainty over all aspects of an analysis.

One source of guidance is empirical research into the judgments required to evaluate analyses. For example, apparent tendencies to overestimate one's knowledge and neglect omissions in problem representations suggest a bias toward putting too much faith in formal analyses. Additional sources include empirical studies of successful analyses and a general error theory for formal analyses (Fischhoff, 1980a) that provides general guidelines as to what errors may enter into analysis, how virulent they are, how they are propagated through the analysis, what can be done to mitigate their impact, and what such errors mean in terms of action.

How adequate are analytic techniques for resolving acceptable-risk problems?

Comprehensive

Decision analysis has the advantage that it can represent whatever fact or value issues interest the decision maker. Cost–benefit analysis runs into trouble when there is a need to accommodate uncertainties or consequences without immediate, tangible economic consequences. On the other hand, the cost–benefit analyst's grounding in economics may enable him or her to provide some substantive guidance as to what issues should be included in an analysis. Purveyors of both methods hope that the conceptual framework and vocabulary they offer will help to identify issues that are omitted and to sharpen the debate around those that are included.

Logically sound

At the core of both cost–benefit analysis and decision analysis lies a coherent theory that describes how to integrate fact and value issues so as to produce recommendations that are in the decision maker's (or society's) best interest. The strength of these prescriptive rules for decision making is limited, in part, by the descriptive validity of their underlying behavioral assumptions. To the extent that market data do not reveal preferences or people reject the axioms of decision theory, the techniques are less trustworthy. The soundness of the methods used to treat some difficult issues (e.g., equity) is still in need of research.

Practical

Although these methods are designed to attack complex problems in great detail, they are not always able to do so. Cost–benefit analysis has no procedures for solving some measurement problems (e.g., value of a life); such issues are either ignored or treated with ad-hoc procedures that may please few knowledgeable consumers. Although decision analysis faces fewer conceptual problems in developing such techniques, workable, validated procedures are not available for all problems (e.g., assessing future values).

Full-blown methods are expensive and time-consuming; even fast, limited analyses may require an abundance of highly trained experts. As a result, the methods are not always thoroughly or competently applied. The possibility that an approach will not be implemented as its designers intended raises a thorny problem for the evaluator. Obviously, formal analysis should not be held accountable for crude and ineffectual analyses done by poorly trained individuals or under severe resource constraints. Or should it? If only a select few can master a craft and the masters do not monitor those acting in its name, then its usefulness is limited. Because the resources needed for a thorough and competent analysis will not always be available, the issue of practicality may depend on how gracefully analyses degrade. Research is needed to tell when a partial analysis is better than a full-blown one or none at all.

Open to evaluation

A strong selling point for formal analysis is not only that it is open to evaluation, but that it provides evaluative techniques such as sensitivity analysis. The analyst is, in principle, saying to critics, Here are the inputs and models that I used. If you don't like them, let's try it your way. However, this potential can only be realized if adequate funds and expert assistance are made available for these reanalyses. Without them, the mass, complexity, and technicality of some analyses may keep observers from seeing whether their point of view was adequately represented. Here, as with other techniques, scrutability is particularly limited when value-laden assumptions are embedded in the problem definition. The judgmental aspect of any application may allow the unscrupulous analyst to alter many inputs in minor ways, changing the result without making any single input clearly objectionable. Fear of such number games may lead to unjustified suspicion or responsible analyses.

A potent aid to evaluating both the contribution of analysis in general and the quality of any particular application is keeping detailed records of assumptions and operations. Both contemporary and future critics will then be better able to judge fairly the adequacy of the analysis.

Scrutability, of course, is not just a sop to critics, but fundamental to the production of competent analyses. Since in many complex problems one cannot get it right the first time, analysis must be an iterative process. Criticisms should not just be filed, noted, or appended to a report, but incorporated in the revisions that they stimulate. Too often, analysts and their clients may adopt a siege mentality, defending their figures against all comers rather than inferring that vigorous critiques may mean that the analysis has succeeded in illuminating the problem.

Politically acceptable

A number of themes emerge from the criticisms that have been made against formal analyses in the political arena. Some critics are concerned about the extent to which analysis transfers societal decision-making power to a technical elite comprising those who perform analyses and interact with the analysts. A member of that elite might respond that the technical nature of the issues and the vagaries of lay judgment render this transfer of power in the public's own best interest: If you let someone competent do the job, we'll all be better off. The counterargument takes several tacks:

1. On questions of value, their superior technical knowledge does not imply that experts' value systems are superior.
2. On questions of fact, the recurrent need to go beyond available data and rely on intuition weakens the experts' advantage. Indeed, lay people may have access to perspectives that the experts lack.
3. Even if an analysis provides the best assurance of maximizing the efficiency of a particular project, there are higher goals that need to be considered. These include developing an informed citizenry, preserving democratic institutions, and making people feel that they have control of their fate.

Other critics argue that the very reasonableness of formal analysis reflects a debatable political-ideological assumption, namely, that society is cohesive enough and has enough common goals that its problems can be resolved by reason and without struggle. Although such a get-on-with-business orientation will be pleasing to many, it will not satisfy all. Those who doubt that society is in a fine-tuning stage may oppose analysis itself, regardless of its content. Even those who accept the value of analysis may also view it as just one more arena of political struggle. Such struggle has its own logic and a rhetoric different from that of formal analysis. If the results do not support one's position, unconstructive criticism may seem eminently fair and rational, as may ridiculing analysts who have ignored vital issues (like income distribution) that were outside their analytic mandate.

Compatible with institutions

Formal analysis not only can but already is being used in many present-day regulatory and administrative institutions. Its future role will depend in part upon how these institutions contend with the resource requirements of the more extensive analyses. Possible strategies are (a) always do incomplete analyses, with no hope or pretense of producing definitive and defensible conclusions; (b) invest all resources in a detailed, initial problem structuring, hoping to derive the maximum educational value; or (c) postpone small analyses until a few landmark cases have been completed in order to establish standards for practice and to develop generally applicable techniques and procedures.

Commissioning analyses is not the same as using them. Both bureaucrats and politicians may be reluctant to publicly endorse the painful, callous-sounding balancing of risks and benefits that these techniques use. In a sense, analysis itself was under attack in the recent trial in which Ford Motor Company was charged with reckless homicide based on its alleged decision to manufacture Pintos with a fuel-tank design known to increase risks in the event of rear-end collisions. People seemed shocked that Ford had used analysis to make explicit tradeoffs between costs and lives.

The openness that serves formal analysis so well in other respects may also make it vulnerable to interminable legal challenges that delay implementation. Recent efforts at regulatory reform seek to shift the burden of proof from risky projects to their regulators by requiring cost–benefit analyses of all proposed regulations. Given the limitations of cost–benefit analysis and the lack of agreement even among its advocates on methodological issues, any analysis could be challenged, thereby postponing new regulations indefinitely.

Conducive to learning

The long-term impact of formal analysis will largely depend upon its success in meeting the preceding criteria. If ways are found to meaningfully involve the public, analysis can improve citizens' ability to cope with future crises. If evaluation is taken seriously, we will have an open and accessible record that facilitates consistent decisions and the accumulation of knowledge. If analyses are well managed, competently performed, and responsibly interpreted, formal analysis may become a fixture rather than be rejected as another (intellectual) technology that promised too much or fell into the wrong hands.

Summary

The great strengths of formal analysis are its openness and soundness. Both cost-benefit and decision analysis have carefully thought out logical foundations and, in principle, the ability to encompass a broad range of issues. In some sense, this thoroughness is also their downfall, for it makes their failings more visible and better documented than those of competing approaches. Good analysts, by detailing every step of their work from problem definition through value and fact assessment to bottom-line calculations, maximize the possibilities for both peer review and political attack.

Formal analysis appeals to some regulators in part because it appears to them as a value-free guide to decision making. However, values are an inherent part of acceptable-risk problems. Compared to other approaches, formal analysis treats values quite explicitly. Yet, like other approaches, formal analysis mixes issues of fact and value in complex and subtle ways. For example, cost-benefit analysis takes a political stand by restricting itself to economic valuations. Although decision analysis can accommodate diverse values, personal predisposition or institutional constraints may make analysts content to work within timid and narrow problem definitions. The explicitness of formal analysis satisfies one necessary condition for clarifying how problem definitions prejudge values issues; additional substantive knowledge is needed to identify options, consequences, and events that have been ignored.

As with other techniques, the promise of openness that formal analysis holds out may not be realized in practice. External reviews are not always elicited; when they are, reviewers may not have the financial or technical resources needed to probe deeply, or, if they do, the original analysts (and their clients) may not be ready to accommodate criticism. Analysts may be tempted to exaggerate the completeness or robustness of analyses, whereas critics may be satisfied with nit picking, unmindful of whether the flaws they find seriously threaten the conclusions of the analysis.

Finally, despite their logical soundness, formal methods were not developed for the problems of acceptable risk. Cost-benefit analysis is most appropriate for private decisions in areas with responsive markets, immediate consequences, and well-informed consumers. Decision analysis presumes the existence of an entity (a single decision maker or group) empowered to speak on behalf of society. Typically, however, it is unclear who is empowered to decide that the necessarily incomplete, inaccurate representation of reality found in even the best analysis has successfully identified the most acceptable option.

7 Comparison of approaches

Most of this report has focused on the extent to which each approach, in and of itself, provides a complete answer to acceptable-risk questions. Given the stringency (and occasional incompatibility) of the seven evaluative criteria, it should be no surprise that no approach has proven entirely adequate when compared with these absolute standards. Because acceptable-risk decisions must still be made, the decision maker's task becomes choosing the most adequate approach (or combination of approaches). As an aid to the metadecision problem of deciding how to decide, this chapter compares the approaches with each other.

In Table 7.1, each approach is rated on each of the seven evaluative criteria, using a scale of 0 to 10 anchored by "completely inadequate" and "completely satisfactory." Comparing a rating with the maximum score of 10 conveys an approach's absolute strength; comparing ratings within rows reveals the approaches' relative strengths. These ratings reflect the authors' best judgment as to how the appraisals of Chapters 4 to 6 should be summarized via-à-vis each approach's ability to cope with the full range of societal hazards. The numbers represent asymptotes, describing the strength of an approach if competently and faithfully applied; inferior performance is always possible. Tables 7.2 to 7.4 make similar evaluations in the context of particular types of decision problems chosen to highlight the strengths or weaknesses of one approach or another.

An explicit evaluative scale was used in an effort to be as specific as possible about our opinions. The numbers themselves should *not* be taken too seriously. Considerable uncertainty surrounds each; the limits of our understanding are compounded by the limits of our ability to express that understanding with even single-digit precision. The absence of extreme ratings also reflects these uncertainties.

Global ratings

The numbers in Table 7.1 are summary measures in several senses. They pool the opinions of the authors, ignore differences among the several approaches grouped under each heading, and make no reference to the various facets of each criterion. However, aggregation at even this level sheds some light on

Table 7.1. Ability to cope with the full range of societal hazards: ratings of approaches on seven criteria

	Approach		
Criterion	Professional	Bootstrapping	Formal
Comprehensive	5	3	8
Logically sound	6	3	7
Practical	8	4	5
Open to evaluation	4	6	8
Politically acceptable	5	4	5
Compatible with institutions	9	4	5
Conducive to learning	4	4	6

Note: Ratings were made on a scale ranging from 0 (completely inadequate) to 10 (completely satisfactory), under the assumption that the approach is applied as well as possible, exploiting all its strengths. A range of possible ratings should be understood to surround each number, both because of the limits of our understanding and because each number summarizes the ability of the several approaches in each category to cope with a broadly defined universe of hazards. Necessary interpretative material is found in the accompanying text.

what each approach was designed to do and how well it might accomplish its goals.

Comprehensive

Formal analyses, particularly decision analyses, are nonsubstantive theories of decision making. By making few assumptions about how problems are to be defined, they promise to accommodate any conception offered by the commissioning client (with the possible exception of noneconomic consequences and equity issues in the case of cost–benefit analysis). The analysts' breadth and depth of vision are limited primarily by their clients' acuity and communicative ability. If communication fails, then clients' desires and substantive experts' knowledge may not be fully expressed in the analysis.

The professional approach makes the most of experts' knowledge by placing them at the center of the decision-making process. Those who employ professionals can, of course, mandate whatever problem definitions they deem appropriate. In practice, however, professionals define and solve problems in habitual ways that may restrict the range of the problems and lead professionals to overemphasize factors within their areas of competence. For example, a civil engineer might neglect the possibility that a highway-safety measure will encourage drivers to increase their speed, thus negating its impact, or the possibility of making roads appear more dangerous than they are in order to outsmart the drivers.

The comprehensiveness of bootstrapping is even further restricted. Each bootstrapping method characterizes technologies according to one particular set of risk (and perhaps benefit) measures. Each derives its standards from one particular past. A broad set of alternative options, consequences, and so forth may have influenced the evolution of those historical standards, but all that remains is what we interpret as a final equilibrium state. A few indicator statistics of that state are then compared with the same few indicators extracted from the present.

Logically sound

From whatever broad or narrow segment of a decision problem it addresses, an approach should produce a recommendation that is timely and defensible. Professional and formal analyses meet the first of these conditions by almost always providing a concrete answer that suggests what to do. However slim its margin, one alternative action emerges as best. The emergence process may be somewhat different in the two cases; the professional may tend to fine-tune an apparently superior option until no further effort seems justified, whereas the formal analyst may tend to look simultaneously at a fixed set of options. Bootstrapping methods fail in this respect by offering acceptability ratings, not preference orderings. If more than one action option passed their threshold of acceptability, some other procedure would be needed to select the best one; the same would happen if no option (even "do nothing") were judged acceptable. Seen in this way, bootstrapping is a screening procedure rather than a decision-making tool.

Each approach embodies an alternative concept of how rational decisions should be made. The arguments by which they justify their recommendations might be characterized as lying along an empirical–theoretical dimension. At the empirical extreme, professional judgment is advocated because it has worked in the past, where *worked* means some combination of: made people happy, identified superior solutions, reflected societal values, and exploited scientific knowledge. The validity of this claim would seem to depend on the context and on the observer. The rating of six in the table suggests that practitioners often do a fairly good job of integrating most relevant concerns in creating their solutions.

At the theoretical extreme lies decision analysis, which identifies the elements of a decision problem with the elements of decision theory as derived from an axiomatic base. The recommendations are then generated according to the rules of formal logic. As a result, the soundness of the recommendations (vis-à-vis the abstracted problem) could be flawed only if one rejected the axioms. Although the axioms are generally uncontroversial (e.g., one's preferences should be transitive), some of their unstated assumptions may be more open to question. One is that a decision-making entity, willing and able to provide information about beliefs and values, can be identified; another is the insistence that beliefs and values are inherently subjective.

The rationales of the bootstrapping methods reflect a mixture of empirical and theoretical arguments. Empirically, they rely on claims that some aspect of the world has functioned superbly, for example, achieving ideal risk-benefit tradeoffs (revealed preferences) or best-adapted species (natural standards). Their argument for preserving these historical relationships in the future is in part empirical (we could do no better if we tried; let us short-circuit the historical process and go immediately to the best answer without recourse to trial and error) and in part political (whatever was, is right; we live in a balanced world and should maintain that balance). The low rating given to bootstrapping (and the lower rating that would be given to cost-benefit analysis within the formal-analysis category) reflects the lack of empirical support and political consensus for the validity of these claims. Within the bootstrapping category, the risk-compendiums method would receive particularly low marks because its interpretations are not altogether clear. Apparently, it represents a form of revealed-preferences analysis but requires additional ad-hoc assumptions.

Practical

One way of being practical is to reduce the scope of the problems that are attacked. Professional judgment tries to restrict its focus to the technical issues with which professionals are most comfortable. The decision-making process centers on selecting and refining concrete options. Because these options undergo some prior screening for feasibility, whatever is expressed on paper is likely to be realizable in reality. Another practical aspect of professional judgment is that the amount of available decision-making personnel is likely to be roughly commensurate with the size of the problems; because professionals often play a role in the creation of a hazard, they are likely to be on hand for its management. This potential practicality is belied to the extent that professionals promise to incorporate society's values without specifying how that is to be done. Even when professionals have a method for getting at society's values, they may be prevented from doing so by clients who want them to concentrate on design issues or by critics who feel that value issues are none of the professionals' business.

Reduced scope enhances the practicality of bootstrapping methods as well. The revealed-preferences analyst who has measured historical risk-benefit tradeoffs needs only two summary statistics, risk and benefit, to decide the fate of any proposed technology. The risk-compendiums method requires only the risk statistic to characterize a technology. Application becomes easier still to the extent that any convenient measure of risk (e.g., per year, per hour of exposure) and any convenient set of statistics on comparison technologies will suffice. The popularity of bootstrapping methods in some circles may indeed reflect a willingness to sacrifice other goals in order to get on with business. Failure to specify exactly which numbers are needed can, however, hinder application when disputes arise about how to define such terms as risk, benefit, relevant past, or comparison technologies. Once agreement on these questions is reached, considerable ingenuity and faith may be needed to produce the requisite data from a past that was unaware of our need for documentation.

Cost–benefit analysts face similar problems in their quest for market indicators of value. However, attempts to get by with ad-hoc numbers may be thwarted by the legions of economists capable of mounting critiques based upon economic theory. The presence of competing analyses of how various quantities should be measured makes it difficult for the practicing analysts to give critics a definitive answer and proceed with implementation. When they do agree about measurement, these economists may show great resourcefulness in getting the most out of whatever data do exist. The new techniques that they generate enhance the practicality of future analyses.

By using subjective judgments, decision analysis is able to translate any concept in the problem definition into operational terms. It can use economic and statistical estimates when they are available (and appropriate) and fall back on judgment when they are not. This judgmental strategy fails when respondents cannot produce the required assessments, as might happen when they do not have a coherent, articulated view on a topic. Such failure can be identified within the context of decision analysis through the judicious use of consistency checks; or, it can be detected from the outside by behavioral research that identifies kinds of judgments that are not to be trusted (e.g., introspections about why one has made particular decisions; see Ericsson & Simon, 1980; Nisbett & Ross, 1980). Continuing research into how to model particular issues signifies both that decision analysis cannot as yet cope with every issue and that its practitioners are concerned about these deficiencies.

Open to evaluation

Professionals exercise their judgment outside the public's view, in offices, laboratories, and construction sites. To the extent that they make their decisions intuitively, the components of those decisions may be outside their own view as well. Making a virtue of a necessity, some would argue that the fallibility of professionals' introspection is a sign of their prowess, for they have mastered inarticulable intellectual habits that can be acquired only through an apprenticeship that begins once one has acquired the knowledge that can be written in books.

Written standards are one way that professionals cope with pressures for accountability. These standards are themselves typically generated by unanalyzable judgment, in which it is hard to know just how risks and benefits have been balanced, or even what options and consequences have been considered. Standards do, however, make it easier to monitor practice, particularly when it is formalized through licensure. As critics are quick to note, licensure is not synonymous with impartial evaluation. Like guilds, professions face a traditional conflict between maintaining enough quality assurance to keep the public's confidence but not so much as to make life too difficult for members or to cast doubt on the profession's claim to efficacy.

By contrast, formal and bootstrapping analyses were designed for ready evaluation. Their numbers and calculations are all laid on the table, open to view and review. Still, analyses must be explicated clearly enough for outsiders to follow their details. Moreover, these outsiders must have both the technical sophistication and the financial means needed to take independent positions. Decision rules may be as well hidden in the bowels of computers as in the minds of professionals. In this respect, the judgmental component of decision analysis may become a liability. Help may be needed particularly when observers try to identify the underlying assumptions about problem definitions, facts, values, human behavior, and decision quality. Although it is not uncommon for analyses to include some discussion of technical uncertainties, it is most uncommon to find discussion of the theoretical uncertainties that render the approaches themselves somewhat inconclusive.

Openness, therefore, may be achieved only by beginning each application with a briefing on the debate about social discount rates, the problems of aggregating over individuals in decision analysis, the unclear relationship between the economists' notion of revealed preferences and that represented in the acceptable-risk procedure of the same name, or the ambiguities of operationalizing concepts like risk and exposure.

Politically acceptable

Even the most open of approaches may not invite criticism. The job of the experts who implement each approach is hard enough without looking for trouble. Outsiders are unlikely to volunteer for critic duty unless it seems worth their while - that is, unless they are out to discredit an approach that has produced a displeasing conclusion. Hence, approaches often enter the political arena in an atmosphere of distrust. The experts had been left alone until they were "caught"; now a shadow falls on the approach itself as well as on the offending decision.

One way to avoid these problems is to make decisions that make everyone relatively happy. Professionals seem to have been able to do that in many of their routinized decisions (e.g., prescribing medical treatment, ascertaining that a girder is strong enough). Through trial and error, they have found out what is pleasing as well as what works. They are aided by the credit afforded to prestigious professions as well as by the absence of organized critics capable of questioning technical decisions. Some recent attacks on the medical profession (e.g., for its practices regarding DES, breast cancer, laetril, and fluoridation) suggest that once professionals are mistrusted, political opposition can form quickly.

When it is impossible to make everybody happy, one way to keep a low profile is to avoid making recommendations that persistently upset one group. Cost–benefit analysis is likely to fail in this regard, as it gives little attention to consequences that do not have readily calculable economic value; witness, for example, the increasing mistrust among workers who feel that their health is given short shrift in analysis after analysis, not, in their view, because the analysts do not care, but because health is hard to measure in dollars.

A more assertive strategy for political popularity is to involve potential critics in the decision-making process, either incorporating their concerns or co-opting their opposition. Decision analysis is particularly amenable to public participation; anyone's perspective can be represented in it. But decision analysis (like any other novel technique) is handicapped by the need to convince participants that they are not being bamboozled in a sophisticated numbers game. Reassuring the skeptical may require extensive briefings, sensitivity analyses, and even the conducting of parallel analyses.

Professionals can listen to a broad range of people before reaching their decisions, but it may be hard to demonstrate that these decisions incorporate particular views. Cost–benefit and bootstrapping analyses are expert rather than participatory tools and can do even less to accommodate outside input, except by allowing various parties to participate in shaping problem definitions (e.g., choosing possible options).

No amount of public participation or public relations can, however, eliminate opposition inspired by the inherent political biases of the different approaches. To the extent that each approach gives experts such a central role, it raises fears of creating a technocratic elite. Those fears may be alleviated only by embedding an approach in a political process that makes lay people as well as experts essential to its application. For the bootstrapping methods, which hold the present and its actors irrelevant except for defining the options to be evaluated, it may be impossible to develop a satisfactory political process. Nor is any process likely to satisfy those who dispute the assumption of most cost–benefit and bootstrapping analyses that current economic and social relations should be preserved in the future.

Compatible with institutions

Professionals and their clients determine the initial safety levels of the technologies they create. Unless problems arise, decision making is likely to remain within the creating organization and to rely on professional judgment. Even when a technology is forced to conform to general standards, professionals are still the main decision-making institution. When decision-making power is given to governmental bodies, professionals' knowledge and willingness to provide summary judgments ensure them an active role. Only when the courts with their adversarial system become the decision-making body might professionals' influence be frustrated. Indeed, one might fault professionals for undue deference to institutional constraints. However, their role as servants, the unclear authorization of their decision-making function, and the penalties for deviating from traditional practices combine to discourage professionals from being too assertive.

Although it is a more recent development, formal analysis has already earned a niche in many institutions. Regulators, industry, professional organizations, labor unions, and consumer groups have all learned to commission at least an occasional analysis to guide their thinking or justify their conclusions. None of these groups, however, would bind itself to the conclusions of these analyses, knowing that ambiguities and omissions make even the best analyses somewhat indeterminate. The broader acceptance of cost–benefit analysis may reflect its seniority to decision analysis and its promise of objectively measuring values. Bureaucrats who hope to avoid both litigation and accountability may be wary of acknowledging the subjectivity that decision analysis holds to be inherent in all decisions.

Bootstrapping's strengths are ease of application and provision of a number that decision makers can grasp; its backward-looking perspective allows users to point to historical or legal precedents as justifications. On the negative side, bootstrapping procedures are new, untested, and not mentioned in enabling legislation. Currently pending legislation calls for the use of "comparative analysis," which appears to be a mixture of bootstrapping and formal analysis. It is unclear how well this proposal will be received by the institutions that would implement it. Uncertainty about how to justify comparative analyses, how to monitor their use, and how to avoid deleterious side effects may make bureaucrats reluctant to try them out.

Conducive to learning

An approach should help us get smarter in the long run as well as help us to get by with reasonable decisions in the short run. One key to enhancing society's sophistication is educating the participants in each decision about the issue in question and decision making in general. A second key is creating a clear, cumulative record for future decision makers to draw on. It is a sign of wisdom if decisions are made with increasing consistency and predictability.

The different approaches reflect rather different time horizons. Bootstrapping promises to skip the cumbersome processes of history and immediately institute safety standards that represent perfected versions of past experience. Any changes in society's standards would be reflected only as gradual shifts in the historical relationships, assuming that they are periodically updated. To those who doubt that society has nothing more to learn about how to make acceptable-risk decisions, this quest for consistency could mean striving for more of a bad thing. By working for consistency with values expressed in more localized marketplace decisions of the immediate past, cost–benefit analysis promises to be somewhat more responsive than bootstrapping to changing values. But as a general rule, highly consistent, historically oriented approaches attempt to produce predictable decisions at the expense of any educative function. Confidence in the wisdom of the past may even make it seem less important to work to create a more enlightened society.

H. G. Wells once predicted that the day would come when statistical thinking would be as necessary a skill as reading or writing. Acquiring that skill requires, among other things, that one acknowledge the subtleties of acceptable-risk decisions and abandon the hope for simplistic solutions. To the extent that they hold out the hope of easy answers, bootstrapping approaches may actually impede learning. By contrast, a theoretically based technique like cost-benefit analysis could enhance a society's understanding if its underlying principles were broadly disseminated to citizens, scientists, and regulators. However, because participatory analyses or educational programs would be a rather new development, one can only speculate as to whether they would lead people to behave rationally – in the economists' sense of that term.

Much of the educational potential of decision analysis lies in the lengthy interactions between analysts and clients, which are designed to help the latter formulate and express coherent beliefs regarding any particular decision. On the other hand, by being atemporal, decision analysis imposes no consistency across decisions. In principle, of course, the result could be chaos, with values and conclusions fluctuating from analysis to analysis or even in replications of the same analysis performed at different times or with a different cast. This threat is reduced when there is stability and consensus in societal values and when analysts turn to the same sources for assessment of those values.

Professional judgment effects a continuous compromise between the decisions of the past and values of the present, achieving relative consistency by gradually adapting traditional standards and solutions. The closed nature of professional judgment, however, reduces opportunities for educating nonprofessionals. It may also prevent a useful cumulative record from being created; even when professionals' conclusions are made explicit, their underlying logic may not be detailed beyond such statements as, "according to standard operating procedure." Both bootstrapping and formal approaches can leave a better record if their deliberations, assumptions, data bases, and so forth are preserved in public view. Indeed, once a bootstrapper has adequately identified and characterized the relevant past, that historical tradeoff may be used again and again. Formal analyses do not aim to establish eternal standards. However, if properly conceived and managed, formal analyses might be modularized so that components could be re-used in subsequent analyses. Serious studies of the value of a life, the way errors compound in an analysis, or the problem of intergenerational equity could inform many analyses.

In hazard management, as elsewhere, short-term pressures are often the enemy of long-term planning. Decision makers press into service techniques that still need theoretical and practical development. The long-term contribution of a technique may decrease to the extent that it promises definitive answers in the short run, thus frustrating its own development.

Choosing an approach

If one took the numbers in Table 7.1 seriously, there would be no contest between bootstrapping and formal analysis: Formal analysis wins out over bootstrapping on every criterion. On the other hand, choosing between professional judgment and formal analysis would require setting priorities among the criteria. If practicality and institutional compatibility are critical, the edge would go to the professionals. A stress on logical soundness or comprehensiveness would tilt the balance back toward formal analysis. Only if openness to evaluation were of overriding importance would one choose bootstrapping over professional judgment.

However accurate these assessments might be, they are aggregated over a hard-to-define universe of possible usages. Tables 7.2 to 7.4 offer speculative characterizations of the approaches' ability to cope with three specific situations in which acceptable-risk questions must be addressed: (a) a routine decision with an individual decision maker (e.g., a woman deciding whether to use an intrauterine device); (b) standard setting for the reliability of one component of a complex technological system (e.g., a valve in a liquid natural gas facility); and (c) deciding whether and how to go ahead with a new technology (e.g., genetic engineering).

These numbers, like those in Table 7.1, are rough summaries of how we rate the various methods in each approach category on a hypothetical sampling of problems drawn from each case category. Unlike the numbers in Table 7.1, these are not estimates of potential, but assessments of how well an approach is likely to perform given the pressures and constraints of actual problems. Except where one approach appears to dominate the others, these estimates do not dictate the choice of an approach. One still has to determine the relative importance of the respective criteria.

Routine individual decisions

Such decisions are usually made by professionals after some consultation with the client, a division of labor whose reasonableness emerges in Table 7.2. Professional judgment shines relative to its competitors and relative to its overall capability (as represented in Table 7.1). Professionals are the decision-making institution and they know how to produce answers that have been shaped by trial-and-error experience. This legacy even offers some opportunity for external evaluation, although that potential may not be exploited very often (Bunker et al., 1977).

Perhaps it makes more sense to explain why professional judgment does not

Table 7.2. Ability to make routine individual decisions: ratings of approaches on seven criteria

	Approach		
Criterion	Professional	Bootstrapping	Formal
Comprehensive	8	2	8
Logically sound	8	2	8
Practical	9	3	3
Open to evaluation	6	5	7
Politically acceptable	7	3	5
Compatible with institutions	9	4	2
Conducive to learning	3	4	8

get perfect marks. Its most glaring weakness is failure to promote long-term management. Even when satisfied with the professionals' solutions to their immediate problem, clients may learn little that would enable them to make more independent decisions or to make better use of professionals in the future. The professionals' own development may be stunted to the extent that inertia, unchanging standards, isolation, or liability worries bind them to the increasingly outdated practices common when they received their schooling. Although routine professional practice is seldom a political topic, it can become very controversial when critics spot a questionable tendency. Recent critiques have accused professionals of not seeing the "whole" client, of treating symptoms rather than problems, of adopting overly cautious practices that protect the professional at the expense of the client, of using their own values even in cases where they conflict with those of the client, and of overpromoting solutions within their own areas of competence.

These problems are minor compared to those that arise in applying bootstrapping approaches to such decisions. Not only must analogous problems be found in the past, but the individual must be convinced that they are personally relevant. One need not follow a course of action just because others have done so; who knows how wise they were or what values they had? Nor need one repeat one's own previous decisions or even maintain the same attitude toward risk that they reflected. It is easy to imagine responses such as, Driving is one thing and health is another, or, I would have chosen a safer alternative if I'd had the opportunity.

Formal analysis may eventually become a useful tool for this sort of decision (Jungermann, 1980; Wheeler & Janis, 1980). Decision analysis, which is designed for situations with an identifiable decision-making entity, has already been proposed for problems like genetic counseling or coronary bypass surgery (Pauker, 1976). The client could be taught something about decision making in the course of treating the immediate problem. Unfortunately, these

Table 7.3. Setting standards for a component of a complex technology: ratings of approaches on seven criteria

Criterion	Approach		
	Professional	Bootstrapping	Formal
Comprehensive	5	3	5
Logically sound	7	2	7
Practical	9	4	6
Open to evaluation	4	6	7
Politically acceptable	5	4	6
Compatible with institutions	9	2	6
Conducive to learning	4	3	6

ideas do not seem likely to be accepted soon. Such a cards-on-the-table approach would be threatening to many professionals, undermining their status, forcing confessions of uncertainty, and demystifying their judgment. Helping clients trust and understand formal analysis may require educational efforts beyond the scope of many counseling settings. Without such efforts, some clients may be so intimidated by the technique that they may prefer to let someone else decide.

Setting standards for a component of a complex technology

Most standard-setting decisions (see Table 7.3) are made by experts or within institutions dominated by experts. Hence, professional judgment is the order of the day, with great deference being shown to consistency with past decisions. The focus on technical issues and the lack of authorization for tackling broader problems lead to minimal emphasis on other aspects of long-term management (e.g., public education), as well as fairly restricted problem definitions. Like other activities conducted outside the public eye, these decisions are likely to be noncontroversial. Even when feelings about a technology run high, attention is likely to focus on overall safety rather than on the reliability of particular components. As a result, when professionals are singled out as the decision makers, attacks may center on the general propriety and competence of their judgment rather than on any specific decisions. The unclear link between component reliability and overall safety may produce frustrating confrontations, with professionals unable to demonstrate that they have addressed the public's concerns and the public unable to explain what they want in terms the professionals can make use of.

Formal analysis is readily adaptable to such decisions and to the institutions that make them. The promise of openness to evaluation may make formal analyses an attractive adjunct to the more closed professional judgments, although the result may be analyses conducted to justify intuitive decisions. In these interactions, the formal analysts' familiarity with a variety of decision problems may compensate for their lack of substantive knowledge and help the professional to transcend unduly narrow problem definitions. A possibly unattractive aspect of formal analysis is directly facing difficult questions of quantifying risks and benefits. For example, just what is the cost saving (in lives or property) of reducing the expected failure rate of a valve from 2×10^{-6} to 1.7×10^{-6}? On the other hand, such aspects are part of the problem regardless of the approach used.

It is difficult to see how bootstrapping approaches can be applied to component decisions. A detailed analysis of the relationship between the component being considered and the technologies that have been managed by society in the past would be required.

Deciding the fate of a new technology

Here, if anywhere, the conditions for applying bootstrapping methods are met (Table 7.4). One may be able to identify comparison technologies and plausibly argue that society should be managing the balance of costs and benefits in a consistent fashion. The statistics for evaluating entire technologies are most likely to be available. To the extent that bootstrapping focuses on overall acceptability and affords a readily explicable decision rule, it may be attractive to those who do not want to be bothered by confusing technical discussions about components. On the other hand, these weighty decisions will tend to draw an intense scrutiny of decision-making processes and methods that is likely to uncover the logical weaknesses of bootstrapping (e.g., failure to consider available alternatives).

Formal analysts could outflank the bootstrappers by using the latter's characterization of society's historical values as inputs to their own analyses. If critics accept bootstrapping's rationale, then the formal analyst may be able to escape such charges as, Just whose values are represented? by modeling options, events, and consequences in a more comprehensive way. Of course, the inevitable omissions and complexity of such models and the uncertainty surrounding their components will still make them ready targets for critics unhappy with their conclusions or mistrustful of their machinations. To some extent, the force of these critiques will reflect how well the analysis has identified key issues. Identifying pockets of uncertainty may also help direct scientists to topics with the greatest policy relevance.

The main limitation of professional judgment is the absence of individuals with demonstrated competence to judge complex and novel technologies. The breadth of the issues in many decisions regarding the fate of technologies prevents any discipline from comprehending the whole problem. With new technologies, there may be no one with hands-on experience and a practical grasp of the problem. Even if there are professionals who can make some claim to such understanding, they may either be politically restrained by those

Table 7.4. Deciding fate of a new technology: ratings of approaches on seven criteria

	Approach		
Criterion	Professional	Bootstrapping	Formal
Comprehensive	4	6	8
Logically sound	4	5	7
Practical	3	5	5
Open to evaluation	3	7	8
Politically acceptable	4	5	5
Compatible with institutions	6	5	6
Conducive to learning	5	5	6

who believe that some problems are too important to be left in the hands of those who know most about them, or they may have financial interests in promoting or eliminating particular technologies.

Summary

When the three generic approaches are compared to one another, several patterns emerge. The professional and formal approaches seem to be much better able to cope with the broad range of acceptable-risk problems than is bootstrapping. The choice between the former two approaches would depend upon the relative importance one attached to those evaluative criteria on which professional judgment scored well (e.g., practicality) and those on which formal analysis scored well (e.g., openness to evaluation). The capabilities of the different approaches and the importance of the different evaluative criteria for specific problems may lead to different choices of the most suitable approach. For example, professional judgment may have some advantages for certain routinized, decentralized decisions, whereas formal analysis (and even, at times, bootstrapping) may provide more insight into decisions about the fate of technologies.

8 What have we learned?

We began this inquiry by asking the seemingly straightforward question, How safe is safe enough? Like others before us, we discovered that there are no easy answers. To understand what some of the possible answers entailed, we had to step back and characterize (a) acceptable-risk problems, (b) the generic approaches available for resolving them, and (c) the things to consider in choosing an approach. The appraisal that followed used this conceptual framework to clarify the strengths and weaknesses of the various approaches. In addition to the guidelines to choosing an approach that were offered, we now make some general suggestions about acceptable-risk problems and their management.

General conclusions about acceptable-risk problems

Acceptable-risk decisions concern the relative desirability of options

All decisions involve a choice among alternative courses of action, including, perhaps, inaction. A sensible decision-making procedure enables one to identify a plausible candidate for the most attractive (or most acceptable) option. Whether or not one follows the procedure's recommendations, one adopts or accepts an option, not a risk. The choice of this option is conditional on the alternatives considered, the evidence consulted, and the consequences weighed. Hence, the most acceptable option could change whenever new evidence comes to light, new options are invented, different values become relevant, or different procedures are used.

One might call the risk associated with the most acceptable option an acceptable risk. That definition would, however, obscure the fact that the choice of an option depends upon all of its features, not just its risk. Whenever the decision maker wants to consider benefits as well as risks, the most acceptable option need not be the one with the least risk. Nor need its risks be considered acceptable in any absolute sense. Since the choice of options is context dependent, there are no universally acceptable risks.

There is no definitive method for choosing the most acceptable option

Selecting an approach to acceptable-risk decisions is complicated by the difficulty of satisfying all seven of the evaluative criteria simultaneously. One frequent conflict between criteria involves comprehensiveness and logical soundness; it is often easier to produce a defensible, or at least plausible answer if one first reduces the scope of a problem. Or, there may be conflict between openness to evaluation and compatibility with institutions; openness may invite outside meddling that interferes with the desire of institutions to get their jobs done.

In order to produce explicit recommendations, each approach restricts itself to a subset of issues that it abstracts from the complex problems. In doing so, it must make simplifying assumptions about the nature of the world (e.g., fully informed consumers, stable and articulated values, identifiable states of societal equilibrium). Unless these limitations are appreciated, the advice produced by an approach may have an undue aura of understanding, analyzability, and finality. On the other hand, if these problems are taken too seriously, these approaches may be crippled. Rejecting all approaches means accepting the marketplace or raw politics, with all their attendant dangers, as the decision-making process.

From a more balanced perspective, these approaches can be seen as decision aids - ways to enhance understanding that need not dictate choices. Much of their usefulness lies in structuring and organizing those parts of the decision problem and those categories of data that each approach addresses. The only reasons for taking the next step and computing a bottom line might be to provide an index useful for sensitivity analyses and to avoid the calculation errors that arise when people make computations in their heads. In this view the advice givers are valued not as the bearers of sophisticated calculuses, but as critical outsiders able to propose and creatively explore alternative representations of complex problems. Their understanding and intuitions are prized, not their numbers. One should always want to know what a cost-benefit analyst, bootstrapper, or professional has to say about a particular problem. One should bear in mind the limits of their viewpoints, however, and never hear any one of them alone. Although these approaches, if used judiciously, can improve our understanding, none is sound enough to serve as a sole guide to policy.

There are no value-free methods for choosing the most acceptable option

A recurrent hope is that we will find a scientific method for objectively resolving acceptable-risk problems, one that protects decision makers from any charges of having imposed their beliefs or values on society. Unfortunately, however, the distinct strengths and weaknesses of the respective approaches mean that the choice of an approach is also a decision to emphasize particular concerns.

In addition, each approach embodies a particular view of what society is and how it should operate. Each represents some view on who should make society's decisions, and thereby lends credibility to some entity such as the market, the regulatory system, the courts, or various technical elites. For example, the limited role of the lay public in professional judgment affects future decisions as well as present ones by reducing the public's opportunities to learn about hazard management. Each approach also prejudges particular value issues that one might want left open to discussion. For example, bootstrapping approaches are biased toward preserving the social-political status quo, whereas some formal analyses give short shrift to equity issues. Choosing an approach means taking a position. One goal of the present analysis is to help all parties to spot the value assumptions implicit in any approach they may consider.

Whatever approach is adopted, honesty requires a serious effort to separate issues of fact from issues of value. It also requires the realization that facts and values are always part of acceptable-risk problems and are often tightly intertwined. They come together in the way we define decision problems, the units we use to measure vital quantities, the alternatives and consequences we consider, the research we sponsor, the standards we use for interpreting evidence, the way we treat divergent views, the respect we afford lay perceptions of risk, and the manner in which we interpret results. The decision-making process cannot proceed without taking a stance on these questions; in doing so, various parties' chances of getting what they want will inevitably be affected. An approach cannot overcome the values built into the problem definition that constrains its activities. In should, however, help users identify these values.

Acceptable-risk decision making takes place throughout society

Common to the approaches considered here is an image of decisions as being made at discrete points in time and space. With many hazards, however, identifiable decisions are largely an idealization. Such heavy stakes ride on the outcomes of decision processes that hard lobbying and even dirty tricks can be expected as the sides jockey to have their facts, values, options, and problem definitions adopted. By the time many "decisions" are reached, they have only symbolic value, legitimating conclusions that have already emerged. The battle then resumes over issues of implementation, monitoring, and revision. Any approach to acceptable-risk decisions may become a pawn in this game, manipulated to sanction choices that have been made for other reasons.

There are many smaller decisions that are made at identifiable points but only have an accretive effect on society's acceptable-risk decisions. Those larger decisions are shaped every time a consumer returns a risky product, a worker enters a risky job, a court awards damages, or a profession decides to censure a member. In one way or another, each of the approaches depends upon the wisdom of these smaller decisions to inform it regarding society's values. Any act that improves these decisions also enhances the larger decision: for example, informing workers better about occupational hazards, providing courts with better guidelines regarding the foreseeability of product defects, or reducing impediments to efficient pricing of safety in the marketplace.

The expertise needed for acceptable-risk decisions is dispersed throughout society

The term *expert* may have a rather different meaning in hazard management than in other spheres. Whereas there are people who know nearly all there is to know about grammar or auto mechanics, for many hazards there is no one who understands their full present and future impact on nature and society. Those who know how a system operates in theory may not know how it operates in practice. Even those who know both theory and practice may not understand how a system interacts with related social and environmental systems. When experts are forced to go beyond the data available to them and rely on educated intuition, their opinions should be treated with some of the same caution given the speculations of lay persons.

Exaggerating the breadth of an individual's expertise can be as dangerous as exaggerating its depth. People familiar with one hazard may not be particularly well equipped to deal with another. Experts in the magnitude of risks need know nothing about their acceptability, nor need they understand what it is like to experience the effects they measure.

If society is to apply its cumulative wisdom effectively, it should "domesticate" acceptable-risk problems to make them accessible to experts in similarly complex problems. Anyone who can shed any light on court-ordered bussing may have something to contribute to understanding nuclear power. Yet leading lights in other intellectual fields may not be able to immediately grasp the subtle wrinkles of hazard issues, with their complicated constituencies, ambiguous problem definitions, and poorly discriminable effects.

Disciplinary training and personal experience teach one how to find a reasonable answer to a fairly small class of narrowly defined problems. Hazard management is too complex for any one individual, group, institution, discipline, or approach to have all the answers or better answers than all others. Some of the worst surprises in hazard management have involved events that were not anticipated by the experts, but which might at least have been suggested by members of other disciplines, operators, people living on site, and so forth. Instead of looking for techniques that will provide the right answer, we might better focus our efforts on avoiding the mistakes to which various perspectives are prone. If each new perspective has some unique contribution, we may want to lend an ear to parties not often heard in policy-making circles – the poor, the philosophers, the artists – in hopes that their life experiences have something illuminating to offer. Even when experts may have a near monopoly on technical facts, they need not have a monopoly on alternative perspectives, and may suffer from ingrained disciplinary blinders.

Acceptable-risk decisions affect as well as reflect the nature of a society

In all societies, the division of power among technical experts, political leaders, and the laity is a persistent source of tension. To some extent, the balance depends on how much the various parties know. People are often willing to surrender some power to those who know more. However, when the knowledge of experts seems limited, one must worry about how much our political processes should be distorted to gain the (possibly limited) insights they possess. If, for example, the best available formal analysis is so sophisticated that only a handful of individuals can monitor it, one may prefer a more modest approach that does not confer as much power on experts and their immediate clients.

Some would argue that an active citizenry is the greatest asset of a democracy. Unless it is well informed, however, even the most involved public may not make decisions in its own best interests. The evidence suggests that, all in all, lay people have done a fairly good job of tracking the risk information that is presented to them. Often, however, the information is given in a way that is confusing, incomplete, biased, and contradictory. As a result, lay people seem to be highly educable but only moderately educated. Approaches to acceptable risk that fail to educate the lay public in the short run also disenfranchise them in the long run.

Once the political decision has been made to adopt an approach that affords a role to "the public," an additional political decision is needed to define that term. There is no all-purpose public. Those who speak in its name may have gained their prominence through a haphazard process. Often the individuals most directly affected are not represented, whether because they were not informed, lacked the skills to gain a hearing, or were not born when the decision was made. Moreover, when the opportunity is provided for public input, it may be exploited by technology promoters and regulators eager to influence our political agenda. Like "the public," promoters and regulators are heterogeneous groups. Just as one can ask, Who appointed Ralph Nader to speak in the public interest (and not just as an anticorporate lobby)? one can ask, Who appointed the Business Roundtable to speak for business (and not just major corporations)? or Who appointed the AFL-CIO to speak for workers (and not just a relatively powerful and politically conscious sector of the labor force)?

Acceptable-risk decisions do (and should) evolve over time

Acceptable-risk decision making is a messy, diffuse, and dynamic process that may frustrate efforts at consistency and expediency. Still, its very unwieldiness may be a virtue as well as a necessity. Only as time goes on do we learn about how a hazard behaves and how much we like or dislike its consequences.

A good decision-making process will contribute to this learning. Thus we must be ready to go through a process more than once, with each iteration being fed by the insights and criticisms arising from its predecessors. Indeed, a sign of a good analysis might be that it deepens one's understanding enough to require an iteration, possibly involving a complete redefinition of the problem. It may be a misallocation of resources to spend, say, 95 percent of a budget on a sophisticated analysis and only 5 percent on an external review followed by begrudging cosmetic revisions. A better division of resources might be 40-40-20 (for the first, second, and third rounds of analysis). One result should be better-informed decisions. Another might be somewhat different kinds of decisions. Admitting our relative ignorance may lead us to wait until better information is available, to avoid actions with irreversible consequences, or to hedge our bets by using tentative and diversified strategies.

The educational potential of an approach is particularly important in situations where it is hard to learn from experience. Too often, life's messages are obscured by the complexity of problems or by the distortions of hindsight, wishful thinking, and overconfidence, all of which can make us underestimate our need to learn. The education of experts can be speeded by subjecting their work to rigorous peer review; the education of hazard managers can be aided by developing improved decision-making methods; the education of a society can be enhanced by treating its citizens as integral parts of the decision-making process. In this light, public participation is not a necessary encumbrance to the decision-making process, but an important element in assuring its validity.

Summary

The appraisal of decision-making methods offered in this book points to several general conclusions.

1. Although the phrase *acceptable risk* is useful for describing a kind of decision-making process, it is not appropriate for describing the results of that process. The risk associated with the most acceptable option is not acceptable in any absolute sense. One accepts options, not risks, which are only one feature of options. Moreover, even the choice of an option is highly contingent on how the problem is defined, what other options are available, and who is doing the deciding.
2. No approach to acceptable-risk decisions addresses more than a portion of complex hazard problems. An approach's greatest contribution may be structuring those issues with which it does deal. If we feel compelled to calculate a bottom-line recommendation, we should not forget the heavy qualifications that should surround it.

3. There are and can be no value-free approaches to acceptable-risk decisions, nor is it possible to completely separate facts and values.
4. Decisions about hazards take place throughout society. Care must be taken to cultivate each component of the decision process.
5. No one knows enough about the management of many hazards. Expertise is best viewed as relative rather than absolute, and may be shared by many in a society.
6. The choice of an approach affects society as a whole as well as the distribution of power and expertise in specific decisions. Confronting those broader political issues is a part of making acceptable-risk decisions.
7. Society will be dealing with hazards for a long time. If our managerial ability is to improve over time, we must recognize the limits of our knowledge and structure our experience to facilitate learning.

9 Recommendations for improving acceptable-risk decision making

As described in Chapter 8, acceptable-risk decisions are often made by a variety of individuals and institutions acting in an uncoordinated, piecemeal fashion. Each of these actors has some unique contribution to make to those decisions. The present chapter offers recommendations for the four major actors of the acceptable-risk world: the technical community, the public, the marketplace, and government. These recommendations are nonexclusive. No attempt is made to establish priorities among them, as their implementation could begin simultaneously. Some, however, could be accomplished overnight, whereas others would take years, even if implemented today (e.g., where education is involved). Where time, resources, or politics might hinder implementation, these constraints must of course be taken into account.

Recommendations for the technical community

The technical community includes all those whose role in the decision-making process is legitimated by some trained expertise. Professionals, formal analysts, and bootstrappers all fall into this category; thus, these recommendations are guidelines for getting the best out of their techniques. To stress the common elements of these diverse approaches, we will use the term *technical analysis* to refer to any advice produced by experts, whether its logic is intuitive, formal, or comparative. The terminology of the chapter will resemble that of formal analysis because that method is both the most comprehensive and the most explicit about what it does. However, the points that are made are of a general character.

The premise of technical analyses is that we can think our way to a better understanding of acceptable-risk conundrums. The case for incorporating one or several, such analyses in every decision-making process is easy to make:

1. However restricted their perspective may be, technical analysts have some insight to offer.
2. Cognitive limitations make it highly unlikely that anyone can perform such analyses intuitively.
3. As long as it is explicit and scrutable, even a flawed analysis may provide a good point of departure.
4. Most analyses can address some of the concerns of many participants and help focus their debates.
5. An analysis may organize and summarize technical details in a form that allows systematic updating as new facts emerge.

This potential is, of course, not always realized in practice. Furthermore, analysis entails risks as well as benefits. These risks include:

1. Obscuring value issues (by burying them in technical language or unstated assumptions).
2. Systematically biasing decisions (by underrepresenting concerns such as equity or less tangible costs and benefits).
3. Disenfranchising lay people (by restricting the participation of citizens, journalists, or legislators).
4. Creating a myth of analyzability (and overconfidence in society's ability to understand and manage hazards).
5. Slowing the decision-making process (by making the analysis, rather than the problem, the focus of debate and litigation).
6. Generating solutions that cannot be implemented (because they have not evolved within the regulatory, professional, industrial, and intervenor communities).

Of course, even with these risks, technical analysis may be preferable to the alternatives of purely political or intuitive decision making.

What should technical analyses contain?

As every politician knows, controlling the agenda in a policy debate is part of a winning strategy. The agenda of an analysis is embodied in its problem statement. The terms of a problem statement can foreclose decision options directly by not raising them as possibilities, or indirectly by neglecting the consequences that those options best serve. Knowing the power of these definitions, experienced warriors in hazard disputes fight hard to have their concerns reflected in the analyst's mandate; if that fails, they may fight hard to impeach the analysis. To the extent that ignored consequences do not go away and overlooked options dominate considered ones, comprehensiveness is crucial to sound advice as well as political acceptability.

Incompleteness is usually justified by limited resources, limited data, or limited authority. Unfortunately, however, components that are out of sight also tend to be out of mind. If analysis is designed to enhance our intuitions by framing the overall acceptable-risk problem, breadth may be more important than depth. All topics listed in Table 9.1 should be given at least minimal consideration before elaborating any one topic with costly numerical or modeling exercises. Any omissions, if unavoidable, should be explicitly noted and their potential impact discussed.

Consider all feasible options. Hazards may be conceptualized as a causal chain leading from general needs to specific wants, to technologies, to initiating events, to intermediate outcomes, to deleterious consequences (see Figure 2.1). Possible actions are associated with each link. One can, in principle, modify wants, alter technologies, mitigate consequences, and so forth. Despite this range of possibilities, many analyses consider only one option (build

Table 9.1. Minimal scope for an analysis

Consider all feasible options	Consider all sources of uncertainty
Modify wants	In scientific knowledge
Modify technology	In society's values
Prevent initiating event	In decision-making methods
Prevent release	In implementation
Prevent exposure	Consider all reasonable values
Prevent consequences	
Mitigate consequences	
Consider all major consequences	
Economics	
Environment	
Societal resilience	
Equity	

the plant), or only variants on one option (build it here or there), or only alternate forms of the same kind of solution (pesticide X or pesticide Y). Even when such narrowness can be attributed to the analyst's limited mandate or to political and economic realities, decision makers and impactees alike should know what possibilities were precluded.

Consider all major consequences. Most analytic methods were developed to help individual or corporate decision makers cope with primarily economic concerns. Over time, they have been extended to economic decisions on a societal level, to decisions with environmental impacts, and to decisions with effects on social structures (e.g., neighborhood deterioration). All legitimate societal concerns should be addressed as consequences in any analysis, if only to list them and then officially ignore them.

Although environmental- and social-impact assessments are designed to expand the range of consequences that are considered, readily monetized effects still get the most attention, to the point where other concerns are often mislabeled intangibles. An economic effect should be thought of as any effect that someone might pay to get or get rid of, regardless of whether the economists have agreed on how to measure it. It would thus include both health impacts and the economic consequences of environmental enhancement or degradation (despite the difficulty of pricing lives, limbs, genetic diversity and scenery). Environmental-impact assessments should deal with the intrinsic value of preserving or enhancing natural systems, whereas social impacts should be thought of as changes in a society's structure, resilience, and ability to cope with future challenges. Such assessments should ask such questions as: Will innovation be hampered? Are future options foreclosed? Will trust in government and one's fellows be eroded? Is understanding being disseminated?

Finally, a comprehensive analysis should review all consequences with an

Table 9.2. How should an analysis be presented?

- Use a standard presentation
- List the behavioral and value assumptions of the analysis
- Detail the comprehensiveness of the analysis
- Qualify inputs and conclusions
- Offer summary statements
- Identify sources of information and potential bias

eye to who gets what. This equity-impact assessment should consider both direct consequences, like money and lives, and indirect ones, like shifts in political power or access to information. Reference groups will vary from problem to problem; they might include present versus future generations, workers versus nonworkers, rich versus poor, or those living close to the hazard versus those living far away.

Consider all sources of uncertainty. Treating all feasible options and all major consequences helps assure that the technical analyst is addressing the right problem. Solving it adequately means considering the uncertainty that arises whenever (a) scientific knowledge is absent, inconclusive, or in dispute; (b) society's values are unarticulated, unstable, or conflicted; (c) political pressures and resource limits threaten to keep options from being implemented as planned; and (d) the analyst's own techniques are fallible. A technical analysis should address all these possibilities, not just by a compartmentalized listing but by working through their implications for the strength of the analysis.

Consider all reasonable values. Because values are a crucial part of every acceptable-risk problem, the values used to weigh possible consequences should be carefully considered and stated. Where societal consensus on values is absent a range of values representing different constituencies should be used, and it should be made clear what recommendations follow from what values. Where only one set of values is used (or allowed to dominate), it should be made clear whom those values are meant to represent.

How should an analysis be presented?

When technical analyses cannot produce binding conclusions, their decision-*aiding* function must be taken very seriously. Table 9.2 summarizes our recommendations for exploiting the user's current sophistication and enhancing it over time.

Use a standard presentation. For most lay consumers, technical analysis is conducted in a foreign language. Learning that tongue is complicated by the terminological and conceptual differences among different forms of technical analysis. The reasons for these differences vary from theoretical disagreements to deliberate relabeling for some strategic purpose (e.g., having a special tool to promote, or escaping the criticism leveled at a familiar technique). However justifiable such shifts might be in the abstract, using similar terms and formats would facilitate learning and comparison across problems. One might even argue against adopting improved techniques unless they represent major steps forward. Aside from confusing users, new techniques have not been tested over time so as to reveal their subtle flaws, create a coterie of critics, and generate an art of implementation.

List the behavioral and value assumptions of the analysis. These assumptions, discussed at length in Chapters 4 to 6, embody the inherent biases and limitations of the techniques. Like the surgeon general's warning on cigarette packs, this listing might be repetitious for the repeat users. However, it will be news for others and an affirmation of frankness for all.

Detail the omissions. When an analysis fails to address the wish list of topics in Table 9.1, the analyst(s) should be forthright about what has been ignored and why. Candidness can allay participants' fears of being deceived, clarify the legitimate topics for discussion, and help explain why agendas need to be restricted.

Qualify the inputs and conclusions. Technical analysts who have explored the various areas of uncertainty need to inform consumers about the robustness of their conclusions. Because responsible qualifications are difficult to make or comprehend, more is needed than a last-minute tack-on or an obligatory "nobody's perfect." In addition to being told where the greatest uncertainties and disagreements lie, the user needs to know whether the whole analytic enterprise is in danger of collapsing under the cumulative weight of the problems the analyst has encountered.

Offer summary statements. Just as summaries are inadequate (thus require qualification), so are they indispensable. The mind cannot comprehend lengthy compendiums of statistics, arguments, tables, and figures. In self-defense, observers will produce their own summaries, risking a higher rate of conceptual and computational errors than one would expect from a trained analyst. One way to get the benefits of expert summaries without having to become unduly reliant on them is to obtain several, each representing different conclusions reached using different problem definitions, inputs, and combination rules.

Identify sources of information and potential bias. In scientific research, incomplete documentation suggests sloppy work; in politicized risk analyses, bias may be suspected as well. Critics may wonder: Were these promoters' or opponents' data? Is the analyst making too much of hot new results? Is the testing laboratory trying to hide some problems? Although awkward, acknowledging such fears may forestall problems in the long run. To protect its panels' conclusions from post-hoc attributions of bias, the National Academy of Sciences asks panelists to disclose their financial interests.

How should technical analyses be managed?

Because analytic resources are limited, attention turns to how to allocate them. Three managerial principles are set out in Table 9.3; their immediate corollaries are discussed in the text.

Ensure adequate problem structuring. The eventual wisdom, comprehensiveness, and responsiveness of an analysis are constrained once its structure or definition is set. When a single analysis is being managed, elaborate calculations should be postponed until an adequate structure has been developed. When several problems are involved, analysts may contribute more by characterizing each briefly than by working out one in detail.

Avoid premature closure. The structuring stage of a good analysis is never completed. The first round should reshape the problem for subsequent iterations, suggesting new solutions, identifying critical issues, and incorporating new insights. To exploit this potential, resources must be allocated for diverse reviews and comprehensive responses.

Coordinate analyses. Time and analytic resources are too limited for studies to be conducted in relative isolation from one another. Thus technical analysts should (a) use the results of previous analyses wherever possible; (b) modularize analyses for easy reuse; (c) make generic decisions; (d) leave a clear, concise record of deliberations and the reasoning underlying decisions; and (e) avoid making the same omissions in analysis after analysis when all aspects cannot be analyzed in depth.

To some extent, using technical analysis to solve particular problems impedes its long-term development. Existing analytic resources may be best exploited by spreading them around to shed some light on many issues. However, advancing the craft itself may require heavy investment in a few analyses thorough enough to recruit scientific talent and to serve as models.

How should technical analysts be prepared?

Public-policy analysts often have more of the rights than the responsibilities of a profession. There are research contracts, publication outlets, and opportunities to speak or testify, but relatively little in the way of standards, licensure, qualifying exams, or peer review. At times, risk issues are needlessly

Table 9.3. How should analyses be managed?

Ensure adequate problem structuring
Avoid premature closure
Coordinate analyses

Table 9.4. Recommendations for preparing technical analysts

Educate technical analysts
Training programs
Texts and workshops
Internships
Improve professional standards
Develop professional codes
Promote public-interest work
Guarantee external review
Formulate guidelines for testimony
Refuse biased mandates
Respect other disciplines
Validate techniques

mystified as phenomena that can only be penetrated by veteran risk buffs; at other times, the subtlety of these issues is underestimated, leading otherwise perceptive individuals to offer simplistic solutions. The recommendations summarized in Table 9.4 are designed to improve analysts' ability to serve society.

Educate technical analysts. Analysis should be a clinical science, grounded in theory but demanding considerable art in practice. Three ways to provide more systematic training might include:

1. Graduate programs combining social and technical theory with applied experience (like Carnegie-Mellon University's Department of Engineering and Public Policy).
2. Advanced texts and workshops to familiarize scientists from various disciplines with risk issues.
3. Internships in government, industry, labor, and public-interest bodies.

Improve professional standards. Risk analysis is in the preprofession stage. That status entails the benefits of openness to other disciplines as well as the liability of weakness on quality assurance. Some ways to develop the positive controls of a profession without falling into the exclusionary trap might include:

1. Develop a code of professional responsibility before it emerges haphazardly from the legal system.
2. Set up a public-interest risk-analysis group like the organization founded by some large U.S. accounting firms to "give accounting away."
3. Insist that a fixed portion of the funds (e.g., 15%) in any analysis contract be allocated to independent external review.
4. Adopt guidelines for experts who must give testimony.
5. Refuse to perform justificatory analyses with predetermined and nonnegotiable conclusions.

ure that analysis teams have multidisciplinary capability.
courage studies of the validity of analytic techniques.

Recommendations for public involvement

Let's dismiss the public – and elect a new one.
Brecht

One popular strategy for dismissing the public is to discredit its intelligence, thereby letting others speak in its stead. There are, however, both practical and political reasons for doubting the wisdom of that strategy. From a practical standpoint, hazard management often requires the cooperation of a large body of lay people. These people must agree to do without some things and accept substitutes for others; they must vote sensibly on ballot measures and choose legislators who will serve as surrogate decision makers; they must obey safety rules and use the legal system responsibly. Even if the experts were much better judges of risk than lay people, giving experts an exclusive franchise for hazard management would mean substituting short-term efficiency for the long-term effort needed to create an informed citizenry.

From a political standpoint, exclusion may breed anger as well as ignorance. Citizens in a democratic society will eventually interfere with decisions in which they do not feel represented. When lay people do force their way into hazard decisions, their vehemence and technical naïveté may leave the paid professionals aghast, reinforcing suspicions that the public is stupid. By avoiding these conflicts, early public involvement may lead to decisions that take longer to make but require less time to implement and are more likely to stick. Where public involvement is called for, the recommendations in Table 9.5 could help make it more satisfying and constructive.

Conditions for involvement

The recurrent appearance of the adjective "meaningful" in discussions of public participation suggests a legacy of less than satisfying experiences. Appropriate involvement may be defined by listing things that work against it: (a) excluding the public from the problem-definition process; (b) making portions of the decision-making process inaccessible to the public; (c) soliciting testimony that will be filed and forgotten; (d) representing public opinion by superficial polls; and (e) defining "education" as manipulation and consensus as the state in which the public agrees with the experts.

Of these pathways to alienation, only (d) may require elaboration. Although public-opinion polls appear to provide a ready albeit expensive way to find out what "the people" think, even methodologically competent surveys have limitations as guides to policy makers. One limitation is that respondents can offer opinions only on questions that interest those who commission the

Table 9.5. Recommendations for public involvement

Avoid	Consider that the public
Predetermined problem definitions	Knows something
Secrecy	Has reasons for skepticism
Lip-service testimony	Is deeply involved
Superficial public-opinion polls	Prepare for involvement
Manipulation of public opinion	By studying the issues
Provide	By recognizing impossible demands
Guides to understanding tools	By understanding broader societal contexts
Financial and technical support	

polls; and the formulation of the questions usually further restricts the range of views that can be expressed. A second is the assumption that people have well-formulated opinions on any question the pollster chooses to ask and that those opinions can be matched to one of a set of multiple-choice answers. Interaction with the interviewer to clarify the meaning of questions and the implications of answers may be necessary to allow respondents a chance to understand and express their own views.

Tools for involvement

Technical experts owe their centrality in acceptable-risk decisions to the power of the tools they wield. To participate responsibly, the public needs to understand those tools. One necessary step is clarifying their strengths and weaknesses. The present book is designed in part as a consumers' guide to decision-making methods. Kindred analyses would explain in plain language what one can reasonably expect of epidemiology, mega-mouse studies, and computer simulations. Offering summaries of such explications whenever techniques are used might defuse suspicions that they are arcane tools for confusing and disenfranchising the public.

A second necessary step is providing the public with the technical and financial support needed to review analyses. Critics are naturally most sensitive to errors and omissions prejudicial to their own interests. If competent reviews are commissioned by only one side in a controversy, only one kind of error will be corrected, leaving the conclusion biased.

These steps should help the public place the wisdom of tools in appropriate contrast to the wisdom of intuition. The right to participate carries with it the responsibility of realizing the limits to one's own knowledge and intellect.

Procedures for conflict resolution

What do we do if disagreements between the experts and the public persist? In a democratic society, "we" don't do anything; the political process resolves the issue, for better or worse. Assume, however, that some wise and dispassionate institution is entrusted with resolving these disagreements (or that our courts, legislatures, or bureaucracies constitute such institutions); could it responsibly act according to the public's fears rather than the experts' facts? The answer could be yes if at least one of the following conditions holds:

1. The lay public knows something that the experts do not; the dispassionate institution should then change its best estimate of what the facts are.
2. The lay public knows nothing special, but has good reason to be unconvinced by the experts' testimony; the institution might leave its best estimate unchanged, but increase the confidence intervals around it. The result might be delay, hedging, or switching to a more certain course of action.
3. The public is unreasonable and unresponsive to evidence, but has a deep emotional investment in its beliefs. There are costs to a society for overriding the strong wishes of its members; these include anomie, resentment, mistrust, sabotage, stress, and psychosomatic effects (whose impact is physical even when their source is illusory). Such costs could tip the balance against the action indicated by the experts' best guess.

Responsibilities of the public

The right to participate in acceptable-risk (or any other) decisions carries certain responsibilities. The first is to make the effort needed to understand the issues that recurrently arise in acceptable-risk problems. Perhaps the most difficult and pervasive of these issues is the probabilistic nature of risk phenomena. Within any specific domain, there are certain basic phenomena that any participant should feel required to know (e.g., that nuclear power plants cannot explode like atomic bombs). A second responsibility is to refrain from demanding infeasible solutions, such as zero risk. Such demands may lead to delays, frustration, and adoption of unsound options whose attractive feature is that they seem to have zero risk. Finally, participants need to consider the broader societal implications of the options they advocate. For example, refusal to allow a risky facility near one's own community may mean imposing it on another. One may feel comfortable with that imposition; but such positions should be taken deliberately.

Recommendations for the marketplace

Acceptable-risk decisions are made every time a worker accepts or rejects a hazardous job assignment, a consumer saves money by buying a slightly defective product, or a manufacturer brings out safety-oriented products. The wisdom of these decisions not only affects the fates of those involved, but also has implications for the validity of the three approaches to acceptable-risk decisions, each of which refers back to how people think and act for guidance as to human values. Those thoughts and actions are conditioned by the interactions between the actors in the marketplace as they exchange information and negotiate exchanges. The recommendations outlined in Table 9.6 should improve those interactions and help ensure that a proper price is paid for safety.

Table 9.6. Recommendations for the marketplace

Acknowledge the experimental nature of technological innovation	Increase market sensitivity to safety issues
Monitor warning signs	Offer safety as an option
Face fallibility	Clarify the costs of safety
Provide better risk information to workers and consumers	Improve the liability system
	Investigate schemes for coping with risks that cannot be borne by their creators

Acknowledge the experimental nature of technological innovation

A common refrain of developers runs something like, We build them safe, We've identified and solved all possible problems, or, We wouldn't sell it if it weren't safe. With complex innovations, such claims tend to be overstatements and to be treated as such by a skeptical public. Admitting the possibility of error would serve not only rhetorical frankness, but also the cause of better acceptable-risk decisions in the following ways:

1. Improving the quality of information and the frequency of safety assessments. A promoter who acknowledges the possibility of problems is presumably more likely to spot early warning signs. This may be particularly important when workers serve as guinea pigs for the rest of society. Substances that workers handle in concentrated doses often reach the public in weaker doses (e.g., PCBs); processes that prove themselves in industrial applications often find domestic uses (e.g., microwaves). Because health effects can most easily be detected when large doses are given to a readily defined population, every effort should be made to learn the most from this bitter lesson in which workers (and, often, their supervisors) partake.
2. Stimulating more explicit discussion of the limits to and costs of safety. Promoters should address the possibility that their technologies are too dangerous or too poorly understood to be promulgated; consumers should face the impossibility of a risk-free existence.
3. Encouraging fuller disclosure of risk information to workers and consumers. Such knowledge would enhance their ability to negotiate fair compensation for hazardous work and fair prices for safety devices. In some situations, better information may lead them to decide that risks are less important than they had thought, or that life really involves a choice among risks. In others, they may demand increased wages or safer products, leading in turn to increased prices that may more accurately reflect the full costs of the product. One beneficial side effect of better information would be that people could better control risks in the machinery and substances they deal with.

Increase market sensitivity to safety issues

To the extent that hazards are regulated by the marketplace, the efficacy of the relevant market mechanisms needs to be strengthened. The following suggestions would make for better acceptable-risk decisions in the marketplace:

Offer safety as an option. At times, people are willing to pay a substantial premium for protection (e.g., organic foods for some people, mountain-climbing equipment); at other times, they are not (e.g., organic foods for other people, reinforced automobile front ends). Because different consumers have different preferences, promoters should offer safety as an option wherever possible. If safety were marketed as fervently as other attributes, people could express their preferences much more accurately.

Clarify the costs of safety. Especially for large-scale developments, the economic costs of safety are often paid in a very indirect manner. Better knowledge will help consumers understand where too much or too little is being paid for safety, and should facilitate comparison of the funds spent on similar risks incurred from different sources.

Improve the liability system. The courts, and more specifically liability suits, provide an important cue to risk creators regarding how much to invest in safety. However, there are some things that impede the courts from providing useful feedback. At present, workers' compensation laws limit the damages an employee can obtain directly from an employer. In addition to reducing the employer's incentive for safety, this arrangement may force workers to sue the manufacturers of tools used (perhaps improperly) in the workplace in order to gain redress for injuries. Some of these suits are justified; other commit one injustice to alleviate another. More generally, promoters, juries, and users need guidelines as to what risks are foreseeable and what uses are reasonable. The Pinto case suggests another problem: Manufacturers may be penalized for keeping good records, thereby making it more desirable to seem or remain ignorant of their products' risks. There should be incentives for collecting data and making conscious decisions, and disincentives for incomplete or fraudulent records.

Investigate schemes for coping with risks that cannot be borne by their creators. Many hazards are capable of creating damages that are larger than the total assets of those who create them. Whereas bankruptcy places an effective limit on liability, public exposure may be unlimited. One possible solution is to make the government an insurer of last resort. This idea, however, would be unpopular with promoters because it invites government meddling in their affairs, and might be unpopular with taxpayers because it represents a public subsidy to private entities. A voluntary alternative might be an industry commitment to cover the damages created by constituent corporations. One side effect would be an increase in the likelihood of firms blowing the whistle on one another for unethical practices, a role for which they would be uniquely suited because of their technical expertise and natural interest in one another's affairs. A court-based scheme might be tried in which corporations would be treated as partnerships for third-party liability, making the resources of their shareholders subject to claims by victims (R. A. How-

Table 9.7. Recommendations for government

Managing individual hazards	Managing many hazards
Give a clear, feasible mandate	Encourage generic decisions
Avoid mandating inadequate decision-making techniques	Establish priorities for hazard regulation
Avoid ad-hoc meddling in specific decisions	Coordinate acceptable-risk decisions
Emphasize due process by law	
Give agencies consistent roles	

ard, 1978). An analogous problem, with no obvious solution, arises when government creates larger risks than it can handle.

Recommendations for government

Barring a dramatic change in political climate, some government involvement in acceptable-risk decisions is inevitable for the foreseeable future. Even staunch opponents of regulation may feel that an efficient free market is an impossibility with sophisticated technologies that naturally foster monopoly conditions, unequal distribution of critical information, and ambiguity as to who is responsible for damages. Moreover, the national interest may make the management of some technologies too important to be left to those who create and use them. On the other hand, even proponents of regulation may feel that government solutions, like other aspects of our society's response to hazards, have evolved without adequate forethought, evaluation, or coordination. The recommendations outlined in Table 9.7 should be useful whenever government has a role in acceptable-risk decisions.

Managing individual hazards

Regulatory agencies can be no more intelligent than their enabling legislation allows them to be. Unwisely formulated mandates spell frustration for all concerned. Five guiding principles are:

Give a clear, feasible mandate. Acceptable-risk decisions require hard choices, especially when it comes to loathsome jobs like setting a value on human life. To avoid responsibility for such decisions, Congress has often passed the buck to regulators without, however, giving them the authority to make binding decisions. As a result, the center of government has shifted toward the courts or those technical analysts bold enough to make such determinations. To make the regulators' task reasonable, Congress must clearly state what it believes the will of the people to be. That goal is not achieved by mandating unrealistic standards like zero risk.

Avoid mandating inadequate decision-making techniques. When legislation or regulations mandate a technique that is unable to produce unimpeachable recommendations, interminable proceedings may result. When one cannot prove anything with, say, a cost-benefit analysis, any action forced to justify its existence by such an analysis could be litigated to death. For example, the National Environmental Policy Act's call for a cost-benefit type of analysis of new projects may have made it impossible for those projects to prove their worth. Conversely, the call for having regulations *prove* that their costs are less than their benefits might, if taken literally, mean the end of regulation. In the end, we must rely on the wisdom of our legislators and regulators to make decisions, informed, but not replaced, by decision-making techniques.

Avoid ad-hoc meddling in specific decisions. Second-guessing through legislative or executive vetoes is likely to make consistent, predictable acceptable-risk decision making impossible. Although some vetoes may stymie unwise regulatory decisions, it is more likely that vetoes will serve powerful vested interests. Even those interests may be hurt in the long run if they destabilize the decision-making processes, making planning impossible. When systematic problems are discovered, new mandates can be drafted to guide the entire process.

Emphasize due process by law. Acceptable-risk decisions rely on a healthy legal system (e.g., for interpreting laws and regulations, for scrutinizing evidence, for holding polluters accountable), but they also place great stress on that system. The high stakes and time pressures may make it tempting to tinker with these seemingly clumsy processes. For example, an Energy Mobilization Board would short-circuit some standing processes to the consternation of environmentalists; attempts to subpoena proprietary information trouble developers. An alternative approach is to look for creative solutions within the current framework – for example, a regulatory appeals court or a clearinghouse might be able to examine sensitive data without prejudicing producers' rights to keep proprietary information secret.

Give agencies consistent roles. The breakup of the Atomic Energy Commission reflected a presumption that no entity can promote and regulate simultaneously. The events at Three Mile Island suggested another pair of incompatible roles: An agency designed for routine decision making may be ill suited to handle crisis situations. The Kemeny Commission's (U.S. Government, 1979) recommendation to replace the current five-person commission with a single commissioner seems to change the priorities between these two roles without disentangling them. An alternative solution might be to structure an agency around one role but to have contingency plans for rapidly shifting from routine to emergency procedures (or vice versa).

Managing many hazards

Improved small-scale decision making is a necessary but not sufficient condition for improved large-scale decision making. The following suggestions apply to allocating resources over the universe of risk problems.

Encourage generic decisions. Some 60,000 chemicals and 50,000 consumer products are used in the United States. If even a small fraction presented the legal and technical complexities of saccharin or flammable sleepwear, the society would need legions of analysts, lawyers, toxicologists, and regulators. Agencies that try to deal with hazards singly are doomed to overwork, frustration, and glaring instances of neglected hazards causing egregious harm. One obvious solution is to concentrate on making sound generic decisions. For this strategy to work, careful thought must be given to the definition of hazard categories. Inevitably, some category members will be treated too leniently and some too harshly relative to their category's ideal type; that, however, may be a tolerable price for society to pay for greater coverage and consistency.

Establish priorities for hazard regulation. A recurrent complaint against the Consumer Product Safety Commission was that it cut its teeth on minor problems (e.g., swimming-pool slides). Although there are possible rationales for this selection (e.g., organizational procedures are best developed with noncontroversial test cases), failure to argue them effectively has made the agency vulnerable. To avoid such criticism and to ensure timely treatment of problems, some decision-making priorities are needed. The following are some alternative (and inconsistent) schemes that might be suitable for different contexts.

Attend first to hazards with:

1. The most visible consequences (to enhance the agency's image and credibility).
2. The least visible consequences, particularly those that affect politically powerless groups (to ensure that they get a hearing).
3. The greatest catastrophic potential, regardless of their likelihood (to assuage fears and reduce threats to societal resilience).
4. The highest ratio of long-term to short-term consequences (to give the former more immediacy than they typically have).
5. The greatest promise of quick, cheap fixes (e.g., childproof drug caps).
6. The widest range of control options, including substitute technologies (to exploit the potential for action).

A radical alternative would be for an agency to set no priorities and to address problems in a random order. Once hazards have been prioritized, those involved with technologies far down the list can relax. Unpredictability will encourage everyone to be wary and to think in terms of safety.

Coordinate acceptable-risk decisions. The following regulatory functions are vital for effective acceptable-risk decision making, but are often treated unsystematically.

1. Resolving jurisdictional disputes between agencies.
2. Assessing the consistency of standards, both across hazards and for the same hazards in different domains (e.g., lead in ambient air and lead in domestic water supplies).
3. Identifying effects involving several hazards (e.g., cumulative doses, synergies).
4. Managing information (e.g., integrating data bases to increase their accessibility, standardizing research reports to improve their interpretability).
5. Promoting research that is relevant to policy; in particular, pooling resources from mission-oriented agencies in order to sponsor basic research on common problems.
6. Monitoring and improving acceptable-risk decisions (e.g., spotting recurrent omissions or oversimplifications).

Such coordination is too important and complex to be handled by occasional ad-hoc committees. A standing committee, such as the Interagency Regulatory Liaison Group, is a step in the right direction. The effectiveness of such committees will be enhanced to the extent that agency representatives have enough permanence to acquire expertise and enough standing to influence their own agencies' operations. Failing that, less voluntary arrangements might be needed. Although it is premature (and somewhat grisly) to think about a hazards czar, that prospect may be with us before too long.

Summary

However flawed our methods might be, acceptable-risk decisions must still be made. The recommendations in this chapter suggest ways to get the most out of the capabilities that we have. Those capabilities are spread throughout society, and effective decision making involves the technical community, the lay public, the marketplace, and government. Suggestions for the technical community stress the comprehensiveness and clarity of their work and the improvement of their training. For the public there is a need to become better informed and more responsible. Suggestions for the marketplace include more careful monitoring and more adequate responding to safety information. Government should establish clearer guidelines and authority for dealing with public risks.

10 What do we need to learn?

A recurrent theme of earlier chapters was that our decision-making tools are not adequate for the challenges that many hazards pose. The result of expecting more of existing tools than they are capable of delivering is a clumsy, unsatisfying decision-making process. This chapter addresses the areas where we are still ignorant by pointing out urgent and promising research projects that may serve to reduce that ignorance. It presents proposals for reducing the uncertainties that arise in each of five general areas of difficulty. The chapter ends with a discussion of the social and intellectual context within which future research has the greatest chance of succeeding. The underlying premise of the chapter is that research can be an effective alternative to trial-and-error learning, especially for institutions (e.g., agencies, corporations) that are so buffeted by political pressures and fire fighting that they cannot adequately reflect on their own experience or experiment with new procedures. In acceptable-risk decision making, additional theory could be very practical.

Research to reduce uncertainty about problem definition

Once a problem is defined, its solution may already be ordained. We have attempted to identify the key issues in problem definition in order to suggest where the different approaches stand in this regard. Additional analysis, as depicted in Table 10.1, would reveal further subtleties of acceptable-risk decisions and the tools available for resolving them.

Extend the present analysis

The three generic approaches we have described are among those most forcefully advocated in acceptable-risk debates. This analysis should be extended to the process-oriented approaches briefly introduced in Chapter 3, those embodying *market* and *procedural* logic. These approaches reject the possibility of centralized, analytic decision making in favor of letting standards evolve through the interactions and experiences of the various actors. This combination of learning by doing and negotiated settlements could occur either in the marketplace or through various social processes (including electoral politics and the workings of a bureaucracy designed for sophisticated muddling through).

The analysis of the three approaches we have focused on is itself necessar-

Table 10.1. Research to reduce uncertainty about problem definition

Extend the present analysis
  Consider additional approaches (e.g., market, procedural)
  Iterate analysis of three approaches
Develop a conceptual framework for hazard definition
  Establish bounds for hazard categories
  Clarify logic of key descriptors (e.g., risk voluntariness)
	Develop guidelines for identifying consequences
	  Construct a compendium of consequences
	  Explore systematic omissions
	Design clearer, more workable options
	  Identify full range of possibilities
	  Develop practical expressions

ily incomplete, pending an iteration that exploits whatever insights it provides and criticisms it provokes. Two particularly useful extensions would be further analysis of the fit between approaches and specific problem types, and of the design of hybrid approaches that incorporate complementary strengths. Another extension might be to investigate the manner in which each approach would best fit into society's existing decision structure.

Develop a conceptual framework for hazard definition

Like any new field, acceptable-risk decision making is hindered by disagreements over the meaning of key terms. Some misunderstandings between experts and lay people seem to arise from inconsistent definitions of risk. Many quantitative criteria, such as, "Reduce the risk of a fatal event from each occupational activity to less than 10^{-5} per year," are rendered indeterminate by uncertainty about what an event or an activity is. In setting air-quality standards, the Environmental Protection Agency must avoid "adverse health effects" without a clear definition of that term. The lack of a taxonomy of hazards impedes the development of generic decisions or priorities for research. Even such simple terms as "voluntary risk" or "exposure" present problems under closer scrutiny: How voluntary is taking a job in a tight labor market, or airplane travel for scientists, or smoking for addicts? Are we always or rarely exposed to the risk of handguns? The power of definitions is such that theoretical disagreements are often suspected of being rooted in vested interests.

A concerted effort is needed to make currently used definitions explicit, to clarify their underlying assumptions, to identify cases that push them to their limits, and to propose standard usages. If a theory of acceptable risk is to be developed, clear definitions of its primitives must come first.

Develop guidelines for identifying consequences

Given the importance of specifying the set of relevant consequences, decision makers should not have to start from scratch each time. They needs lists of the effects of particular hazards and a theory of usage that would describe, for example, which consequences are important to which constituencies, what higher-order and synergistic effects should be borne in mind, where one runs the risk of double counting, and where indicator consequences can be used to represent a larger set of possible outcomes. One way to start developing this guide would be to conduct retrospective technology assessments that would identify systematically neglected consequences (Tarr, 1977). Another would be to create a generic structure for objectives and consequences, such as for siting any energy facility (Keeney, 1980b).

Design clearer, more workable options

Guidelines are needed for identifying the set of possible options, along with some notion of the strengths and weaknesses of each. Such guidelines would help decision makers to know what they can conceivably do and their critics to know what options are being ignored. They would show how to express options in terms that are explicit and operational enough to keep the options from being implemented in arbitrary and inconsistent ways. As before, the ways to begin would be with a theory of hazards (e.g., Figure 2.1) and a review of current practice. It would be of particular interest to take a look at those options that are now mandated: How specific are the mandates? Do some hazards require less specific legislation? How do laws cope with the possibility of lax enforcement?

Research to reduce uncertainty about the facts

We are only better off with knowledge when we know how to use it. Without a framework for integrating new knowledge with old and for understanding its limits, confidence may increase faster than wisdom. Although the need for substantive knowledge varies from problem to problem, research into some general questions of applied epistemology could help clarify areas of uncertainty. Table 10.2 summarizes these opportunities.

Explore the limits of knowledge

When making uncertain decisions, and particularly in deciding when to decide, it is important to have some idea of how quickly our ignorance is going to be reduced. Research here would ask such questions as: When does it pay to wait for a few more data points or a scientific breakthrough? How fast will various frontiers of knowledge push forward? Which technological innovations are more and less likely? To what extent is the reliability of technical systems limited by their complexity, with actions designed to solve one problem inadvertently leading to others (e.g., more alarm systems leading to more false alarms leading to reduced vigilance)? A more sociological assessment might try to estimate the extent to which scientists and technology promoters

Table 10.2. Research to reduce uncertainty about the facts

Explore the limits of knowledge
  Characterize its extent and growth rate in different areas
  Devise general rules for when it pays to wait for better knowledge
Understand expert judgment
  Investigate the cognitive processes of experts
  Assess experts' ability to assess the limits of their own knowledge
	Improve society's ability to accommodate evidence
	  Develop better procedures for expert witnesses
	  Develop more adequate formats for public participation
	Develop better summary measures
	  Perform theoretical analyses of possible risk statistics
	  Conduct empirical tests of experts' ability to provide inputs and lay people's ability to understand them

are pressured to make impossible promises in order to gain time and resources for their work. Do they, like lay people, tend to underestimate the time needed to complete tasks?

How much will be known is often bounded by practical limits on how much can be known. An understanding of the ultimate resolvability of different scientific questions would give decision makers a more realistic appraisal of what science can and cannot do. Products of this project might explain the limits of epidemiology for untangling complex causal relationships, of theory and experience for assessing very low probabilities, or of clinical trials for establishing the effectiveness of drugs.

Understand expert judgment

Decision makers often rely heavily on the intuitions of experts to tell them what the available data cannot. Particularly when it is difficult to get an independent second opinion, guidance is needed in interpreting those judgments. Although the intellectual processes of the highly trained are seldom studied, existing research methodologies could readily be applied to such questions as: Can one generalize to experts from research conducted with lay people, or are their judgmental processes too dissimilar? Does professional training encourage or discourage particular misperceptions? How independent can the opinions of two experts be when they have gone through similar training? How well do experts understand the limits of their own knowledge? Further research questions arise if one considers experts not as dispassionate interpreters of results, but as individuals strongly motivated to confirm pet theories or satisfy clients.

Improve society's ability to accommodate evidence

The two recognized founts of wisdom in our society are the people and the experts. Unfortunately, our legal and political institutions seem ill equipped to exploit the insights that either group offers. The adversarial context of legal settings may not elicit experts' knowledge in a thorough and balanced fashion, particularly when statistical evidence is involved. Public input, although a vaunted ideal, is often solicited by powerless junior officials who offer little technical assistance. Some ways to get more out of these human resources might include instituting a science court, having panels that include "representative" citizens accompany decision-making processes, using alternative procedures for expert testimony, and conducting regular polls of attitudes toward risks. These proposals merit theoretical analysis and field testing. They should be supplemented by procedures that have been used for other social problems or for acceptable-risk problems in other countries.

Develop better summary measures

To be useful, scientific results must be understood. When states of nature (e.g., air quality) are described on several dimensions, each characterized by various statistics and having different effects on each of several populations, comprehension may be next to impossible. Rather than have the consumers or producers of such statistics produce ad-hoc intuitive summaries, systematically developed risk indices are needed. Like approaches to acceptable risk, these indices should be comprehensive, defensible, and comprehensible.

A different sort of summary measure is an expert's judgmental summary of his or her experience with a hazard. That experience may not always be cognitively organized in the form desired by the risk analyst. For example, a

"Meaningless statistics were up one-point-five per cent this month over last month."

Drawing by Dana Fradon. Reprinted with permission of The New Yorker Magazine Inc.

mechanic, accustomed to seeing problems as they arise, may be unable to estimate failure rates or the likelihood of various malfunctions occurring together. Summary measures that have theoretical appeal are of little use if no one can produce them. The development of judgmental procedures requires expertise in both statistics and cognition.

Research to reduce uncertainty about values

Acceptable-risk decisions require people to assess their values on complex, subtle, and novel issues. Table 10.3 suggests research that should help people develop and express coherent, articulated value judgments.

Develop improved methods for eliciting values

The naïve view of survey research is that pollsters can find out what the public thinks about any and every question that interests a decision maker. This view is reinforced by the low rates of no-opinion responses encountered even in surveys that address diverse and obscure topics. Although capable of providing some answer to whatever question is put to them, people may often express a desire to be counted rather than deeply held opinions.

A research program for improving value elicitation might include structured interactions in which the interviewer offers alternative perspectives; iterative procedures, which review the issues until a feeling of closure is reached (or rejected); and unstructured sessions in which respondents are allowed to choose the questions. Although procedures that have many of these features have been used to elicit the values of single individuals (Keeney, 1977; Keeney & Raiffa, 1976), there has been little collective experience with such procedures. Especially when public values are to be assessed, substantive experts (e.g., philosophers, economists) would be needed to help ensure that questions are well conceived, and communications specialists to help ensure that they are clearly expressed.

Survey public attitudes toward risk evaluation

When the voice of "the public" as expressed in surveys appears confused or irrational, the trouble may be with the transmitter or the receiver. The methods described in the preceding section could help make the latter possibility less likely. Their application requires some strategic decisions about whom and what to ask.

"The public" is usually defined as whatever population is represented by a probability sample of adults who can be found and will respond. When the issue is so obscure or complex that even the most sensitive and interactive interview cannot sufficiently educate the average layperson, the public weal may be better served by questioning existing groups already interested in the

Table 10.3. Research to reduce uncertainty about values

Develop improved methods for eliciting values	Conduct theoretical analyses of value issues that arise in acceptable-risk decisions
Find better ways to formulate questions	Identify possible perspectives
Create more suitable interviewer-interviewee relationships	Work out their implications
Survey public attitudes toward risk acceptability	Identify hidden agendas
Identify relevant respondent populations	Isolate concerns that are not directly addressed
Conduct appropriate surveys	Understand how they might nonetheless be incorporated

topic – or, by paying a representative group of citizens to follow the issue over a period of time. It may also be useful to conduct repeated surveys in the hope that they would reveal increased sophistication in thinking about hazards, greater consistency between attitudes and behavior (as their logical links are learned), and the stability of values over time.

When eliciting public values, another important strategic decision is whether or not to ask about specific policy recommendations, such as where to site an energy facility, what kind of containment structure is needed, or what land-use regulations are needed. At times, people may be able to develop articulated positions at this level. At other times, they may feel more comfortable answering questions of principle from which specific recommendations could be derived, such as: Should equity be a goal in acceptable-risk decisions (or left to other processes)? Should there be a different standard for the safety of voluntary and involuntary activities? Should policy decisions be guided by what our values are or by what they should be?

Conduct theoretical analyses of value issues in acceptable-risk decisions

Successful decisions and surveys depend on knowing what value questions to ask and understanding the societal implications of different answers. Thus interviewers or technical analysts intent on helping people develop positions consistent with their underlying values need some substantive knowledge of the issues. Rather than relying on whatever general formulations have evolved, they should have the benefit of theoretical analyses of these issues by multidisciplinary teams of philosophers, economists, psychologists, sociologists, and others. These analyses could explore in detail such questions as: What would it mean if a society failed to place a premium on avoiding catastrophic losses of life? What hazard policies would violate our social contract? If equity is important, should it be sought merely in economic effects, or also in political power, knowledge, and feelings of entitlement? Such analyses should be informed by how these issues have been addressed in different political and cultural settings and by how they would be viewed from the perspective of alternative world outlooks. Even nonbelievers might learn something from seeing a coherent libertarian, Marxist, Hindu, Christian, hippie, or Dadaist analysis of acceptable-risk questions.

Identify hidden agendas

When participants in a decision-making process find that its official problem definition precludes issues important to them, they may resort to diversionary strategies. Lacking a forum to discuss what really concerns them, foes of growth may choose to fight the siting of particular power-generating facilities using whatever arguments prove convenient. Companies may feel compelled to fight regulations that they consider reasonable as part of their struggle against regulation in general. An anxiousness to demonstrate competence may infect the work of analysts eager to be consulted or pundits and professors eager for the limelight. When social policies are decided piecemeal, it is natural to exert leverage wherever one can. Nonetheless, the level of the discussion of the official problem would be raised if such hidden agendas were to be clarified. What the actors might lose by exposing their biases they might gain by being shown to be less irrational than they may have originally seemed.

The existence of hidden agendas suggests that legitimate concerns are not being addressed. Research into ways of handling such neglected issues may be timely and useful. For example, although a forum for directly affecting national energy policy might be expensive and unwieldy, it might more than pay for itself by taking the pressure off smaller, more technical decisions such as plant siting.

Research to reduce uncertainty about the human element

The way people perceive and respond to risks is central to acceptable-risk decisions. Our present understanding of these processes is based on a small body of psychological work that uses techniques of varying sophistication and a large body of speculation by experts. The research suggested in Table 10.4 would help experts to understand and serve the public.

Develop research methods for studying perceptions of risk

The straightforward approach to assessing the public's risk perceptions is to elicit risk estimates that can be compared with the best available technical estimates; discrepancies are interpreted as measuring the respondents' ignorance. Although direct, this research strategy prejudges a variety of empirical issues in ways likely to increase the public's apparent stupidity. As a step toward developing more sophisticated methods, these assumptions need to be explored. They include: (a) People are able to translate their knowledge into

Table 10.4. Research to reduce uncertainty about the human element

Develop methods for studying risk perception	Develop educational procedures
Understand the terms in which people conceptualize risk	Produce curricular materials
Produce elicitation procedures for different populations	Identify dangers of opinion manipulation
Survey public perceptions of risk	Discover what decision makers believe about the public's risk perceptions
Question both general public and interest groups	Determine the perceived substance of public beliefs and desires
Identify educational needs	Determine the perceived extent of public understanding and competence

whatever terms interest the interviewer. Will alternative formulations using more comfortable terms enable people to acquit themselves better in expressing what they know? (b) Providing summary statistics is the only way to demonstrate competence. Would proficiency in describing the maximum credible accident or the range of ameliorative strategies be a better test? (c) The public has concentrated on the same aspects of risk as the experts. Does their expertise lie in assessing personal risk rather than risk to the U.S. adult population? Do they worry about catastrophic potential and morbidity rather than yearly fatalities? (d) Errors reflect poorly on lay people's intellect. Is inaccuracy due to the quality of the information provided by the media and by experts' testimony? Would inconsistencies disappear with modest educational efforts, perhaps using multiple perspectives feedback to respondents? Investigating these issues is essential to understanding what people know and how to go about helping them to know more.

Survey public perceptions of risk

Once developed, improved methods for studying risk perceptions should be applied to both the general population and special-interest groups. Surveys of the former should show ambient levels of interest and knowledge; studies of the latter should show the potential for understanding. Only after these surveys can statements be made as to the public's real attitudes toward risks. What do people know? What information do they want? What sources do they trust? What does *risk* mean to them? How do they set their priorities? How do they define such terms as event, responsibility, foreseeability, controllability, voluntariness? Where do they need help? Where could their perspectives enrich or even supplant those of experts?

Develop educational procedures

When it is clear that people need to know more, it is also clear that education is needed. People will readily change their minds when given clear-cut evidence from credible sources expressed in psychologically meaningful terms. Procedures for providing such evidence need to be developed, based on the findings of the research described in the two previous sections. Among the special groups for whom curriculums are needed are workers exposed to occupational hazards, science writers, general journalists, prescription-drug users, and young people (perhaps focusing on recreational drugs and contraception). Given the deep-seated nature of cognitive processes, starting young may provide the best hope for inculcating the intellectual skills for understanding risks. Given the important role of expert judgment, techniques should be developed to help experts make better use of what they know. As with any other study of human behavior, educational research could be used to enhance the public's decision-making ability or to exploit its weaknesses for manipulative purposes. Researchers have an obligation to provide convenient guides that alert people to how messages about risk can be distorted.

Discover what decision makers believe about the public

Many risk decisions are based upon policy makers' images of what the public believes and wants. These images, however, are not necessarily accurate, and may lead to misguided policies. A general misunderstanding of how much (or little) lay people know or wish to know may distort the role given them in the political process. Research is needed into what decision makers know about risks as well as into what they think the public knows.

Research to reduce uncertainty about decision quality

In each approach to acceptable-risk decisions, wisdom about risk issues is seen as emerging from a particular source, whether the educated intuitions of substantive experts, the synthetic recommendations of normative experts, or the natural functioning of historical processes. Understanding how these putative sources of wisdom function would help one gauge the soundness of the decisions they produce. Table 10.5 summarizes research that would serve this end.

Study subjective aspects of professional judgment

Professional judgment takes part in the decision-making process in three ways: filling in missing data, deciding what the client wants, and defining the problem. Roughly speaking, these functions belong, respectively, to the domains of fact, value, and the meeting ground of fact and value. Earlier we made recommendations for research into the first of these functions, we will now turn to the latter two.

Professionals can represent their clients' interests only to the extent that they understand what those interests are. With vague mandates, labile values and competing concerns, more than one interpretation of those interests is often possible, making it easier for professionals to either deliberately or inadvertently impose their own values (when in doubt, do what makes sense

Table 10.5. Research to reduce uncertainty about decision quality

Study subjective aspects of professional judgment	Clarify the effectiveness of market mechanisms
Identify where subjective elements enter professionals' decisions	Assess the validity of perfect-market assumptions in acceptable-risk cases
Assess size and direction of potential biases	Assess the threat that failure of these assumptions poses to the interpretation of market data
Improve the accountability of formal analysis	Clarify implementation of proposed decisions
Develop professional standards and evaluation tools	Characterize changes in options due to exploitation of loopholes and ambiguities
Assess the quality of existing analyses to establish track record	Anticipate side effects

to you). Systematic study is needed to identify the tradeoffs (e.g., between dollars and safety) implicit in professionals' decisions, as well as political analysis of the appropriateness of these tradeoffs. Analogous studies are needed to reveal the psychological and political processes that come into play as professionals develop a workable definition of hazard problems. What consequences do they consider and neglect? Where do they turn for advice on feasibility? What control strategies are they likely to ignore? In what ways are they the captives of untested theories or of the failure of researchers to study potentially useful topics?

Improve the accountability of formal analysis

Any pursuit that fails to evaluate its own performance is likely to raise some suspicions. Technical risk analysis, like other forms of policy analysis, is often justified by such claims as, We're doing the best we can, or, My clients like my work. The modest success of such arguments in forestalling criticism may reflect both their kernel of truth and the difficulty of countering them.

The sophisticated evaluation methodologies of professions such as psychotherapy that have similarly complicated problems suggest that better answers are possible. One thrust of such research should be retrospective case studies. Was criticism solicited from other analysts? Were analyses updated to accommodate new information and insights? Were all relevant perspectives consulted? Were the technical details in order? A second thrust should be experimental tests of the effectiveness of approaches. These might involve standardization of techniques to facilitate comparisons, random assignment of problems to different kinds of treatment, a deliberate effort to leave a clear audit trail, and the formulation of recommendations that can be readily evaluated. A third thrust would be theoretical analyses of the vulnerability of procedures to particular problems and their suitability to particular situations.

Clarify the effectiveness of market mechanisms

The adequacy of both revealed-preferences methods and cost–benefit analyses depends upon the adequacy of market mechanisms. Each assumes an unrestrained and responsive market that serves fully informed and rational decision makers – a picture of both the market and its denizens that is known to be somewhat inaccurate. Although it can be argued that some inaccuracy is tolerable, it is unclear just how much of it these approaches can get away with before they lose their validity. Research into the veracity of public risk perceptions is one key to this puzzle; research into market failures is another. Theoretical analyses are needed to assess the implications of this research for the interpretation of marketplace data.

Acceptable-risk debates often center around thinly substantiated assertions about economic issues. Better studies are needed to help answer such questions as: Are people really unwilling to pay for safety (or have unpopular safety features been designed for rejection)? Do companies flee developed countries with strict environmental standards (or do they assume that developing countries will eventually adopt standards from the developed countries)? Have workers negotiated compensation for the risks they assume (or have their unions concentrated on other issues)? Do regulations tend to invigorate industries by prompting technological innovations (or do they give an undue advantage to foreign or larger firms, thereby reducing competitiveness)?

Clarify implementation of proposed decisions

A recurrent source of insecurity in decision making is concern over what decisions will look like once implemented in the real world. Research is needed to clarify our chances of getting what we wanted or more than we bargained for. There is a particular need to know more about presumptions about implementation that guide current practices. For example, one such presumption is that as soon as rules are made, the affected parties begin to explore ways to ensure themselves maximum freedom and advantage. The need to reduce the opportunities for such creative interpretation is one argument for relying on technical rather than performance standards: Although they stifle engineering creativity, technical standards offer ready measures of compliance. But is this argument sound? What opportunities are lost by adhering to it? Other areas of acceptable-risk decision making that are in need of research include the liberties that are taken with measurement of regulated pollutants, procrastination, nuisance litigation, and manipulating the definition of a technology (e.g., disaggregating a major technology into several smaller ones, each below the threshold of serious regulation).

Other problems in implementation that could be studied, anticipated, and prevented arise whenever acceptable-risk decisions confront other social systems. These confrontations tend to raise such questions as: What happens when workers' rights to protection conflict with employers' rights to privacy? To what extent does allowing some pollution affect the property rights of impactees? How seriously do government reporting requirements threaten proprietary information? Does the protection of nuclear plants and materials really constitute a threat to civil liberties?

An experimenting academe

The projects described above entail research skills beyond the capabilities of any individual scientist. What is needed is a deliberate effort to create a research community with the right mix of disciplines, including both basic and applied perspectives. The following recommendations are designed to aid in that effort. Each constitutes something of a departure from current practices, suggesting the need for risk taking by academic organizations.

Broaden the ranks of the risk community. Few of today's "experts" in acceptable-risk decision making were trained in the field, simply because little such training was (or is) available. Instead they were trained in traditional disciplines and wound up in the risk business because of intellectual curiosity or involvement in some substantive problem. As a result, various disciplines are unevenly and often poorly represented. To the extent that risk issues affect all of society, there is a role for members of all disciplines. But the invitation should be accompanied by some warning to the effect that although acceptable-risk decisions are more similar to other complex social problems than has been recognized, they still hold some unique subtleties; even intelligent observers are unlikely to produce viable proposals right away.

Create a profession of risk management. One reason why few people take the interdisciplinary plunge is that there are often rather meager rewards for doing so. University departments prefer individuals who can teach the traditional courses and be evaluated by the usual criteria. Joint appointments often leave one doubly orphaned. The notion that those who can't hack it in basic research tackle applied problems is widespread. The quality of some past interdisciplinary research has strengthened these views. At times, scientists have borrowed tools from other disciplines without the full appreciation of limitations that comes from extended experience with them. When scientists from different disciplines do work together, they may be tempted to oversell their own wares in order to get a hearing, particularly when corrective criticism from colleagues of the same discipline is absent. Quality-control problems are exacerbated by the dearth of systematic peer review for interdisciplinary and applied products. Although creating a risk-analysis profession with all the familiar trappings (journals, appointments, standards, etc.) would not solve all of these problems, it may be a step in the right direction.

Involve representatives of different professions in the awarding and monitoring of research projects. Academic and research institutions typically evolve into a de-facto hierarchy of disciplines, reflecting political clout. Real-life problems are often restricted to just one discipline (e.g., economics, climatology), which is reluctant to share attention or resources. If complex issues are to be understood, however, mutually respectful interaction among disciplines is essential. Little intellectual progress can be expected if, say, political scientists are invited only when toxicologists hope to add a touch of "social relevance" to their own fixed research agenda. One recurrent prejudice that contributes to disciplinary imbalance is that technology holds the solution to economic health. A social scientist might believe that the most effective way to increase productivity is to improve social control of existing technologies, thereby getting more out of the tools we already have. Mixing these positions may generate both heat and light.

An experimenting society

Acceptable-risk decisions are leading our society into a large uncoordinated experiment with unprecedented stakes. It behooves us to learn as much as we can from this experience. Research is one strategy. Acknowledging the uncertainty in our actions and designing them to enhance learning is another. Without such efforts, it is difficult to tell what we are doing and what is happening to us; many aspects of the situation vary at once, systematic data are not collected, processes are curtailed or redesigned midway through, and so forth. Even when the stakes would seem to preclude deliberate experimentation, our collective stake in learning may justify efforts such as the ones about to be proposed.

Perform model analyses. One lesson to be learned from the Reactor Safety Study is that through massive investments of talent and resources techniques can be tested, illuminated, and improved. Comparable investments might show what, if anything, can be learned from other approaches when they are given maximal scope, full opportunity for iteration, stringent peer review, and so forth.

Sponsor exemplary public-participation processes. Clearly, halfhearted hearings with junior officials listening to poorly informed lay people may be of benefit to no one involved. Carefully designed and monitored efforts are needed to establish the potential of real public participation that involves people meaningfully in the earliest stages of problem definition, allows them to follow the process, and provides them with technical support.

Establish an "ideal" hazard-monitoring system. The Food and Drug Administration, Consumer Product Safety Commission, Center for Disease Control, and Occupational Safety and Health Administration all have systems for detecting incipient hazards. Each is plagued, however, by such problems as incomplete reporting, proprietary data, and ambiguous evidence. The potential and difficulties of monitoring may best be understood by a concen trated effort. The workplace might be a sensible place to start, as the risks are relatively high and those at risk are generally identifiable. Useful steps might include hiring industrial hygienists to screen workers, protecting companies from increased liability due solely to keeping better records, and concentrating on cases where workers are heavily exposed to hazards that may eventually reach the general public in smaller doses.

Summary

Given the enormous stakes riding on acceptable-risk decisions, our investment in research seems very small. For example, if we consider the cost of a day's delay in returning a nuclear facility to service or in approving a pipeline proposal, it becomes clear that a research project that offered a 0.1 chance of responsibly shortening the decision-making period would have an enormous expected return on investment. Similar bargains would accrue from research to improve public involvement in project planning (so as to avoid mid-construction surprises), or identify generic categories of new chemicals (so as to reduce testing costs), or decrease the uncertainty in drug licensing (so as to encourage innovative research and development), or inform workers about occupational risks (so as to enable them to make better decisions on their own behalf). Such research could be a good place to invest some of society's venture capital.

References

Acton, J. *Evaluating public programs to save lives: The case of heart attacks (R-950-RC)*. Santa Monica, Calif.: Rand Corporation, 1973.

Agricola, G. *De re metallica*, 1556.

A look at human error. *Chemical and Engineering News*, 1980, *58*(18), 82.

American Public Health Association. *Statement on S.2153 Occupational Safety and Health Improvement Act of 1980*. Washington, D.C.: Author, 1980.

Ames, B. N. Identifying environmental chemicals causing mutations and cancer. *Science*, 1979, *204*, 587-593.

Appelbaum, R. P. The future is made, not predicted: Technocratic planners vs. public interests. *Society*, May/June 1977, pp. 49-53.

Armstrong, J. S. Tom Swift and his electric regression analysis machine: 1973. *Psychological Reports*, 1975, *36*, 806.

Ashcraft, R. Economic metaphors, behavioralism, and political theory: Some observations on the ideological uses of language. *Western Political Quarterly*, 1977, *30*, 313-328.

Atomic Industrial Forum. *Committee on Reactor Licensing and Safety Statement on Licensing Reform*. New York: Author, 1976.

Barber, W. C. Controversy plagues setting of environmental standards. *Chemical and Engineering News*, 1979, *57*(17), 34-37.

Bazelon, D. L. Risk and responsibility. *Science*, 1979, *205*, 277-280.

Bazelon, D. L. Science, technology, and the court. *Science*, 1980, *208*, 661.

Berkson, J., Magath, T. B., & Hurn, M. The error of estimate of the blood cell count as made with the Hemocytometer. *American Journal of Physiology*, 1939-1940, *128*, 309-323.

Bick, T., Hohenemser, C., & Kates, R. Target: Highway risks. *Environment*, 1979, *21*(2), 7-15, 29-38.

Bøe, C. Risk management:The realization of safety. *Proceedings of the 11th Congress of the International Association of Bridge and Structural Engineers*, 1979, 237-245.

Boffey, P. M. Nuclear war: Federation disputes Academy on how bad effects would be. *Science*, 1975, *190*, 248-250.

Borch, K. *The economics of uncertainty*. Princeton, N.J.: Princeton University Press, 1968.

Bradley, M. H. Zero - what does it mean? *Science*, 1980, *208*, 7.

Brooks, A., & Bailar, B. A. *An error profile: Employment as measured by the current population survey* (Statistical Policy Working Paper 3). Washington, D.C.: U.S. Department of Commerce, 1978.

Brown, R. *Social psychology*. Glencoe, Ill.: The Free Press, 1965.

Bunker, J., Barnes, B., & Mosteller, F. *Costs, risks, and benefits of surgery*. New York: Oxford University Press, 1977.

Burch, P. R. J. Smoking and lung cancer: The problem of inferring cause (with discussion). *Journal of the Royal Statistical Society, Series A (General)*, 1978, *141*, 437-477.

Burton, I., Kates, R. W., & White, G. F. *The environment as hazard*. New York: Oxford University Press, 1978.

Calabrese, E. J. *Methodological approaches to deriving environmental and occupational health standards*. New York: Wiley, 1978.

Calabresi, G. *The costs of accidents*. New Haven, Conn.: Yale University Press, 1970.

Callen, E. The science court. *Science,* 1976, *193,* 950–951.
Campbell, D. T. Degrees of freedom and the case study. *Comparative Political Studies,* 1975, *8,* 178–193.
Campbell, D. T., & Erlebacher, A. How regression artifacts in quasi-experimental evaluations can mistakenly make compensatory education look harmful. In J. Hellmuth (Ed.), *Compensatory education: A national debate.* Vol. 3. *Disadvantaged child.* New York: Brunner/Mazel, 1970.
Canadian Standards Association. *Background paper concerning the selection and implementation of the CSA quality program standards* (CSA Special Publication QA1-1978). Rexdale, Ontario: Author, 1978.
Carter, L. J. Alaskan gas: The feds umpire another confused pipeline debate. *Science,* 1975, *190,* 362, 364.
Carter, L. J. How to assess cancer risks. *Science,* 1979, *204,* 811–816.
Chapman, L. J., & Chapman, J. P. Illusory correlation as an obstacle to the use of valid psychodiagnostic signs. *Journal of Abnormal Psychology,* 1969, *74,* 271–280.
Cohen, A. Personal communication, 1980.
Cohen, B., & Lee, I. S. A catalog of risks. *Health Physics,* 1979, *36,* 707–722.
Cohen, J. The statistical power of abnormal-social psychological research: A review. *Journal of Abnormal and Social Psychology,* 1962, *65,* 145–153.
Cohen, J. *Statistical power analysis for the behavioral sciences.* New York: Academic Press, 1969.
Comar, C. L. Risk: A pragmatic de minimis approach. *Science,* 1979, *203,* 319. (a)
Comar, C. L. SO_2 regulation ignores costs, poor science base. *Chemical and Engineering News,* 1979, *57*(17), 42–46. (b)
Combs, B., & Slovic, P. Newspaper coverage of causes of death. *Journalism Quarterly,* 1979, *56*(4), 837–843.
Commoner, B. *The politics of energy.* New York: Knopf, 1979.
Corbin, R. Decisions that might not get made. In T. Wallsten (Ed.), *Cognitive processes in choice and decision behavior.* Hillsdale, N.J.: Erlbaum, 1980.
Crask, M. R., & Perreault, W. D., Jr. Validation of discriminant analysis in marketing research. *Journal of Marketing Research,* 1977, *14,* 60–68.
Crouch, E., & Wilson, R. *Estimates of risks.* Unpublished manuscript, Energy and Environmental Policy Center, Harvard University, 1979.
David, E. E. One-armed scientists? *Science,* 1975, *189,* 891.
Dawes, R. M., & Corrigan, B. Linear models in decision making. *Psychological Bulletin,* 1974, *81,* 95–106.
De Groot, A. D. *Thought and choice in chess.* The Hague: Mouton, 1965.
Doern, G. B. Science and technology in the nuclear regulatory process: The case of Canadian uranium miners. *Canadian Public Administration,* 1978, *21,* 51–82.
Dorfan, D. Personal communication, 1980.
Doubts linger on cyclamate risks. *Eugene Register-Guard,* January 14, 1976, p. 9A.
Dunlap, T. R. Science as a guide in regulating technology: The case of DDT in the United States. *Social Studies of Science,* 1978, *8,* 265–285.
Dyson, F. J. The hidden cost of saying no! *Bulletin of the Atomic Scientists,* 1975, *31,* 23–27.
Einhorn, H. J. Decision errors and fallible judgment: Implications for social policy. In K. R. Hammond (Ed.), *Judgment and decision in public policy formulation.* Boulder, Colo.: Westview, 1978.
Ellul, J. *Propaganda.* New York: Knopf, 1969.
Elstein, A. Personal communication, 1979.
Ericsson, A., & Simon, H. Verbal reports as data. *Psychological Review,* 1980, *87,* 215–251.
Fairfax, S. K. A disaster in the environmental movement. *Science,* 1978, *199,* 743–748.

Fairley, W. B. Evaluating the "small" probability of a catastrophic accident from the marine transportation of liquefied natural gas. In W. B. Fairley & F. Mosteller (Eds.), *Statistics and public policy*. Reading Mass.: Addison-Wesley, 1977.

Farmer, F. R. Siting criteria:A new approach. In *Containment and siting of nuclear power plants*. Vienna: International Atomic Energy Agency, 1967, 303–318.

Fay, A. J. *A public interest point of view*. Paper presented at the Risk-Benefit Methodology and Application Conference, Asilomar, California, September 1975.

Feagans, T. B., & Biller, W. F. *A method for assessing the health risks associated with alternative air quality standards*. Research Triangle Park, N.C.: U.S. EPA Office of Air Quality Planning and Standards, 1979.

Ferreira, J., & Slesin, L. *Observations on the social impact of large accidents* (Technical Report No. 122). Cambridge, Mass.: MIT, Operations Research Center, 1976.

Fischhoff, B. Hindsight ≠ Foresight: The effect of outcome knowledge on judgment under uncertainty. *Journal of Experimental Psychology: Human Perception and Performance,* 1975, *1,* 288–299.

Fischhoff, B. Clinical decision analysis. *Operations Research,* 1980, *28,* 28–43. (a)

Fischhoff, B. For those condemned to study the past: Reflections on historical judgment. In R. A. Shweder & D. W. Fiske (Eds.), *New directions for methodology of behavior science: Fallible judgment in behavioral research.* San Francisco: Jossey-Bass, 1980. (b).

Fischhoff, B., Slovic, P., & Lichenstein, S. Knowing with certainty: The appropriateness of extreme confidence. *Journal of Experimental Psychology: Human Perception and Performance,* 1977, *3,* 552–564.

Fischhoff, B., Slovic, P., & Lichtenstein, S. Fault trees: Sensitivity of estimated failure probabilities to problem representation. *Journal of Experimental Psychology: Human Perception and Performance,* 1978, *4,* 330–344.

Fischhoff, B., Slovic, P., & Lichtenstein, S. Weighing the risks. *Environment,* 1979, *21*(4), 17–20, 32–38.

Fischhoff, B., Slovic, P., & Lichtenstein, S. Knowing what you want: Measuring labile values. In T. Wallsten (Ed.), *Cognitive processes in choice and decision behavior*. Hillsdale, N.J.: Erlbaum, 1980.

Fischhoff, B., Slovic, P., & Lichtenstein, S. Lay foibles and expert fables in judgments about risk. In T. O'Riordan & R. K. Turner (Eds.), *Progress in resource management and environmental planning* (Vol. 3). Chichester, U.K.: Wiley, 1981.

Fischhoff, B., Slovic, P., Lichtenstein, S., Layman, M., & Combs, B. Judged frequency of lethal events. *Journal of Experimental Psychology: Human Learning and Memory,* 1978, *4,* 551–578.

Fischhoff, B., & Whipple, C. *Assessing health risks associated with ambient air quality standards*. Research Triangle Park, N.C.: EPA, Office of Air Quality Planning and Standards, 1980.

Fishbein, M., & Ajzen, I. *Belief, attitude, intention and behavior*. Reading, Mass.: Addison-Wesley, 1975.

Fitts, P., & Posner, M. *Human performance*. Belmont, Calif.: Brooks/Cole, 1965.

Florman, S. C. Pomp and civil engineering: Image advertising. *Harper's,* November 1979, pp. 100, 104.

Forrester, J. W. *World dynamics*. Cambridge, Mass.: Wright-Allen, 1973.

Gamble, D. J. The Berger inquiry: An impact assessment process. *Science,* 1978, *199,* 946–951.

Gardiner, P. J., & Edwards, W. Public values: Multiattribute-utility measurement for social decision making. In M. F. Kaplan & S. Schwartz (Eds.), *Human judgment and decision processes*. New York: Academic Press, 1975.

Green, A. E., & Bourne, A. J. *Reliability technology*. New York: Wiley Interscience, 1972.

Greene, G. *Doctor Fischer of Geneva. Or, The Bomb Party*. New York: Simon & Schuster, 1980.

Hammer, W. *Product safety and management engineering*. Englewood Cliffs, N.J.: Prentice-Hall, 1980.

Hammond, K. R., & Adelman, L. Science, values and human judgment. *Science,* 1976, *194,* 389-396.

Handler, P. Public doubts about science. *Science,* 1980, *208,* 1093.

Hanley, J. The silence of scientists. *Chemical and Engineering News,* 1980, *58*(12), 5.

Henshel, R. L. Effects of disciplinary prestige on predictive accuracy: Distortions from feedback loops. *Futures,* 1975, *7,* 92-106.

Hexter, J. H. *The history primer*. New York: Basic Books, 1971.

Hoffman, S. D. *Unreasonable risk of injury revisited*. Chicago: Underwriters Laboratories, 1976.

Hohenemser, K. H. The failsafe risk. *Environment,* 1975, *17*(1), 6-10.

Holden, C. FDA tells senators of doctors who fake data in clinical drug trials. *Science,* 1979, *206,* 432-433.

Holden, C. Love Canal residents under stress. *Science,* 1980, *208,* 1242-1244.

Holdren, J. P., Smith, K. R., & Morris, G. Letter to the editor. *Science,* 1979, *204,* 564.

Holmes, R. On the economic welfare of victims of automobile accidents. *American Economic Review,* 1970, *60,* 143-152.

Howard, N., & Antilla, S. What price safety? The "zero-risk" debate. *Dun's Review,* 1979, *14*(3), 48-57.

Howard, P. Personal communication, 1978.

Howard, R. A. The foundation of decision analysis. *IEEE Transactions on Systems, Science and Cybernetics,* 1968, *SSC-4*(3), 393-401.

Howard, R. A. Life and death decision analysis. *Proceedings of the Second Lawrence Symposium on Systems and Decision Sciences,* 1978, 271-277.

Howard, R. A., Matheson, J. E., & Miller, K. L. *Readings in decision analysis*. Menlo Park, Calif.: Decision Analysis Group, Stanford Research Institute, 1976.

Howard, R. A., Matheson, J. E., & Owen, D. The value of life and nuclear design. *Proceedings of the Topical Meeting on Probabilistic Analysis of Nuclear Reactor Safety, 1978, 2,* IV.2-1-IV.2-9.

Hyman, R. Scientists and psychics. In S. O. Abell & B. Singer (Eds.), *Science of the paranormal*. New York: Scribner's, 1980.

Hynes, M., & Vanmarcke, E. Reliability of embankment performance prediction. In *Proceedings of the ASCE Engineering Mechanics Division Specialty Conference*. Waterloo, Ontario, Canada: University of Waterloo Press, 1976.

Ingram, M. J., Underhill, D. J., & Wigley, T. M. L. Historical climatology. *Nature,* 1978, *276,* 329-334.

Inhaber, H. Risk with energy from conventional and nonconventional sources. *Science,* 1979, *203,* 718-723.

International Commission on Radiological Protection. *Implications of commission recommendations that doses be kept as low as readily achievable* (ICRP Publication 22). Oxford: Pergamon Press, 1973.

Janis, I. *Victims of groupthink*. Boston: Houghton Mifflin, 1972.

Jennergren, L. P., & Keeney, R. L. Risk assessment. In *Handbook of applied systems analysis*. Laxenburg, Austria: International Institute of Applied Systems Analysis, in press.

Johnson, B. B. *Selected federal legislation on technological hazards 1957-1978*. Unpublished doctoral dissertation, Clark University, 1980.

Johnson, W. G. Compensation for occupational illness. In R. Nicholson (Ed.), *Carcinogenic risk assessment*. New York: New York Academy of Sciences, 1980.

Jones-Lee, M. W. *The value of life: An economic analysis*. Chicago: University of Chicago Press, 1976.

Jungermann, H. Speculations about decision-theoretics aids for personal decision making. *Acta Psychologica,* 1980, *45,* 7–34.

Kahneman, D., & Tversky, A. On the psychology of prediction. *Psychological Review,* 1973, *80,* 237–251.

Kahneman, D., & Tversky, A. Prospect theory. *Econometrica,* 1979, *47,* 263–292.

Kastenberg, W., McKone, T., & Okrent, D. *On risk assessment in the absence of complete data* (UCLA report No. ENG-7677). Los Angeles: UCLA, 1976.

Kates, R. W. *Hazard and choice perception in flood plain management* (Research Paper No. 78). Chicago: University of Chicago, Department of Geography, 1962.

Keeney, R. L. The art of assessing multiattribute utility functions. *Organizational Behavior and Human Performance,* 1977, *4,* 267–310.

Keeney, R. L. Equity and public risk. *Operations Research,* 1980, *28,* 527–534.(a)

Keeney, R. L. *Siting energy facilities.* New York: Academic Press, 1980.(b)

Keeney, R. L., & Raiffa, H. *Decisions with multiple objectives: Preferences and value tradeoffs.* New York: Wiley, 1976.

Kletz, T. A. What risks should we run? *New Scientist,* 1977, *74,* 320–322.

Knapka, J. J. The issues in diet contamination control. *Lab Animal,* 1980, *9*(2), 25.

Knoll, F. Safety, building codes and human reality. *Proceedings of the 11th Congress of the International Association of Bridge and Structural Engineers,* 1979, 247–258.

Kolata, G. B. Love Canal: False alarm caused by botched study. *Science,* 1980, *208,* 1239–1242.

Kozlowski, L. T., Herman, C. P., & Frecker, R. C. What researchers make of what cigarette smokers say: Filtering smokers' hot air. *Lancet,* 1980, *1*(8170), 699–700.

Krass, A. Personal communication, 1980.

Kunce, J. T., Cook, D. W., & Miller, D. E. Random variables and correlational overkill. *Educational and Psychological Measurement,* 1975, *35,* 529–534.

Kunreuther, H., Ginsberg, R., Miller, L., Sagi, P., Slovic, P., Borkin, B., & Katz, N. *Disaster insurance protection: Public policy lessons.* New York: Wiley, 1978.

Kyburg, H. E., Jr., & Smokler, H. E. *Studies in subjective probability.* New York: Wiley, 1964.

Lanir, Z. *Critical reevaluation of the strategic intelligence methodology.* Tel Aviv: Center for Strategic Studies, Tel Aviv University, 1978.

Larkin, J., McDermott, J., Simon, D. P., & Simon, H. A. Expert and novice performance in solving physics problems. *Science,* 1980, *208,* 1335–1342.

Lave, L. B. Ambiguity and inconsistency in attitudes toward risk: A simple model. *Proceedings of the Society for General Systems Research Annual Meeting,* 1978, *00,* 108–114.

Layard, R. *Cost-benefit analysis.* New York: Penguin, 1974.

Lepkowski, W. Appropriate technology prods science policy. *Chemical and Engineering News,* 1980, *58*(24), 31–35.

Levine, M. Scientific method and the adversary model: Some preliminary thoughts. *American Psychologist,* 1974, *29,* 661–716.

Lichtenstein, S., Fischhoff, B., & Phillips, L. D. Calibration of probabilities: The state of the art. In H. Jungermann & G. deZeeuw (Eds.), *Decision making and change in human affairs.* Amsterdam: D. Reidel, 1977.

Lichtenstein, S., & Slovic, P. Response-induced reversals of preference in gambling: An extended replication in Las Vegas. *Journal of Experimental Psychology,* 1973, *101,* 16–20.

Lindblom, C. E. *The intelligence of democracy.* New York: The Free Press, 1965.

Linnerooth, J. *A review of recent modelling efforts to determine the value of a human life* (Research Memorandum RM-75-67). Laxenburg, Austria: International Institute for Applied Systems Analysis, 1975.

Linnerooth, J. Methods for evaluating mortality risk. *Futures,* 1976, *8,* 293–304.

Lovins, A. B. Cost-risk-benefit assessments in energy policy. *George Washington Law Review,* 1977, *45,* 911–943.

Mahoney, M. J. Psychology of the scientist: An evaluative review. *Social Studies of Science,* 1979, *9,* 349–375.

March, J., & Shapira, Z. Behavioral decision theory and organizational decision theory, In G. Ungson & D. Braunstein (Eds.), *New directions in decision making.* New York: Kent, in press.

Markovic, M. Social determinism and freedom. In H. E. Kelfer & M. K. Munitz (Eds.), *Mind, science and history.* Albany: State University of New York Press, 1970.

Marks, B. A. Decision under uncertainty: The narrative sense. *Administration and Society,* 1977, *9,* 379–394.

Marsh, C. *How would you say you felt about political opinion surveys? Would you say you were very happy, fairly happy or not too happy?* Paper presented at BSA/SSRC Conference on Methodology and Techniques of Sociology, Lancaster, U.K., Nov., 1979.

Marx, J. L. Low-level radiation: Just how bad is it? *Science,* 1979, *204,* 160–164.

Maxey, M. N. Radiation health protection and risk assessment: Bioethical considerations. *Proceedings of the 15th Annual Meeting of the National Council on Radiation Protection and Measurements,* 1979, 18–33.

Mazur, A. Disputes between experts. *Minerva,* 1973, *11,* 243–262.

Mazur, A., Marino, A. A., & Becker, R. O. Separating factual disputes from value disputes in controversies over technology. *Technology in Society,* 1979, *1,* 229–237.

McNeil, B. J., Weichselbaum, R., & Pauker, S. G. Fallacy of the 5-year survival rate in lung cancer. *New England Journal of Medicine,* 1978, *299,* 1397–1401.

McNown, R. F. A mechanism for revealing consumer preferences towards public goods. *Review of Social Economy,* 1978, *36,* 2.

Meadows, D. H., Meadows, D. L., Randers, J., & Behrens, W. W. *The limits to growth.* New York: Signet, 1972.

Meehl, P. E. Nuisance variables and the ex post facto design. In M. Radner & S. Winokur (Eds.), *Minnesota studies in the philosophy of science.* Minneapolis: University of Minnesota Press, 1970.

Menkes, J. *Epistemological issues of technology assessment.* Unpublished manuscript, 1978.

Mishan, E. J. Flexibility and consistency in project evaluation. *Economica,* 1974, *41,* 81–96.

Mishan, E. J. *Cost-benefit analysis.* New York: Praeger, 1976.

Mishan, E. J., & Page, T. *The methodology of cost-benefit analysis: With particular reference to the ozone problem* (Social Studies Working Paper 249). Pasadena, Calif.: California Institute of Technology, 1979.

Moreau, D. H. *Quantitative risk assessment of non-carcinogenic ambient air quality standards.* Research Triangle Park, N.C.: U.S. EPA, Office of Air Quality Planning and Standards, 1980.

Morgan, K. Z. Present status of recommendations of the International Commission on Radiological Protection. In A. M. F. Duhamel (Ed.), *Health physics.* New York: Pergamon Press, 1969.

Morgan, M. G., Rish, W. R., Morris, S. C., & Meier, A. K. Sulfur control in coal fired power plants: A probabilistic approach to policy analysis. *Air Pollution Control Association Journal,* 1978, *28,* 993–997.

Morris, P. A. Decision analysis expert use. *Management Science,* 1974, *20,* 1233–1241.

National Academy of Sciences. *The effects on populations of exposure to low levels of ionizing radiation.* Washington, D.C.: Author, 1972.

National Academy of Sciences. *Decision making for regulating chemicals in the environment.* Washington, D.C.: Author, 1975, Appendix H.

National Academy of Sciences. *Surveying crime.* Washington, D.C.: Author, 1976.

Neyman, J. *Probability models in medicine and biology: Avenues for their validation for humans in real life.* Berkeley, Calif.: University of California, Statistical Laboratory, 1979.

Nisbett, R. E., & Ross, L. *Human inference: Strategies and shortcomings of social judgment.* Englewood Cliffs, N.J.: Prentice-Hall, 1980.

Nisbett, R. E., & Wilson, T. D. Telling more than we can know: Verbal reports on mental processes. *Psychological Review,* 1977, *84*(3), 231–259.

Norman, D. A. Post-Freudian slips. *Psychology Today,* 1980, *13*(11), 42–50.

Okrent, D., & Whipple, C. *An approach to societal risk acceptance criteria and risk management* (Report UCLA-ENG-7746). Los Angeles: UCLA, School of Engineering and Applied Sciences, 1977.

O'Leary, M. K., Coplin, W. D., Shapiro, H. B., & Dean, D. The quest for relevance. *International Studies Quarterly,* 1974, *18,* 211–237.

Otway, H. J., & Cohen, J. J. *Revealed preferences: Comments on the Starr benefit-risk relationships* (Research Memorandum 75-5). Laxenburg, Austria: International Institute for Applied Systems Analysis, 1975.

Owen, P. A. Discount rates for social cost benefit analysis of nuclear energy. *Proceedings of the Topical Meeting on Probabilistic Analysis of Nuclear Reactor Safety,* 1978, *2,* IV.5-1–IV.5-12.

Page, T. A generic view of toxic chemicals and similar risks. *Ecology Law Quarterly,* 1978, *7,* 207–243.

Page, T. A framework for unreasonable risk in the Toxic Substances Control Act. In R. Nicholson (Ed.), *Carcinogenic risk assessment.* New York: New York Academy of Sciences, 1981.

Parish, R. M. The scope of benefit-cost analysis. *Journal of the Economic Society of Australia and New Zealand,* 1976, *52,* 302–314.

Pauker, S. G. Coronary artery surgery: The use of decision analysis. *Annals of Internal Medicine,* 1976, *85,* 8–18.

Payne, S. L. *The art of asking questions.* Princeton: Princeton University Press, 1952.

Pearce, D. W. Social cost-benefit analysis and nuclear futures. In G. T. Goodman & W. D. Rowe (Eds.), *Energy risk management.* New York: Academic Press, 1979.

Peters, T. J. Leadership: Sad facts and silver linings. *Harvard Business Review,* 1979, *57*(6), 164–172.

Peto, R. Distorting the epidemiology of cancer. *Nature,* 1980, *284,* 297–300.

Piehler, H. R., Twerski, A. D. Weinstein, A., & Donaher, W. A. Product liability and the technical expert. *Science,* 1974, *186,* 1089–1093.

Polanyi, M. *Personal knowledge.* London: Routledge & Kegan Paul, 1962.

Poulton, E. C. The new psychophysics: Six models for magnitude estimation. *Psychological Bulletin,* 1968, *69,* 1–19.

Poulton, E. C. Quantitative subjective assessments are almost always biased, sometimes completely misleading. *British Journal of Psychology,* 1977, *68,* 409–425.

Raiffa, H. *Decision analysis.* Reading, Mass.: Addison-Wesley, 1968.

Rappoport, E. Unpublished doctoral dissertion, Department of Economics, UCLA, 1981.

Rethans, A. *An investigation of consumer perceptions of product hazards.* Unpublished doctoral dissertation, University of Oregon, 1979.

Riesman, D. *The lonely crowd.* New Haven, Conn.: Yale University Press, 1961.

Rokeach, M. *The nature of human values.* New York: The Free Press, 1973.

Rosencranz, A., & Wetstone, G. S. Acid precipitation: National and international responses. *Environment,* 1980, *22*(5), 6–20, 40–41.

Rothschild, N. M. Rothschild: An antidote to panic. *Nature,* 1978, *276,* 555.

Rothschild's numerate arrogance. *Nature,* 1978, *276,* 429.

Rotow, D., Cochran, T., & Tamplin, A. NRDC comments on criteria for radioactive waste proposed by the Environmental Protection Agency. *Federal Register,* 1978, 43(226). Issued January 5, 1979 by the Natural Resources Defense Council.

Rowe, W. D. *An anatomy of risk*. New York: Wiley, 1977.(a)

Rowe, W. D. Governmental regulations of societal risks. *George Washington Law Review*, 1977, *45*, 944–968.(b)

Savage, L. J. *The foundations of statistics*. New York: Wiley, 1954.

Schelling, T. C. The life you save may be your own. In S. B. Chase (Ed.), *Problems in public expenditure analysis*. Washington, D.C.: Brookings Institution, 1968.

Schlaifer, R. O. *Analysis of decisions under uncertainty*. New York: McGraw-Hill, 1969.

Schneider, S. H., & Mesirow, L. E. *The genesis strategy*. New York: Plenum, 1976.

Schneider, T. H. Safety concepts. *Proceedings of the 11th Congress of the International Association of Bridge and Structural Engineers*, 1979, 225–236.

Schneiderman, M. A. The uncertain risks we run: Hazardous material. In R. C. Schwing & W. A. Albers, Jr. (Eds.), *Societal risk assessment: How safe is safe enough?* New York: Plenum, 1980.

Schulze, W. Social welfare functions for the future. *American Economist*, 1974, *18*(1), 70–81.

Schuman, H., & Johnson, M. Attitudes and behavior. *Annual Review of Sociology*, 1976, *2*, 161–207.

Schuman, H., & Presser, S. Question wording as an independent variable in survey analysis. *Sociological Research and Methods*, 1977, *6*, 151–170.

Segnar, S. F. *Placing your bets on technology. . . sure thing or long shot?* Paper presented at the American Institute of Chemical Engineers, New York, June 1980.

Settle, D. M., & Patterson, C. C. Lead in albacore: Guide to lead pollution in Americans. *Science*, 1980, *207*, 1167–1176.

Sheridan, T. B. Human error in nuclear power plants. *Technology Review*, 1980, *82*(4), 23–33.

Shroyer, T. Toward a critical theory for advanced industrial society. In H. P. Drietzel (Ed.), *Recent sociology*. Vol. 2. *Patterns of communicative behavior*. London: Macmillan, 1970.

Sinclair, C., Marstrand, P., & Newick, P. *Innovation and human risk*. London: Centre for the Study of Industrial Innovation, 1972.

Sjöberg, L. The risks of risk analysis. *Acta Psychologica*, 1980, *45*, 301–321.

Slovic, P., Fischhoff, B., & Lichtenstein, S. Behavioral decision theory. *Annual Review of Psychology*, 1977, *28*, 1–39.

Slovic, P., Fischhoff, B., & Lichtenstein, S. Rating the risks. *Environment*, 1979, *21*(3), 14–20, 36–39.

Slovic, P., Fischhoff, B., & Lichtenstein, S. Perceived risk. In R. C. Schwing & W. A. Albers, Jr. (Eds.), *Societal risk assessment: How safe is safe enough?* New York: Plenum, 1980.

Smith, R. J. NCI bioassays yield a trail of blunders. *Science*, 1979, *204*, 1287–1292.

Sowby, F. D. Radiation and other risks. *Health Physics*, 1965, *11*, 879–887.

Spetzler, C. S., & Staël von Holstein, C.-A. Probability encoding in decision analysis. *Management Science*, 1975, *22*, 340–358.

Staël von Holstein, C.-A., & Matheson, J. E. *A manual for encoding probability distributions*. Menlo Park, Calif.: SRI International, 1978.

Starr, C. Social benefit versus technological risk. *Science*, 1969, *165*, 1232–1238.

Starr, C. Benefit-cost studies in sociotechnical systems. In *Perspective on benefit-risk decision making*. Washington, D.C.: Committee on Public Engineering Policy, National Academy of Engineering, 1972.

Starr, C., & Whipple, C. Risks of risk decisions. *Science*, 1980, *208*, 1114–1119.

Stech, F. J. *Political and military intention estimation: A taxonometric analysis*. Bethesda, Md.: Mathtech, 1979.

Stokey, E., & Zeckhauser, R. *A primer for policy analysis*. New York: Norton, 1978.

Svenson, O. Risks of road transportation in a psychological perspective. *Accident Analysis and Prevention*, 1978, *10*, 267–280.

Svenson, O. *A vulnerable or resilient society? Some reflections on a problem area* (Report No. 19). Stockholm: Swedish Council for Social Science Research, 1979.

Tarr, J. *Retrospective technology assessment*. San Francisco: University of San Francisco Press, 1977.

Taylor, B. N. Physical constants. *Encyclopedia Britannica: Macropaedia,* 1974, *5,* 75–84.

Teger, A. I. Too much invested to quit. New York: Pergamon Press, 1980.

Thaler, R., & Rosen, S. The value of saving a life: Evidence from the labor market. In N. Terleckyj (Ed.), *Household production and consumption*. New York: Columbia University Press, 1976.

Tihansky, D. Confidence assessment of military air frame cost predictions. *Operations Research,* 1976, *24,* 26–43.

Tribe, L. H. Policy science: Analysis or ideology? *Philosophy and Public Affairs,* 1972, *2,* 66–110.

Tribe, L. H. Technology assessment and the fourth discontinuity: The limits of instrumental rationality. *Southern California Law Review,* 1973, *46,* 617–660.

Tukey, J. W. Some thoughts on clinical trials, especially problems of multiplicity. *Science,* 1977, *198,* 678–690.

Turner, C. F., & Krauss, E. Fallible indicators of the subjective state of the nation. *American Psychologist,* 1978, *33,* 456–470.

Tversky, A., & Kahneman, D. Belief in the law of small numbers. *Psychological Bulletin,* 1971, *76,* 105–110.

Tversky, A., & Kahneman, D. Judgment under uncertainty: Heuristics and biases. *Science,* 1974, *185,* 1124–1131.

Tversky, A., & Kahneman, D. The framing of decisions and the psychology of choice. *Science,* 1981, *211,* 453–458.

U.S. Atomic Energy Commission. *Comparative risk-cost-benefit study of alternative sources of electrical energy* (USAEC WASH-1224). Washington, D.C.: Author, 1974.

U.S. Department of Energy. *Carbon dioxide effects research and assessment program* (DOE/EV-0071). Washington, D.C.: Author, 1979.

U.S. Government. *Hearings, 94th Congress, 1st Session. Browns Ferry Nuclear Plant Fire, September 16, 1975*. Washington, D.C.: U.S. Government Printing Office, 1975.

U.S. Government. *Teton Dam disaster*. Washington, D.C.: Committee on Government Operations, 1976.

U.S. Government. *Report of the President's Commission on the Accident at Three Mile Island*. Washington, D.C.: U.S. Government Printing Office, 1979.

U.S. Nuclear Regulatory Commission. *Reactor safety study: An assessment of accident risks in U.S. commercial nuclear power plants* (WASH 1400 [NUREG-75/014]). Washington, D.C.: Author, 1975.

U.S. Nuclear Regulatory Commission. *Risk assessment review group to the U.S. Nuclear Regulatory Commission* (NUREG/CR-0400). Washington, D.C.: Author, 1978.

Vanmarcke, E. H. *Risk and decision analysis in soil engineering*. Paper presented at the 9th International Conference on Soil Mechanics and Foundation Engineering, Tokyo, July 1977.

Viscusi, W. K. Job hazards and worker quit rates: An analysis of adaptive worker behavior. *International Economic Review,* 1979, *20,* 29–58.

von Neumann, J., & Morgenstern, O. *Theory of games and economic behavior*. Princeton, N.J.: Princeton University Press, 1947.

von Winterfeldt, D. *Modelling standard setting decisions: An illustrative application to chronic oil discharges*. (Research Memorandum RM-78-27). Laxenburg, Austria: International Institute for Applied Systems Analysis, 1978.

von Winterfeldt, D., & Edwards, W. *Evaluation of complex stimuli using multiattribute utility procedures* (Technical Report 011313-2-T). Ann Arbor: Engineering Psychology Lab, University of Michigan, 1973.

Walgate, R. EEC rules soon. *Nature,* 1980, *285,* 432–433.

Walker, R., & Bayley, S. Quantitative assessment of natural values in benefit-cost analysis. *Journal of Environmental Systems,* 1977–1978, *7*(2), 131–147.

Weaver, S. The passionate risk debate. *The Oregon Journal,* April 24, 1979.

Weinberg, A. M. Salvaging the atomic age. *The Wilson Quarterly,* Summer 1979, pp. 88–112.

Weinstein, N. D. Seeking reassuring or threatening information about environmental cancer. *Journal of Behavioral Medicine,* 1979, *16,* 220–224.

Wheeler, D. D., & Janis, I. L. *A practical guide for making decisions.* New York: The Free Press, 1980.

White, I. L. Interdisciplinarity. *The Environmental Professional,* 1979, *1,* 51–55.

Wildavsky, A. The political economy of efficiency: Cost-benefit analysis, systems analysis and program budgeting. *Public Administration Review,* 1966.

Willson, V. L. Estimating changes in accident statistics due to reporting requirement changes. *Journal of Safety Research,* 1980, *12*(1), 36–42.

Wilson, B. Explosives report may rock a new town. *The Observer* (London), January 13, 1980.

Wilson, R. Examples in risk-benefit analysis. *Chemtech,* 1975, *6,* (Oct.), 604–607.

Wilson, R. Analyzing the daily risks of life. *Technology Review,* 1979, *81*(4), 40–46.

Wohlstetter, R. *Pearl Harbor: Warning and decision.* Stanford, Calif.: Stanford University Press, 1962.

World Meteorological Organization. *World Climate Conference.* Geneva: Author, 1978.

Wortman, P. M. Evaluation research: A psychological perspective. *American Psychologist,* 1975, *30,* 562–575.

Zeckhauser, R., & Shepard, D. Where now for saving lives? *Law and Contemporary Problems,* 1976, *40,* 5–45.

Zeisel, H. Lawmaking and public opinion research: The president and Patrick Caddell. *American Bar Foundation Research Journal,* 1980, *1,* 133–139.

Zentner, R. D. Hazards in the chemical industry. *Chemical and Engineering News,* 1979, *57*(45), 25–27, 30–34.

Zuniga, R. B. The experimenting society and radical social reform. *American Psychology,* 1975, *30,* 99–115.

Additional readings

Readers interested in additional material on this topic are encouraged to consult the following general sources.

Clark, E. M., & Van Horn, A. J. *Risk-benefit analysis and public policy: A bibliography* (Updated and extended by L. Hedal & E. A. C. Crouch). Cambridge, Mass.: Energy and Environmental Policy Center, Harvard University, 1978.

Committee on Public Engineering Policy. *Perspectives on benefit-risk decision making.* Washington, D.C.: National Academy of Engineering, 1972.

Conrad, J. (Ed.). *Society, technology and risk.* London: Academic Press, 1980.

Council for Science and Society. *The acceptability of risks.* London: Barry Rose, 1977.

Health and Safety Executive. *Canvey: Summary of an investigation of potential hazards from operations in the Canvey Island/Thurrock area.* London: Her Majesty's Stationery Office, 1978.

Hohenemser, C., & Kasperson, J. (Eds.). *Risk in the technological society.* Boulder, Colo.: Westview, in press.

Jennergren, L. P., & Keeney, R. L. Risk assessment. In *Handbook of applied systems analysis.* Laxenburg, Austria: International Institute of Applied Systems Analysis, in press.

Kates, R. W. *Risk assessment of environmental hazard.* Chichester, U.K.: Wiley, 1978.

Lawless, E. W. *Technology and social shock.* New Brunswick, N.J.: Rutgers University Press, 1977.

Lowrance, W. W. *Of acceptable risk.* Los Altos, Calif.: Kaufmann, 1976.

National Academy of Sciences. *Decision making for regulating chemicals in the environment.* Washington, D.C.: Author, 1977.

Nelkin, D. *Technological decisions and democracy.* Beverly Hills, Calif: Sage, 1977.

The risk equations: What risks should we run? Acceptability versus democracy; the subjective side of assessing risks; Virtue in compromise; The political economy of risk. *New Scientist,* 1977, *74,* (May 12, May 18, May 26, September 8).

Rowe, W. D. *An anatomy of risk.* New York: Wiley, 1977.

Schwing, R. C., & Albers, W. A. (Eds.) *Societal risk assessment: How safe is safe enough?* New York: Plenum, 1980.

Starr, C., Rudman, R., & Whipple, C. Philosophical basis for risk analysis. *Annual Review of Energy,* 1976, *1,* 629-662.

Index